WITHDRAWN

Emerson in His Sermons

251.0092
R54e

Emerson
in His Sermons

A MAN-MADE SELF

Susan L. Roberson

UNIVERSITY OF MISSOURI PRESS

COLUMBIA AND LONDON

Copyright © 1995 by
The Curators of the University of Missouri
University of Missouri Press, Columbia, Missouri 65201
Printed and bound in the United States of America
All rights reserved
5   4   3   2   1   99   98   97   96   95

Library of Congress Cataloging-in-Publication Data

Roberson, Susan L., 1950-
  Emerson in his sermons : a man-made self / Susan L. Roberson.
    p.   cm.
  Includes index.
  ISBN 0-8262-0983-1
  1. Emerson, Ralph Waldo, 1803–1882 — Criticism and interpretation.
2. Sermons, American — History and criticism.   3. Self in literature.
  I. Title.
  PS1623.S47R63   1995   94-32937
  251'.0092 — dc20   CIP

For permissions to reproduce copyrighted material,
see the last printed page of the book.

♾This paper meets the requirements of the
American National Standard for Permanence of Paper
for Printed Library Materials, Z39.48, 1984.

Designer: Kristie Lee
Typesetter: Graphic Composition
Printer and Binder: Thomson-Shore, Inc.
Typefaces: Galliard, Shelly Allegro

I dedicate this book with love
to Wally
to Brad and Cameron

CAT May27 97

ALLEGHENY COLLEGE LIBRARY

Contents

Acknowledgments

This book has been a long time in the making. It began first as a dissertation under the direction of Jerome Loving and with the assistance of W. Bedford Clark, both of whom gave my initial work careful readings and offered me helpful advice. Since that time, I have added a daughter, Cameron, to my family. And I have completely reworked the project, taking to heart hints offered by Norman Grabo that I look more closely at the cultural materials and by Timothy Crusius that I consider the work of Hans-Georg Gadamer. In addition to these early influences on the book, I want to thank the American Antiquarian Society for providing me an opportunity to use their fine library during a History of the Book seminar and the Houghton Library at Harvard University for allowing me access to the Emerson Sermon Manuscripts. Patricia Gaston, Carol Roberson, and Patrick Morrow read intermediate drafts of the manuscript and assured me that I was on the right track. I would also like to thank Clair Willcox, acquisitions editor for the University of Missouri Press, for his faith in the project and the anonymous readers for the Press, who gave me both criticism and encouragement during the crucial last drafts of the manuscript. Finally, I want to thank my husband, Wally Moon, for his love, moral support, and very real assistance with operating my Macintosh.

Abbreviations

For convenience, the following abbreviations are used in the text to identify sources of material often cited:

CS   *The Complete Sermons of Ralph Waldo Emerson*. Edited by Albert J. von Frank et al. 4 vols. Columbia: University of Missouri Press, 1989–1992.

Textual and manuscript notes in *Complete Sermons* are indicated as follows:

< > Indicates a cancellation made by Emerson. Matter that immediately follows a cancellation without a space or symbol of insertion, as in "<i>It" or "<we>you," should be understood as having been written directly over the canceled matter.

↑ ↓ Indicates an insertion.

J   *The Journals of Ralph Waldo Emerson*. Edited by Edward Waldo Emerson and Waldo Emerson Forbes. 10 vols. Boston and New York: Houghton Mifflin, 1909–1914.

JMN   *The Journals and Miscellaneous Notebooks of Ralph Waldo Emerson*. Edited by William H. Gilman et al. 16 vols. Cambridge: Harvard University Press, 1960–1982.

Symbols representing textual and manuscript notes are the same as for *Complete Sermons*.

L   *The Letters of Ralph Waldo Emerson.* Edited by Ralph L. Rusk. 6
        vols. New York: Columbia University Press, 1939.

MS   Manuscript Sermons of Ralph Waldo Emerson. Houghton Li-
        brary, Harvard University.

Emerson in His Sermons

Emerson's Homiletic Narrative

"My trust is that my profession shall be my regeneration of mind, manners, inward & outward estate." (*JMN* 2:242)

"*I will* is a strong word that moves mountains." (*CS* 1:386)

"Be assured we shall not always set so great a price on a few texts, on a few lives. When we were young, we repeated by rote the words of our grandames, of our tutors, — &, as we grew older, of the men of talents & character we met, & painfully recollected & recited the exact words they spake." (*JMN* 7:150)

When Ralph Waldo Emerson delivered Sermon No. CLXIV on October 21, 1832, he had already announced his intention to quit the pastoral duties of the Second Unitarian Church of Boston. Having entered the ministry in part to effect a personal "regeneration of mind, manners, inward & outward estate," the young Emerson had undergone so complete a metamorphosis of character that by 1832 he strained at the cords of tradition and ritual, finding in his dissatisfaction with the administration of the Lord's Supper the issue by which to declare himself.[1] Convinced that Jesus had not meant the festival of breaking bread to be-

---

1. See David Robinson, *Apostle of Culture: Emerson as Preacher and Lecturer,* one of the first and best to trace Emerson's ministerial career and examine the sermons, "the form through which he learned his craft of words" (2).

come "an institution for perpetual observance," Emerson insisted that each person should be free to form his own beliefs.[2] "Freedom," he told his congregation in the famous "Lord's Supper" Sermon, "is the essence of Christianity" (*CS* 4:186, 193).

As he knew from his own experience, freedom entailed not just the liberty to believe and practice according to the dictates of the conscience, but the liberty to invent a new self, true and authentic, from the resources of the self. Having tested his convictions during the six years since he was first approbated to preach, Emerson in 1832 had reached a crisis point in his faith, self-identity, and vocation that demanded decision. That he opted to remain true to his vision at whatever cost attests to the work of those six years in forming a new character and an original philosophy of the self, both of which derived from the passional impulse to empower himself. When Friedrich Nietzsche wrote that "Thoughts are the shadows of our feelings, always darker, emptier, and simpler,"[3] he must have known what Emerson had experienced: that philosophy derives from personal strategies for surviving the psychic and physical maelstroms of life.

Indeed, the story that lies behind Emerson's rejection of the Lord's Supper tradition and his resignation from the Second Church pulpit demonstrates the personal and passional foundation of his thought. Driven to assert his power and position in a universe both tamed by convention and inherently hostile, Emerson shaped his own thought and invented the character who inhabits the narrative of his farewell sermon, the "genuine man" (*CS* 4:203), a fictive character who points the way to Emerson's metamorphosis of self. In a sense, the controversy over the administration of the Lord's Supper is really the epilogue of a longer narrative that traces the progress of a being in search of himself, for woven between the lines of Christian dogma and philosophy in Emerson's sermons is a kind of autobiographical text that unfolds the story of its author and "the crises of [his] fate" (*JMN* 4:29).

Of course, the sermons can be read as separate discourse units, as

2. The use of the masculine pronominal is appropriate for discussing Emerson's thought since, for him, the ideal or empowered self is indeed a masculine self.
3. *The Complete Works of Friedrich Nietzsche,* edited by Oscar Levy, 10:192.

examples of nineteenth-century Unitarian preaching, and as fore-ground for Emerson's more "important" work. For Transcendentalist bookseller Elizabeth Peabody, the sermons' proximity to Emerson's later, more famous work imbued them with a significance apparently unattainable in their own right. Peabody wrote that they were "as truly transcendental as any of his later lectures and writings in prose or verse" and declared that "if a volume of them could be printed to-day in their own form, it would interpret his later revelations, of which they are but a varied expression."[4] Indeed, the sermons are usually read for their historical value and through the lenses of the tradition of American literary criticism that finds Emerson's *Nature* and early essays to be his central work, with other texts peripheral to them. The sermons, when they have been considered at all by critics, have been embedded in an oeuvre shaped by history and by the prevailing interpretations of past and present readers who, like Peabody, have determined their value rel-evant to other texts and historical situations. The persistence of the in-terpretive tradition articulated by Peabody is represented in the work of Arthur McGiffert, whose early collection of the sermons, *Young Em-erson Speaks*, encourages a piecemeal reading of the sermons as separate texts and as forerunners of the later work; of Jerome Loving, who con-siders sermons such as "Summer" (No. XXXIX) as "foreground" for *Nature*; and of David Robinson, who considers them in the context of Unitarian self-cultivation and declares that "the roots of all his great lectures and essays are in the sermon." Perhaps Wesley Mott and Mary Kupiec Cayton come the closest to reading the sermons as "a genuine drama of ideas" that catapults "Emerson's Emergence," to use Stephen Whicher's words.[5]

---

4. Quoted from Wesley T. Mott, *"Strains of Eloquence": Emerson and His Ser-mons*, 1–2.

5. See Arthur C. McGiffert, ed., *Young Emerson Speaks: Unpublished Discourses on Many Subjects;* Jerome Loving, *Emerson, Whitman, and the American Muse;* and Robinson, *Apostle of Culture*, 1–2. Mott, *"Strains of Eloquence,"* announces, "The ser-mons are a brilliant young man's encounter with personal doubt and ambition and with urgent issues of theology, power, and expression, all carried out before a very real audience, an encounter that indelibly stamped the shape of Emerson's mind and career" (4). Stephen Whicher, in *Freedom and Fate: An Inner Life of Ralph Waldo Emerson*, explores the "push and pull of contrary directions" in Emerson's thought,

Intriguing as they are as foundational material for the later thought, the sermons also form a narrative of a young man's encounter with his world and with himself, and of his willful shaping of his thought and life from the crucible of experience. The sermons demonstrate the cohesiveness of an autobiography, for the chronological collection is characterized by direction, invention, and a dialectic with the self and with the culture at large. Emerson's text demonstrates the same "rage for order" that Wallace Stevens finds to be the poet's creative impulse and that James Barcus finds to be an endemic quality of autobiography. And as with autobiography, Emerson fashions a self or writes into being a self who is both himself and a fictive invention. But where the design of more conventional autobiography is imposed from without by the self-conscious author, Emerson's narrative assumes its shape and direction from within the text, making negligible the "collusion between past and present" that is so much a part of more standard autobiography.[6] The desire to recapture the past through the acts of memory and writing is nonexistent in the Emerson text, since the event and the moment of writing are so closely connected. The sermons, which form a serial autobiographical narrative marked by "organic and perpetual motion," have the immediacy of a daily record without the "incoherent realia" of the unedited diary.[7] Perhaps this odd sort of "auto-biography" is truer to the self than the more polished narrative,

---

the dialectic between faith and skepticism (vii). Mary Kupiec Cayton, who draws a fine picture of Boston society in the 1820s and 1830s, is interested in Emerson's rejection of the "customs, ceremonies, and ethos of social organicism that held Federalist society together" and his discovery of what she calls a "natural organicism" (*Emerson's Emergence: Self and Society in the Transformation of New England, 1800–1845,* 57.)

6. James E. Barcus, "Structuring the Rage Within: The Spiritual Autobiographies of Newman and Orestes Brownson," 45–46. Barcus argues that autobiography seeks to create order out of the mass of experience. Roy Pascal, *Design and Truth in Autobiography,* 11. Pascal's study emphasizes the "power of the personality over circumstance" as the writer selects and arranges incidents from the life into a cohesive text (10–11).

7. Judy Nolte Lensink, *"A Secret to Be Buried": The Diary and Life of Emily Hawley Gillespie, 1858–1888.* In her work on the diary of Gillespie, an ordinary woman of the Iowa farmland, Lensink considers the diary as female autobiography and summarizes some of the recent discussions of women's writing and the characteristics of the personal diary.

for the acts of being and writing are more simultaneous than they are in the reminiscence.

The Auto-Biographical Strain

Discussing 164 sermons as autobiography may seem an unusual proposition, but as James Olney has observed, there is a certain ambiguity about what constitutes autobiography. Unlike some genres, say the sonnet, whose form is constrained by long-standing convention, autobiography, Olney suggests, is allowed freer play in the hands of its various creators: "Perhaps this is so because there are no rules or formal requirements binding the prospective autobiographer—no restraints, no necessary models, no obligatory observances gradually shaped out of a long developing tradition and imposed by that tradition on the individual talent who would translate a life into writing."[8] Taking Olney at his word, we can consider Emerson's sermons as autobiography with, certainly, some provisions about their autobiographical quality. Of course, the sermons can be read as just that, sermons written and delivered under specific conditions, for Emerson's obvious and immediate purpose in writing them was occasioned by the often pressing need on Saturday to have a text ready to read on Sunday. But the reader of the entire homiletic narrative discovers what the reader of autobiography discovers—a life translated through time and in the act of writing, an impulse to order experience and invent a self particular to the author and beyond the expectations of his immediate, public audience.

There is, then, something about the sermons that asks that they be read as something more, as a whole discourse rather than only as discrete, oratorical performances. To read the sermons as auto-biography requires, it is true, a Dickinsonian "Slant of light" to uncover an "internal difference. / Where the Meanings are."[9] Even so, to come at the sermons willy-nilly robs them of the story they unfold and the direction

---

8. Quoted in Paul Jay, *Being in the Text: Self-Representation from Wordsworth to Barthes,* 15. For further discussion of autobiography, see James Olney, *Autobiography: Essays Theoretical and Critical,* from which Jay borrowed this quote on page 3.
9. Thomas H. Johnson, ed., *Final Harvest: Emily Dickinson's Poems,* 36.

and progression evident when one looks beyond the immediate situation of a particular sermon to consider its relation to the whole body of the homiletic text. Indeed, the "Meaning" in the sermons resides not only in the literal transcription of Emerson's words but also in the spaces between the words and behind the text, in what is "unsaid and nevertheless made present" and in what is concealed in language.[10] In the sermons, we find both conscious and unconscious material prompted by the dual purposes of composition, to teach others and to inscribe the self, as Emerson attempts through the medium of language to uncover and construct meaning for both of his audiences, the Unitarian congregation and himself. Our reading and understanding thus reach beyond the individual discourses to the whole unit, a multitext document in which the letters and journals become personal footnotes to the sermons, for in the auto-biographical text Emerson and his reader find a meaning that transcends and finally subverts the original occasion of composition as Emerson translates a life *through* (rather than *into*) writing. The auto-biographical text of the sermons is no mere formal, performative occasion of the Christian Church but, like the true Communion, derives meaning from the unseen spirit that forms and informs the body of the text.

Although they are quite peculiar as autobiography, Emerson's sermons evidence the kind of movement and rhetorical self-representation found in more standard autobiographies. Like the "conversion" narratives of British contemporaries William Wordsworth and Thomas Carlyle, Emerson's personal tale "consists in rejecting, with full risks, the inherited modes of experience" and demonstrates a recovery from despair and crisis that involves not merely a return to a previous state of equilibrium but also the invention of a new faith and a new self.[11] Like Wordsworth's *Prelude,* Emerson's narrative is marked by a crisis of identity and the dramatic discovery of his poetic voice; like Carlyle's semiau-

10. Hans-Georg Gadamer, *Philosophical Hermeneutics,* trans. and ed. David E. Linge, 88.

11. Jacques Barzun, *Classic, Romantic, and Modern,* 88. See also M. H. Abrams's discussion of Romantic conversion narratives in *Natural Supernaturalism: Tradition and Revolution in Romantic Literature,* 77, 114, and Daniel B. Shea, *Spiritual Autobiography in Early America.*

tobiographical character Teufelsdrockh, Emerson confronted despair and fear in a kind of "Baphometic fire-baptism" by which he defied the Everlasting Nay and affirmed the self.[12] As with the conversion narratives of Wordsworth and Carlyle, the central figure of Emerson's narrative is an invented, fictionalized representation of the author's truer self; he is the "New Man" (*CS* 4:203) who is "born again" and "possessed of a new hold on existence" (*CS* 4:127), a man who experienced a "conversion from a moral to a religious character" (*JMN* 3:186).

Like other spiritual autobiographies, Emerson's narrative unfolds an exploration of traditional doctrine, crisis, rejection, and creation of a new self. The first stage of his narrative shows him entrenched in the doctrine and tradition that were his inheritance and his culture and that provided the "blueprint" for his own thinking and sermonizing. Indeed, we understand ourselves first in terms provided by our culture or "horizon," as Hans-Georg Gadamer would put it: "Long before we understand ourselves through the process of self-examination, we understand ourselves in a self-evident way in the family, society and state in which we live."[13] In this first stage of his narrative, we hear Emerson echoing the concerns of his culture about man's sinfulness, God's omnipotence, and the divine retributions to come. We hear also the national concern with progress, civilization, and self-cultivation.

While the individual — Emerson included — never escapes, nor can escape, these cultural programs, the way he understands himself and his world can become more individual and idiosyncratic. Indeed, the act of self-representation, so inherently complicated in the auto-

---

12. Thomas Carlyle, *Sartor Resartus: The Life and Opinions of Herr Teufelsdrockh,* 168.

13. Clifford Geertz maintains, "Culture patterns — religious, philosophical, aesthetic, ideological — are 'programs'; they provide a template or blueprint for the organization of social and psychological processes" (*The Interpretation of Cultures: Selected Essays by Clifford Geertz,* 216). For Geertz man is not human without culture and culture is that complex of behavior patterns that shapes and controls human behavior and thought. Gadamer, *Truth and Method,* 245. For Gadamer as well as for Geertz, self-understanding or beingness depends, in very real ways, upon the individual's culture or position in history. For Gadamer, self-interpretation involves a dialectic between the individual and his horizon, each changing the other in a series of dialectical understandings and reformations.

biographical impulse, derives in part from the strain to identify the self with and apart from the communal other, from moods of attachment and abandonment. This strain, the second stage of the narrative, is particularly evident in the sermons of the last few years of Emerson's ministry. These sermons demonstrate the dynamics of both a self in process and autobiographical writing, for they reveal a man, scarred by confrontation with personal disaster, who re-forms his thought and his self in patterns that parallel more authorial, conscious self-representations. If M. H. Abrams is right, the structure of Romantic conversion narratives imitates the larger Christian apocalyptic narrative of crisis and renewal.[14] In this context, the movement of Emerson's narrative and personal experience participates in the larger human (Christian) drama.

Nonetheless, the critical experience of Emerson's narrative was peculiarly and particularly personal, for with his young wife's persistent and degenerating ill health and his corresponding depression, Emerson made tentative explorations into the questions of morality, compensation, and self-reliance. With Ellen Louisa Tucker Emerson's death on February 8, 1831, Emerson more steadily and confidently constructed his own version of self-reliance and the compensating correspondence between the realms of humanity and God. What becomes evident is that the persistent need to find strategies for psychic survival in the face of his personal catastrophe crystallized the philosophical and vocational crisis of the last years of his ministry into his rejection of ready-made institutions and beliefs. While he had made forays into these topics in the years previous to Ellen's death, he seems to have circled around them without settling down to a perspective that made sense to him. But once he found his angle of vision, he grew restless with the constraints of his profession and his era. This third stage, then, marks Emerson's rejection not only of traditional ritual but also of the rationalist, profit-motivated frame of mind that shaped much of contemporary thought. Having examined the "blueprint" of conventional thought and being compelled by his passional need to empower himself, Emerson transcended the prescribed texts and interpretations of his culture

14. See particularly chapter 1 of Abrams, *Natural Supernaturalism*.

to find authority within the self. With his reformation of thought, Emerson formed himself anew and became more thoroughly a self-made man than could his fellows sold on the myth of success, because he created from the internal resources of being a man-made self, a "genuine man" who acts from his thought.

Thus like the autobiography in fiction (James Joyce's *Portrait of an Artist as a Young Man* comes to mind), the hero of Emerson's narrative is both himself and a fictional character. Created by Emerson, this hero is a ferociously self-assured being who wills himself into being by a belief in the divinity of the self and the victory of the ME over the NOT ME, over all the forces — societal and universal — that threaten to bind or crush the realization of the self's potential. He is one with whom Emerson identifies and whom Emerson attempts to emulate in his own life and philosophy, though not always with success. Whereas Joyce set out deliberately to fictionalize the self, Emerson the Unitarian minister came at his fictionalized self in an unconscious, intuitive "curve of an emotion,"[15] out of the testing and contesting of the contrary impulses of his being. This uneasy relationship with himself and between his public and private voices prompts Emerson to neutralize, rather than assert, his own voice and identity in the sermons, often substituting the more distant third person for first- or second-person pronouns. For example, in Sermon No. CXVII he substitutes "they" for "you": "In proportion as <you> ↑they have↓ raised <yourself> ↑themselves↓ to extraordinary acquirements & extraordinary virtues <you> ↑they have↓ outstripped the affections of <your> ↑their↓ fellowmen." Despite (and under) Emerson's purposeful neutralizing in this passage, the reader catches the personal curve of his argument; at the same time that he speaks of past heroes, he challenges himself (the "you" that is his alter ego) to achieve "extraordinary acquirements." The private Emerson, an ambitious young man who longs for greatness and yet is plagued with doubt and anxiety, lies always just behind the public minister's pronouncements about character and genius. When the minister

---

15. Quoted in Jay, *Being in the Text,* 125. In his 1904 "Portrait" essay, James Joyce noted that "a portrait is not an identificative paper but rather the curve of an emotion."

creates the "genuine man" in his farewell sermon, we not only hear the resonance of Emerson's own aspiration to greatness, but we also witness, as he puts his thought into words and then into action, his imitation of the invented hero who "acts his thought" (*CS* 4:206).

Where Wordsworth, like more conventional autobiographers, translated his life *into* writing, retrospectively unfolding the growth of the mind, Emerson translated his life *through* writing, electrifying the emotional edge of the narrative because the risks encountered are alive with danger and the self in process is as yet untested. While the more conventional autobiographer knows how the story he is telling turns out, Emerson does not. The young man, worried that "little is yet done to establish my consideration among my contemporaries & less to get a memory when I am gone" (*JMN* 3:15), does not know that he will become the Sage of Concord. And while the conventional autobiographer can shape the life he recounts to his purposes, Emerson is shaping the life as it is lived without the advantage of hindsight. He does not know, for instance, how or even if he will challenge the Second Church congregation about the administration of the Lord's Supper; indeed, his doubts about the wisdom of such a move and his apprehension about the consequences of being without a livelihood are real and present to him. His narrative, charged as it is with dialectic and with tension and urgency, has an immediacy not always found in autobiographies written from the perspective of distance. This sort of writing of one's biography simultaneous to the event charges it also with the idiosyncrasies of the present moment, of the self actually in formation, and with rhetorical subterfuge as Emerson by starts and stops reveals himself, or his potential self, to himself and his audience. If the Emerson narrative lacks the polish of other autobiographies that have a clearer sense of direction, it resonates with the voice of a dynamic self "a-being" (*JMN* 4:18), a self between times and empowered by ongoing redefinition.

The Strain of Auto-Biography

The autobiographical quality of Emerson's sermons is further complicated by the dual purposes of composition — the discursive and symbolic, the conscious and the unconscious, the public and the private. As a Unitarian minister striving to meet the immediate needs of the pulpit, Emerson had the obvious task of writing sermons that interpreted the Word of God, taught lessons of morality, and inspired purposeful living and self-cultivation. This was no easy task; the journals attest to Emerson's early concern with getting a "sermonbarrelfull" before settling in a church home (*L* 1:234), his relentless search for topics, and his persistent drafting. With his appointment to the Second Church, Emerson was expected to conduct two worship services every Sunday, complete with sermon, prayers, Scripture readings, and hymns, as well as occasional weekday lectures. In addition, he was responsible for baptisms, marriages, funerals, and visitations to his parishioners, a schedule that must have kept in the fore of his mind the immediate tasks of composition, his duties as minister, and the needs and responses of his congregation. Ever careful to make a strong "present effect," Emerson gauged his audience's reactions and strove to "*appeal* to the audience," something he criticized his brother Charles for not doing (*L* 1:211, 238–39).[16]

But Emerson's symbolic, and finally more pertinent, task in writing centered around his need to redefine meaning and to redefine, or invent, the self. In conjunction with and at the same time in conflict with the public discourse is a subversive discourse that cut away traditional readings of God and the self, revealing and hiding a minister who would empower the self at the expense of conventional meaning, at the expense of God, even. In her study of the journal kept by Anna Tilden, a young woman of Boston who often heard and recorded Emerson's sermons, Sara Wider notes that in his early sermons "the more radical thought was rarely introduced by one of the conventional formulas" of Unitarian preaching. Rather, his "divergence from Unitarian tenets appeared primarily in the sections between the formulaic statements — in the very places where the congregation's attention was most likely to

16. See *The Complete Sermons of Ralph Waldo Emerson* for Emerson's Preaching Record and volume 4 for the Records of Second Church. See David Robinson's description of Emerson's pastoral duties in his introductory essay to *CS*, 1:15–16. See also Sara Wider's "What Did the Minister Mean: Emerson's Sermons and Their Audience."

flag." Wider's study may help to explain why his congregation apparently was not alarmed by some of his radical theses and how Emerson subverted the Unitarian sermon at the same time that he used it to posit a new self and a new religion.[17]

Much that is symbolic and transformative in the sermons lies in the interstices between the public and private concerns, for it is here that the project of self-formation is played out, giving the sermons a narrative edge and dialectic tension as Emerson attempts to balance his ministerial duties and inherited beliefs with an emerging new philosophy and self. Indeed, the symbolic level of discourse seems to be more necessary in a public text than in a private one, such as a personal journal, precisely because of the kind of precarious balance the author must maintain to make order of the colliding materials and, at the same time, sustain personal psychic stability. The manuscript sermons offer the reader a rare and privileged look at the rhetorical juggling act — at the subterfuges, emendations, and cancellations that reveal the private Emerson in conflict with the public minister and with conventional thought. For it is between and behind the lines of the public text that the drama of transfiguration is enacted as he struggles to find his own voice and self. Interestingly, while Emerson's private self eventually won the day when he resigned as pastor of Second Church and declared himself in the first person, the individual emendations within the sermons indicate the hold of Emerson's sense of his public duties and voice on his self-identity, for quite often the private "I" is cancelled and the public "you" asserted.

Even more intriguing is Emerson's use of the public document to symbolically work out the depression, anxiety, and grief attendant with Ellen's illness — emotions that are sometimes surprisingly absent in the private journals and letters. It may be that such supercharged emotions were disarmed for him through the symbolic transformation required to present them in a public document, and that with the transformation they became more manageable than the material of the conscious self. As Judy Nolte Lensink notes of the representation of death in nineteenth-century women's diaries, metaphor and "sanctioned im-

17. Wider, "What Did the Minister Mean," 13.

ages" "obscure rather than inscribe true emotion" and "stop raw emotion from pouring out onto the page."[18] In similar ways, Emerson obscures his raw emotion by transforming the scene of Ellen's death into a sentimentalized version informed by culturally approved images and language, as when he speaks in Sermon No. CVII (on the occasion of her death) of "the pious dead" who "went down to the tomb with prayer and praise on their lips" (*CS* 3:103). Here and in similar journal accounts, the private grief appears to be absent when actually it has been camouflaged by conventional, sentimental metaphor. Moreover, much of Emerson's personal conflict is carried out in the sermons at a symbolic level that disguises the real, personal situation from the audience and the symbol maker. For instance, when he turns to the discussion of public issues such as slavery and dueling in the autumn of 1830, he finds a release for the depression that he is unable or unwilling to articulate on a more literal level. It appears on the surface that the two have nothing in common; certainly Emerson left no explicit clues to direct the reader (or himself) to read the public jeremiads as personal testaments of anxiety. Yet they both derive from common moods and motivations and provide Emerson an acceptable way to subconsciously and symbolically sublimate and manage his inner conflict. But Emerson uses metaphor and symbol in even more subtle ways, for symbol becomes not only representational but transformative as well. In Emerson's hands, the person of Ellen becomes a figure he manipulates in his own project of transformation. She becomes a cipher by which and on which he writes his own selfhood, finding his vision and identity through the agency of her figure. For Emerson, "truth and sex are linked," as indeed Michel Foucault suggests they are for everyone; the task of knowing who he is, of becoming and self-fashioning, is complicated by his love for and loss of Ellen.[19] Thus, the homiletic narrative is complicated by gender, by Emerson's masculinized reflection of Ellen, and by his construction of his own selfhood (the man-made self) from her presence and absence. Moreover, as a symbol maker and user, he increases his own power to the extent that he is able to control and

18. Lensink, *"A Secret to Be Buried,"* 381.

19. Michel Foucault, *The History of Sexuality: An Introduction,* 1:61.

manipulate the narrative of his life, to write himself, and to construct a self and a system.

Although they may provide the "moods and motivations"[20] for much that happens in the homiletic narrative, the private life and personal impulses of the minister are not the stuff of the sermons. Rather than reconstituting his personal history, of which very little is mentioned directly, Emerson derives the explicit material for his narrative from his confrontation with texts, linguistic and cultural. Events in Emerson's life that lie behind his sermons are more explicitly expressed in the layers of the journals and letters. Yet even here, the reader must often read behind and between the lines and piece together the strands from the subtexts to get at the "Meaning." When his wife lay ill and dying, an event that I believe greatly influenced his philosophy, the sermons (and sometimes the personal documents) give little *direct* evidence of his suffering. Nonetheless, Ellen's death is translated through a symbolic sublimation of the annihilation, universal and personal, that her death represents into a compensatory affirmation that puts death and pain at a distance, "depriving death of its sting" (*CS* 3:105) by asserting the immortality of the spirit in the unity of all being.

Even though Ellen's presence lies behind much that appears in Emerson's sermons and philosophy, his discourse, given its explicit and implicit purposes, is not concerned with recounting historical or biographical events. Although he later took preachers like Barzillai Frost to task for neglecting to infuse their sermons with their personal lives, Emerson himself abstained from the anecdotal and personal in his own sermons. Indeed, the historicity of Emerson's text lies not so much in the past events of his own life as in the contemporization of texts. As the sermons reveal, meaning for Emerson is a discursive and rhetorical event more than it is a historical event. Although his personal life affected his thought and writing and provided motivation for redefin-

20. Geertz's definition for a religion describes also the process of Emerson's own religion making. Geertz defines a religion as "(1) a system of symbols which acts to (2) establish powerful, pervasive, and long-lasting moods and motivations in man by (3) formulating conceptions of a general order of existence and (4) clothing these conceptions with such an aura of factuality that (5) the moods and motivations seem uniquely realistic" (*Interpretation of Cultures,* 90).

ing meaning, God, and the self, that process occurred through a hermeneutical reading and writing of texts. After all, Emerson's business was
to interpret sacred texts for his congregation and inspire them to right
living.

The Hermeneutics of Interpretation

In the late eighteenth and early nineteenth centuries a new approach
to biblical exegesis, historical hermeneutics, came into vogue among
scholars of the Bible, especially in the German universities. Influenced
by Friedrich Schliermacher, Gotthold Ephraim Lessing, Johann Gottfried Herder, and Johann Gottfried Eichhorn, this new school of biblical interpretation adopted a rationalist, objective stance as it regarded
the historical and literary dimensions of Scripture. Often called the
Higher Criticism, "the art of avoiding misunderstanding" attempted to
solve the riddles of the Bible through impartial, objective research and
to interpret Scripture in ways by which any other book would be interpreted. Herder's *Spirit of Hebrew Poetry,* for example, proposed "to set
in their true light, the obscure and misinterpreted histories of Paradise,
of the fall, of the tower of Babel, of the wrestling with the Elohim
&c." Indeed, questions of authority were posed by the Higher Critics
as they searched for the origins of such problematic texts as the Synoptic Gospels. Their conclusions were to a degree unsettling, compelling
many to rethink their theological positions. Schliermacher, for one, finally rejected the absolute authority of the Bible and emphasized the
humanity of Jesus.[21]

Into this intellectual atmosphere stepped several young men from
Harvard College, excited at the prospects for religion offered by the
German thinkers. Joseph Stevens Buckminster, Andrews Norton, The-

---

21. Gadamer, *Truth and Method,* 163. Quoted in Barbara Packer, "Origin and Au-
thority: Emerson and the Higher Criticism," 73. For a more detailed discussion
of Higher Criticism, see also Richard A. Grusin, *Transcendentalist Hermeneutics:
Institutional Authority and the Higher Criticism of the Bible;* Daniel Walker Howe,
The Unitarian Conscience: Harvard Moral Philosophy, 1805–1861; and David Robinson,
The Unitarians and the Universalists.

ALLEGHENY COLLEGE LIBRARY

odore Parker, Henry Ware Jr., and Edward Everett were among those Americans affected by the new school. Convinced that "the most important corruptions which have crept into the records of our faith have been of a character to favor an opposing system" (Trinitarianism), the young American scholars, bent on proving the validity of the Unitarian position, asserted that "the Bible is a book written for men in the language of men" and that methods to judge its authenticity should follow methods used to correctly edit and evaluate other ancient texts. William Ellery Channing declared in his 1819 Baltimore Sermon that "the existence and veracity of God, and the divine original of Christianity, are conclusions of reason, and must stand or fall with it. If revelation be at war with this faculty, it subverts itself, for the great question of its truth is left by God to be decided at the bar of reason."

Among the Americans going abroad to study was young William Emerson, older brother of Ralph Waldo, who went to pursue divinity studies under Eichhorn from 1823 to 1825. Excited about the new revolution in biblical exegesis, William wrote to Waldo on August 15, 1824: "The effect of even these few months of study I feel in every nerve of the moral frame. My moral horizon seems incredibly widened." Twelve days later he wrote again, urging Waldo to "read all of Herder you can get, and Eichhorn's critical, but not his historical works. If you have a taste for Hebrew, cherish it — if not, borrow it from Herder." But what he learned made him more a skeptic than a believer, and he eventually discontinued his theological studies when he returned home. In fact, for several thinkers, the Unitarian interpretive principles led to Transcendentalism or to what Moses Stuart called "infidelity." Nonetheless, William's letters home to Ralph Waldo, next in line for a ministerial career; the intellectual atmosphere at Harvard; and reports in the *Christian Examiner* and *Monthly Anthology* influenced young Waldo's interpretive stance toward Scripture.[22] Indeed, during the course of his min-

---

22. Howe, *The Unitarian Conscience,* cites Henry Ware Jr. (*Works* 2:238), and William Ellery Channing (*Works* 3:61) on page 91. Conrad Wright, *Three Prophets of Religious Liberalism: Channing — Emerson — Parker,* 53. Quoted in Packer, "Origin and Authority," 73. Packer cites William Emerson's letters from Germany from Karen Lynn Kalinevitch, "Ralph Waldo Emerson's Older Brother: The Letters and Journal of William Emerson." Quoted in Grusin, *Transcendentalist Hermeneutics,*

istry, Emerson's readings of the Bible became more and more radically hermeneutical.

Certainly Emerson was adept at using the interpretive principles of the Harvard Unitarians. In Sermon No. LVIII, for instance, he approaches the biblical text as if in fact it were a literary and historical document. Emerson begins this sermon about Jesus' Sermon on the Mount by asking the congregation to imagine with him the original occasion, to re-create imaginatively the historical moment at which Jesus spoke. He invites the Boston congregation to look with Jesus: "He beheld perhaps in the wide landscape the distant mountain towns, and he said a city that is set on a hill cannot be hid." Emerson is also aware that the historical situation of the author and the original audience may be lost for a later audience, thereby hindering accurate interpretation. When he explains the abrupt transitions of the Sermon, he suggests that Jesus and the multitude actually may have heard the distant "blast of a proclaiming trumpet," prompting Jesus to remark, "When thou doest thine alms do not sound a trumpet as the hypocrites do in the streets." Or that when Jesus advised, "Lay not up for yourselves treasures upon earth," he may have "alluded to recent events known to all, or perhaps to some occurrence at the moment." Emerson also considers the Sermon on the Mount as a type of literary genre, the parable, which characteristically "speaks to the most familiar relations and duties of human life in language of unquestionable authority and directness" (CS 2:97). Emerson thus appears to have assimilated the interpretive methods of the Higher Criticism, treating Scripture as a historical, cultural, and literary text whose meaning becomes clearer the more one attempts to re-create the original historical moment. This seems to be the method of his "Lord's Supper" Sermon, in which he marshals rational evidence to argue the discontinuation of the celebration of the Lord's Supper. Actually, however, Emerson is subverting both the Unitarian theological position and its interpretive method,

---

60. See Mott, *"Strains of Eloquence,"* 80, and Packer, "Origin and Authority," 72. Mott explores as crucial for Emerson's thought the problematics of authority regarding Scripture, eloquence, and the location of authority with the indwelling God.

for he uses the Higher Criticism against Unitarianism and dismisses as irrelevant belief that does not derive from his own heart. He announces to his auditors what counts for him as evidence; in so doing, he topples the structure of historical, rational hermeneutics and points the way to a hermeneutics whose aim is the interpretation not simply of texts but of the self.

As the modern thinker Hans-Georg Gadamer contends, hermeneutics is not just about the historical uncovering of texts; more important, it has to do with self-understanding, ontology, being, and the invention of new texts and new beings. While Schliermacher, Eichhorn, Herder, and the Higher Critics were concerned with correcting any misunderstanding of texts by approaching them through a scientific and objective methodology, Gadamer is concerned with the dialogue between text and interpreter and the impact that the text has on the interpreter's understanding not only of the text but also of himself. Whereas the Higher Critics perceived the task of understanding as being the recovery of the original life-world, Gadamer and Emerson illustrate that understanding is not only reconstruction but a mediation or a translation of past meaning into the present situation.[23] Unlike the kind of ultimate Ur-text that the Higher Critics believed to reside somewhere in the past, the text for Gadamer and for Emerson is a dynamic entity whose meaning changes in the dialogue between text and interpreter. For Emerson meaning, like nature, is alive, fluctuant, and symbolic. An early sermon, No. XXXIX, which invites the congregation to view the "beauty of the external world," displaces the Bible as sole or even primary text of the eternal truths and compares the work of written Scripture with that of nature. In No. XXXIX, Emerson declares that "all nature is a book on which one lesson is written, and blessed are the eyes that can read it." He suggests that meaning, like a garden, is in "constant natural process" and is derived from "some thing in us," that idiosyncratic angle of vision of the inward eye (CS 1:296–99). Both Emerson and Gadamer object to reading texts as if they were dead and their meaning unchangeable by the modern reader. In *The American*

23. Linge makes the point on page xvi of his Introduction to Gadamer's *Philosophical Hermeneutics*.

Scholar, Emerson, in his cryptic fashion, pronounced, "Each age, it is found, must write its own books." And in *Truth and Method,* Gadamer similarly notes, "Every age has to understand a transmitted text in its own way, for the text is part of the whole of the tradition in which the age takes an objective interest and in which it seeks to understand itself." For Gadamer and Emerson, then, to understand a text "does not mean primarily to reason one's way back into the past, but to have a present involvement in what is said."[24]

Moreover, the dialectic between text and interpreter is itself dynamic, experiential, and, according to Gadamer, "always involves an element of self-knowledge and constitutes a necessary side of what we call experience in the proper sense." Indeed, the auto-biographical experience that constitutes the narrative of the sermons is this kind of hermeneutical interplay between Emerson the interpreter and the texts that compose his intellectual and cultural blueprint for meaning and behavior. What becomes evident is that as the homiletic narrative progresses, the meaning of these fundamental texts changes for Emerson as he comes to newer levels of self-understanding and experiences a "change of heart." As "he belongs to the text[s] that he is reading," they belong to him in special, proprietary ways. The crucial text, "The kingdom of God is within you" (Luke 17:21) is just such a one, for in Emerson's hand, it becomes a personal and revolutionary text, and under the text's influence Emerson becomes a new being convinced of the divinity of his own nature. From his dialogue with this germinal text, a new meaning arises as he develops a philosophy of self-reliance that locates authority within the self and a new self-understanding as a potent member of the cosmos. Evidencing the kind of expanded text that hermeneutics implies, the person of Jesus becomes in Emerson's hands a "text" to be read. Like many of his fellow Unitarians, Emerson looked to the historical, and not the divine, Jesus, who served modern man as a model of moral perfection. But for Emerson, Jesus becomes also a symbol of the self's authority and eloquence. As such, Jesus is both "an end and an instrument," not only symbolizing the self's potential but also partak-

---

24. *The Complete Works of Ralph Waldo Emerson,* 1:88. Gadamer, *Truth and Method,* 263, 353.

ing transformationally in the creation or invention of a new self in Emerson's own act of (self) interpretation.[25] Imaginatively projecting the self and himself on the greater image of Jesus, Emerson seeks a translation of power from Jesus to the self, discovering in himself a new being.

Emerson's hermeneutical project in the sermons is thus twofold: to uncover the meaning of texts through a conscious methodology, and to project a new self through the fusion of his present situation with the horizon of the text in an unceasing hermeneutical circle in which understanding changes and becomes ever more self-conscious. This project of understanding is every bit as much an "event" in a life as are more physical kinds of undertakings often described in more conventional autobiographies. Emerson's text demonstrates what Gadamer means, that "reality happens . . . *within* language," for in the autobiographical narrative, reality (the tensions and resolutions of meaning and self) is contained within the circle of language and is constituted by a language-based experience that, for Emerson, was more real, finally, than physical activity. Gadamer again tells us, "To understand what the work of art [or text] says to us is therefore a self-encounter . . . [an] *experience* in a real sense and [the experience of art] must master ever anew the task that experience involves: the task of integrating it into the whole of one's own orientation to a world and one's own self-understanding."[26] As with more conventional autobiographies, Emerson's homiletic auto-biography discloses self-representation derived both from understanding and from an imaginative creation of the self. But part of what marks the difference in Emerson's auto-biography is that the experience that constitutes his personal tale is rhetorical

25. Gadamer, *Truth and Method,* 320. Insight, Gadamer claims, involves more than "the knowledge of this or that situation" but must involve self-knowledge to properly constitute an element of experience. Stanley Cavell, *In Quest of the Ordinary: Lines of Skepticism and Romanticism,* 24. Gadamer, *Truth and Method,* 304. Susanne K. Langer, *Philosophy in a New Key: A Study of the Symbolism of Reason, Rite, and Art,* 53. Langer finds the symbolic transformation of experience, by which activity is given meaning through symbols and ritual, to be an act essential to thought and that which differentiates humans from other animals. What I am suggesting, following Gadamer's lead, is that the symbol participates in the transformation of the symbol maker.

26. Gadamer, *Philosophical Hermeneutics,* 35, 101–2.

rather than historical. While the personal and passional lie behind it, providing the moods and motivations for interpretive exploration in Emerson's auto-biography, the "action" of the narrative itself is text-based.

Even so, the hermeneutical, dialectical self-transformation of Emerson's auto-biography is a risky undertaking. While conventional autobiographers have the safety of retrospection because the self-transformation recounted is an event of the past, for Emerson the self being formed is still in question. In the fluctuant process of forming a self out of the never-ending dialectic with texts, in the tentativeness, searching, questing, and questioning, the self is ever at risk, never sure of the outcome of the life story. As readers distanced by more than 160 years from the life events of Emerson's narrative, we know the degree of success that he attained via his new self. But in 1832, Emerson had no idea where his new self, his new beginnings, would lead him. The consequences of leaving the vocational and financial security of the Second Church pulpit were real to him. At stake as well throughout the narrative, not just at the end, were Emerson's "preunderstandings," which he found himself forced by his new understandings to question, reformulate, or surrender. At risk was not so much his physical well-being, though that was at times crucially fragile, as his emotional and intellectual well-being. Indeed, the very project of dialectical self-transformation entails a degree of psychic anxiety derived from the clash of personal motivations and moods with the cultural ideological program, from the moments when thought is caught between times while belief and understanding are held in temporary abeyance. The self in such a project encounters "a shattering and a demolition of the familiar," leaving the individual to flounder for a time between possible new intellectual homes. While the course of the sermons may demonstrate the foregrounding of Emerson's later Transcendentalist thought, it demonstrates also a being in search of meaning, tentatively trying out for himself and for his audience various angles of interpretation on such monumentally important questions as the life of the soul and the place of the individual in the universe. The sermons are marked by a tension of voices and purposes as Emerson not only wrestles the givens of his time but also grapples with and within himself, between the self convinced of his potential and the self convinced of his abject wretchedness. At the same time that Emerson engages in a dialectic with "texts," his own text is marked by a dialectical questioning and transformation of new understanding and new being up to the point when he can at last resolve the tenuousness of his intellectual and emotional position and declare himself a "New Man." This dramatic encounter with the textual and personal dialectics, Gadamer claims, "is not only the 'This art thou!' disclosed in a joyous and frightening shock; it also says to us; 'Thou must alter thy life!'"[27]

The following chapters offer a more detailed reading of the Emerson text, the multidimensional, auto-biographical text that reveals a being in formation. As Gadamer knew, interpretation/self-interpretation is complicated by a layering of narratives that participate in describing the constitution of the self and in constituting the self. Indeed, the Emerson manuscript demonstrates such a layering of narratives and discourses — of the body, success, self-formation, and of love and loss — that both mirror and intersect each other. Thus grief, consolation, self-formation, and self-reliance all participate in the discourse of the body and dance in their own ways around themes of attachment, union, loss, and independence. And thus public texts, the sermons themselves, and the sacred and secular texts that inform them are intersected by the private texts and moods that charge them with meaning for the reading eye. By watching, then, the changing themes and tenor of the sermons as Emerson explores the nature of evil, compensation and death, freedom, self-reliance, and character, we witness his personal transformation.

My method is hermeneutical in the old, historical sense, for I attempt to re-create the original situation by bringing together Emerson's homiletic text and the cultural and personal texts that provided him means and motivation for interpretation and self-transformation. While I certainly have come to some degree of self-understanding during this project of interpretation, my personal insight is not of interest here; it is Emerson's encounter with himself that concerns me.

27. Ibid., 38, 104.

$\mathcal{S}$in, Retribution, and the Body

"All things are double one against another. What is taken from a man in one way is made up to him in another. Nothing is given or taken without an equivalent." (*CS* 1:78)

The narrative of Emerson's journey to renewal and rebirth begins in the dark wood of the self, a landscape shaped and shaded by the hunger artists of his time and of times previous whose vision was of man's depravity and moral weakness. Emerson's own vision of man's propensity to evil and of the consequences of moral or immoral living is complicated by not only his personal sense of human nature, but also contemporary secular and sacred views that in turn were influenced by the New England Puritan heritage. Even so, Emerson learned during his quest for identity that the individual human will "moves mountains" as he willed himself to a perception of human nature vastly different from that of his early ministerial years. When Emerson told Harvard Divinity students in 1838 that "Evil is merely privative, not absolute," he not only demonstrated the power of his will but also opened the door for pervasive evaluations within the history of Emerson criticism that he had no sense of evil. Henry James Jr. said that Emerson "had no great sense of wrong—a strangely limited one, indeed for a moralist—no sense of the dark, the foul, the base." And Emerson's neighbor, Nathaniel Hawthorne, described him as a "mystic, stretching his hand out of the cloudland, in vain search for something real."[1]

What Hawthorne did not know was that the Emerson of the sermons had a sense of evil and sin almost as pervasive as his own. By the time Emerson delivered the "Divinity School Address," he had come a long way in overcoming his inherited sense of man's weakness and of the nature of the battle between good and evil. Indeed, Emerson's 1838 address demonstrates his willed re-vision as he looks beyond the temporal evidences of evil and corruption to the wider, cosmic arena in which such distinctions blur. But his sermons, particularly the earlier ones, evidence Emerson's grounding in a very old theology that preached the open warfare of the soul against the demeaning temptations of the flesh. When the young minister asked in 1826, "Whence then is evil?" in Sermon No. II (*CS* 1:64), he knew that it resided in the human heart, blighting and marking it as with a brand, and he warned the congregation of the temptations and consequences of sin that were very real to him, both personally and theologically. Emerson not only could declare in his journal, "There *is* a huge & disproportionate abundance of *evil* on earth" (*JMN* 2:115), but also could find the proclivity to moral weakness in himself. In 1824 when he described himself as "the Neophyte who wears this garment of scarlet sin," as "a lover of indolence, & of the belly," and dedicated himself to "the service of God & the War against Sin" (*JMN* 2:241), he acknowledged the darker side of human existence, the perversions of human nature, that he enlisted to combat in his ministry and in his own soul. The outcome of this confrontation was the self-willed formation of not just character, but also a new, empowered self that looked beyond evil to the infinite possibilities of the self. The transformation of his attitude about evil

1. *Complete Works,* 1:124. Quoted in Newton Arvin, "The House of Pain," 47. Arvin makes a similar comparison between Emerson and Hawthorne but concludes that Emerson's "animadversions on human wickedness, like his allusions to human suffering, are closer to the circumference than to the center of Emerson's thought" (51–53). What Arvin misses is that it is only by an act of will that Emerson's sense of evil is pushed outward to the circumference of his vision. On this troublesome issue of Emerson's concept of evil, Joel Porte finds his "quasi-orthodox adherence to notions of innate depravity and the Fall" to be "a bothersome undertone" (*Representative Man: Ralph Waldo Emerson in His Time,* 171).

and compensation from the 1826 remarks to those of 1838 demonstrates in part the transformation of his vision and sense of self revealed in the auto-biographical narrative.

The "Bosom Sin"

Unknown to most readers of his later essays who, like James, find a "strangely limited" sense of wrong, there is an Emerson who lurks in the dimness of forgotten sermons, not daring to wander into the savage silence of the forest, afraid of the unrestrained passions and of facing the "bosom sin" (CS 3:60) that he knew to reside in each person. Had he been a storyteller instead of a minister as a young man, he might have written a tale of two lovers whose sin burned in their hearts. Like the scarlet A embroidered on the gown of Hester Prynne for all to see and the scarlet A secretly branded on the bosom of the Reverend Dimmesdale, there is for Emerson a brand that tells the guilt and punishes the sin of moral transgressors, for a "record of each transaction is faithfully transcribed in the bosom" of the guilty (CS 1:80). Sharing with Hawthorne an inheritance that understood the innate weakness of the human will, Emerson also understood the grim consequences of sin, that its mark was a brand not only on the heart but also on the character, searing and disfiguring it. As if he were speaking of Dimmesdale, in the sermon of June 17, 1827, Emerson declares:

> Alas, he did not see that in the moment he reached out his hand to that evil act that moment his transgression was visited upon him. He was forsaken by his own innocence, which was a wall of defence about him. The barrier which was built between him and destruction is broken down and he is free to walk in the broad road of Ruin. Alas, my friends, a deep, a dire compensation is made for every transgression, for every unjust advantage that man can take of man. The compensation is this, that the strong checks of religion have lost their force and though he believes he shall not sin again, . . . he will prosecute his downward course till it is plain to man as to the angels of God that he is fallen. (CS 1:81)

In his sermons, Emerson, like Hawthorne, understands the individual's liability to sin, to give in to the passions, and just as well, to commit the same error again. His remarks to his congregation are reminiscent not only of the forest scene before the beginning of *The Scarlet Letter* but also of the scene when Hester and Dimmesdale, for a moment, wildly propose to flee the confines of the community and commit again the sin for which they have already been branded. And just as it is plain, Emerson says, to the angels that man is fallen, so in Hawthorne's tale it is plain to Pearl that the Black Man set his mark on Dimmesdale's heart. The intemperate passions of the body, at war with the restraints of religion and society, constitute the drama of Hawthorne's tale just as surely as they constitute the human drama that perplexed the young Emerson.

Emerson played out this drama on the terrain of the body, through a nineteenth-century public rhetoric of the body that both shaped and mirrored his own sense of sin. For Emerson and his contemporaries, the body, with its passions and appetites, constituted both the agency and the register of sin. Wary of the untamed terrain of the self (as well as of the environment), Emerson followed his contemporaries in advocating a morality of control and self-denial. As Carroll Smith-Rosenberg argues, the American nineteenth century was a time of obsession with "categorizing the physical, and especially the sexual" and an "ocean of sexual words . . . rhythmically beat" against discussion of the self. While this discourse may in fact emphasize a language of the body, the aim was not so much erotic as prescriptive, to advocate control, denial, and negation of the body. In doing so, "the opinion setters, . . . male physicians, publishers, educators, and religious leaders," constructed a theology and morality that focused on the body, finding the bosom sin to be one of appetite and indulgence, and morality to be a matter largely of temperance and self-control. Thus when Emerson preaches, "Temptation never ceases. Our passions never relax their hold. Our appetites are never satisfied" (CS 1:167), he is reiterating not only the Puritan inheritance but also the message heard from various sources that the body and its appetites are to be distrusted, that he who gratifies his appetites commits a sin and will receive due compensation, whether in this world or in the one to come. Part of the blueprint for reading the self, this rhetoric of self-distrust, restraint, and reform echoed and managed Emerson's own rhetoric and sense of self. Like the moral advisers of the day, Emerson urged not only resistance to temptation but also a practiced self-denial and the development of habits that would form a character lean and spare and strong. Although, as David Robinson argues, the Unitarians' awareness of evil informed a reading of life as trial and probation and the corresponding call for self-culture, it is also apparent that many liberal Christians shared with their more Calvinistic contemporaries a wider range of discomfort encoded in metaphors of the untamed self.[2]

Advice literature of the early nineteenth century suggests that the body and its appetites presented a clear threat to all that was deemed rational and spiritual, and threatened to "chain . . . down . . . the noble appetites of the soul" (*JMN* 2:88). This sort of "dualistic habit of thought," which dichotomized human nature into binary oppositions and a subsequent war against the self, articulated a version of human nature that privileged and valorized human characteristics that the male opinion setters took to be theirs. Within this rhetoric of control, public and private assessments of morality and selfhood were shaped in gendered terms. A masculinist reading of human nature, it preached the gendered dichotomy of mind and body. Rather than involve the self in an integration of human powers and properties, it sought spiritual affirmation through the negation of the body. This is a masculinist theology not simply because it derives from a male-dominated religious tradition, but also because it so explicitly equates that which is deemed positive, spirit and mind, with the masculine and that which is deemed negative, the body and moral weakness, with the feminine. Feminist thealogian Carol Christ argues that "men have organized dualisms hierarchically and have associated themselves with the positive sides of the dualisms — spirit, freedom, reason, and soul — while relegating women to the negative sides of the dualisms — nature, emotion, irrationality, and the body."[3] By associating themselves with the positive sides, men perpetuate and justify their position of power in social and spiritual matters, in part by celebrating manliness. In characteristic fashion, Em-

2. Carroll Smith-Rosenberg, *Disorderly Conduct: Visions of Gender in Victorian America*, 91, 25. CS 1:4.

3. Carol P. Christ, *Laughter of Aphrodite: Reflections on a Journey to the Goddess*, 142. Carol P. Christ, *Diving Deep and Surfacing: Women Writers on Spiritual Quest*, 25. The term *thealogian* is one Christ uses to define herself as a female theologian, from the Greek thea, meaning goddess.

erson, too, associates self-denial and bravery with manliness and godliness, and denotes the weak and self-serving impulse that keeps individuals from Sabbath worship as a "degenerate effeminacy" (*CS* 1:106).

Into this dualistic frame of mind, which informed cultural and hence individual formulations of the self and of the dynamics of morality, Unitarians like Emerson embedded their own notions of the self, character formation, and compensation. Writing first to himself in his journal and then to the Second Church Congregation in Sermon No. LXIII, Emerson noted, "Self Denial is only one form of expression for perfection of the moral character" (*JMN* 3:175, *CS* 2:129). Such a spirit of negation urged more than just the transcendence of the body and nature; it also involved individuals in a program of self-denial that was often deleterious to their health but that promised sanctity, moral power, and an empowering self-concept.

Like his contemporaries, Emerson publicly and privately equated human appetite with weakness, and self-control with sanctity. Throughout his journal run not only a distrust of the "Belly," the locus of so much "lust" and "bad direction" (*JMN* 3:277), and diatribes against the debilitating influence of temptation and pleasure, but also scattered experiments at curbing his own dinner in an attempt to raise his intellectual or spiritual sensibilities. Playing out the rhetoric of morality on his own body, Emerson's anorexic reaction to his physical self registers in his efforts to disengage himself from the body and to define and fashion himself as a man of the mind. In April 1824, he reminded himself "to curtail my dinner & supper sensibly & rise from table each day with an appetite; & see if it be fact that I can understand more clearly" (*JMN* 2:240). Here he suggests that clear thinking is inconsistent or even impossible with a full belly. Later, in March and April 1832, he again experimented in mastering his appetite by diminishing his food intake, this time in a gambit to gain "personal purity":

> 28 March my food per diem weighed 14 1/4 oz
> 29---   ---13 oz
>   2 April   12 1/2
>   (*JMN* 4:6)[4]

---

4. Grusin, *Transcendentalist Hermeneutics,* also discusses this "diet plan for the self" in terms of Emerson's efforts to avoid excess and gain a clearer understanding

Though his trial did not last long, it demonstrates his conviction that moral worth and character are equated with self-mastery and the individual's ability to transcend the unmanning appetites of the flesh. Finding that "a man's enemies are those of his own household. . . . slothful sensual indulgence . . . and that when he has overleaped this, God has set no bounds to his progress" (*JMN* 2:112), Emerson practiced and preached a version of the self that pitted "the man of passion" against "the man of principle" (*JMN* 3:129).

Interconnected with this dichotomization of the human being, then, is a strategy to shape an empowered self, and in the lexicon of success — spiritual and material — the terms "body," "temptation," and "sin" are correlated with weakness, while "mind," "soul," "virtue," and "sanctity" are associated with manliness and power. Indeed, manliness and power are themselves compensations for self-denial and virtue. The word "power" (and its derivatives such as "energy" and "strength") is one of the most frequently used words in the literature of morality and success, appearing, for instance, eight times in two paragraphs of Emerson's Sermon No. IX, about the nature of man and the "power of the soul" (*CS* 1:116). Dancing around issues of attachment and detachment, Emerson makes clear the correlation between the body and power/ sanctity when he asks "whether the greatest pleasure was not found to consist in overcoming pleasure" (*CS* 1:118). As in No. IX, morality and the consequent compensations for living either a life of "passion" or a life of "principle" are both worked out on the terrain of the body, the self one shapes, and in the rhetoric of the body.

The "Master Narrative"

It is apparent, then, that Emerson's personal sense of weakness and his public pronouncements about sin, especially in the early years of his ministry, were informed and shaped by the cultural texts and definitions of sin, compensation, manliness, and power. What will become equally

---

and purity. As I do in chapter 3, Grusin also notes its proximity to Emerson's visit to Ellen's tomb and suggests, "In the mirror of his wife's remains, Emerson was reminded that a ledgered temperance is one 'whose root is intemperance'" (33–39).

apparent is that by the end of his ministry, Emerson had reshaped to some extent those definitions, freeing himself not only from the body but also from the rhetoric of the body.[5] As David Reynolds has suggested, "during the American Renaissance literariness resulted not from a *rejection* of socioliterary context but rather from a full *assimilation* and *transformation* of key images and devices from this context." The extent of Emerson's participation in this kind of assimilation and translation of the "master narrative"[6] is evinced in the sermons as he first echoes the conventionalities of his time and then transforms them according to his vision of universal correspondences and the potential of the man-made self.

This master narrative told over and over again a gendered and bodied story of morality and compensation, of the difficulties and consequences of engagement and disengagement with the physical self. In language that is at the same time moral and masculine, this cultural narrative provided a pervasive discourse of the body that figures in the texts of individual authors. A few examples from the early nineteenth century demonstrate the terms and perimeter of this discourse, which combines practical and moral advice about successful living. Archibald Alexander warned in Edwardsian strains of the "deep depravity" of the human heart with its "innumerable evils" and of "the horrible pit" that awaits the sinner. Advising his audience of young men, "Set your affections on things above and not on things on the earth," he suggested that they "cultivate humble penitence, and exercise daily self-denial." Similarly, Joseph Allen, in an 1829 lecture titled "The Sources of

5. Though as Robinson, *Apostle of Culture,* points out, Emerson never escaped the dualism of body and spirit even as he devised a theology of unity. Nor did he ever escape a conviction of his own imperfection (26, 29). See also Porte, *Representative Man,* 295, for a similar analysis of the role of duality and self-distrust in Emerson's thought.

6. David Reynolds, *Beneath the American Renaissance: The Subversive Imagination in the Age of Emerson and Melville,* 7. Reynolds demonstrates that "far from being estranged from their context," American authors "were in large part created by it" (3). Fredric Jameson, *The Political Unconscious: Narrative as a Socially Symbolic Act,* 34, argues that "master narratives have inscribed themselves in the texts as well as in our thinking about them" and are "a persistent dimension of literary and cultural texts precisely because they reflect a fundamental dimension of our collective thinking and our collective fantasies about history and reality."

Public Prosperity," warned his congregation of the "torments of a guilty conscience, and the wrath of a just and holy God." He also advised them to establish "regular habits of industry and thrift" as means to leading a virtuous, happy, and useful life and avoiding "effeminacy and corruption of morals." Regular habits of self-denial will save the individual not only from a debilitating "effeminacy," which is likened here to moral corruption, but also from the torments of the conscience and the wrath of God. Indeed, Alexander paints a grisly picture of the guilty man's moral callousness when he says that repeated transgression has caused the conscience to be "seared as with a hot iron."[7] Like Alexander, other moralists figure the conscience as one of God's mechanisms for guiding and enforcing virtue, as an internal agent whose task is to deliver the "higher" self from the gross consumption of and by the physical self.

While William Ellery Channing, the spokesman for Unitarianism, preached man's likeness to God, encouraging the individual to be true to his "own highest convictions" and to unfold his spiritual nature "by right and vigorous exertion," the *Christian Examiner,* Unitarianism's official journal, reported "that we are so affected by our constitution, that we sin as soon as we can, and do nothing else." Sounding more Calvinistic than Unitarian, the reviewer for the *Christian Examiner* argued that we suffer by our inheritance from Adam. His seems not to be an idiosyncratic view of human nature, for throughout the *Christian Examiner* during the period of Emerson's ministry, the journal's contributors, despite Channing's optimism, demonstrate a distrust of inherent human nature, urging the vigilant avoidance of sin and the cultivation of habits of self-discipline and self-denial. An article appearing in the July 1830 issue of the *Christian Examiner* makes clear the distrust of the human impulses and the power of sublimation, themes pervasive in the literature of the period:

> *Conscience,* then, is that principle in man, which is manifested, first, by an impulse or desire to exert all the strength of his will, in pre-

7. Archibald Alexander, *A Sermon, preached to the Chapel of Nassau Hall,* 27–28, 35. Joseph Allen, *The Sources of Public Prosperity, a Discourse Delivered in Northborough, April 9, 1829, on the Day of the Public Fast,* 10–11, 15. Alexander, *A Sermon,* 11.

venting his *appetites* from interfering with the attainment of the greatest perfection and happiness, and then, by feelings of pain and pleasure adapted to the degree in which that impulse has been obeyed or neglected. The appetites, so far as they are opposed to the monitions of conscience, we call temptations. The willing obedience of man to his own conscience, we call virtue; and the willful disobedience, we call sin.

Conscience, then, in bidding us to restrict the animal propensities by voluntary effort, does not tend to impair, but to enlarge our real power and freedom.[8]

Clearly the author of this piece links virtue and sin to the denial or gratification of the body's appetites and employs the conscience as the monitor and judge of wrongdoing. Just as clear, he finds the sublimation of the body to be self-willed and empowering. The individual not only avoids or effects either retribution or reward as a result of moral decisions, but also participates in the formation of his own character by individual decisions to deny or gratify the appetites. Indeed, the character formed through the series of moral decisions is in and of itself ample compensation, one way or another. As a later article makes more evident, "We all are, under God, intellectually, the makers of ourselves."[9] Like the economic myth of the self-made man, which stressed the individual's ability to form his material success, the religious version emphasized man's role as maker of his own character and hence of his spiritual success. In both versions, success derives from individual effort and is achieved through similar means of self-discipline and regular habits of industry and temperance. And with both, the bottom line is power, the power that money buys and "our real power" that the life of the mind purchases at the cost of the natural self.

This conflation of morality and economics in the popular literature is evident in the advice that Joel Hawes gives his readers. Hawes, a Presbyterian minister and author of success manuals for young men, warned his readers against the temptations and dangers that young men

8. William Ellery Channing, *William Ellery Channing: Selected Writing,* 244, 146. *Christian Examiner* 4:1 (1827): 78. *Christian Examiner* New Series, 9 (1830): 270.

9. *Christian Examiner* New Series, 6 (1832): 299.

meet, especially in the city. In his book *Lectures to Young Men, on the Formation of Character* (1829), Hawes asserts that those who do not have the firmness to resist temptation "fall in with the mass of corruption around them, and go to swell the monstrous tide of depravity and dissipation, which is rolling, as a mighty desolation, over the cities of our land." He insists on the necessity of establishing an "unbending regard to rectitude and duty" and the need to resist such temptations as pleasure: "It is utterly inconsistent with all manliness of thought and action" and "forms a character of effeminacy and feebleness." For Hawes, as for the other writers of advice manuals, the pleasures of the body are to be firmly resisted by adhering to habits of self-discipline.[10]

The anonymous author of *The Young Man's Own Book,* a more thoroughly secular and business-oriented advice manual, articulates in less religious language the same precepts: the need for habits of industry and thrift and the unmanning consequences of pleasure and indolence. In rather practical terms, he advises his young readers to establish habits of temperance regarding drink, food, dress, conversation, and economics. He tells his readers to "banish sloth, and an inordinate love of ease; active minds only being fit for employments, and none but the industrious either deserving, or having a possibility to thrive."[11] Here he converts the religious message of virtue into an economic one of getting ahead in the world. But the idea is the same: success, which is equated with power and manliness, is self-made and involves, more than anything, self-denial and right principles of living.

Indeed, as another advice writer, Hubbard Winslow, asserts, principles "are your only protection against the exposures incident to the passions and temptations of youth." Furthermore, adherence to moral and industrious principles will develop character, which, as Isaac Taylor notes, is "of more value than luck, fortune, or even talent." In the world of business, character has a market value, for it opens "the gates of opportunity" and "is a ready passport into society." Hawes makes even clearer both the immediate and future compensations for a good character when he says, "Character is power; character is influence; . . . [it]

10. Joel Hawes, *Lectures to Young Men, on the Formation of Character,* 41, 80, 69, 84.
11. *The Young Man's Own Book,* 134.

opens for him a sure and easy way to wealth, to honor and happiness. . . . On the character you are now forming hangs your own eternal destiny."[12] According to these writers, character is a redeemable commodity, good for influence, money, power, and even eternal salvation. The compensation for living a life of abstinence and hard work is success, temporal and eternal.

The Fragmented Self

These descriptions of the self and prescriptions for morality and success also made their way into the private domain of the self, contributing to a bifurcated and anxiety-ridden sense of self and to a self-identity shaped to some degree by the public discourse. That the messages from these cultural texts impinged on individual self-concept is attested to by the level of anxiety and self-doubt in private texts. Young men warring with passion and indolence in the race to success, Donald Scott observes, paid a "heavy tax of anxiety" and felt psychically whipped about by the world and by their "acute self-preoccupation."[13]

This anxiety resonates in the journals of Waldo Emerson as he questions his own place in the world. Urged by his era to seek material success, he worries that his abilities are below his ambition. But wary of the physical quality of that success, he also questions his embroilment in worldly concerns, which, he wrote, "are choked with evils" (*JMN* 3:103). His ardent search for success and subsequent feelings of inadequacy, as well as his doubts about ambition, are framed in the discourse of morality and figured on the image of the body — the human body and the social body. A passage in his journal dated September 1823 clearly shows the link in Emerson's mind between success and

12. Hubbard Winslow, *The Young Man's Aid to Knowledge, Virtue, and Happiness*, 73. Isaac Taylor, *Character Essential to Success in Life. Addressed to those Who Are Approaching Manhood*, 36, 38, 49. Hawes, *Lectures to Young Men*, 111–16.

13. Donald M. Scott, *From Office to Profession: The New England Ministry, 1750–1850*, 79–80. Scott tells us that the generation coming of age after 1815 was a "dislocated generation, forced to strike out on its own" without the resources of family or clear-cut institutions to guide them. They were a troubled generation who often referred to life "as a scramble, a treacherous maze, a whirlwind" (78–79).

self-denial and the potent force of the public rhetoric. In a much-quoted section of the entry's first paragraph, Emerson muses, "The dreams of my childhood are all fading away & giving place to some very sober & very disgusting views of a quiet mediocrity of talents & condition." Here he appears to be a young man high on ambition, longing to make his mark in the world, who discovers that his talents are at best mediocre. He seems to blame his talents and inherent abilities for his lack of success. Yet it goes against the democratic grain and the cult of the self-made man to rely on inherited goods and advantages rather than those of one's own making.[14] And in the next paragraph, Emerson commences a diatribe against young men who forfeit their place in the world, their "rights & claims on the universe," because "the ordinary temptations of indolence, of sensual gratification, return upon them. . . . They forget for a long & weary interval that to eat, & to drink, & to lie down in sleep is not the life of man but the life of swine" (*JMN* 2:153–54). Attempting to assert his claim on the universe, Emerson paradoxically seeks to empower the self by splitting it, setting the mind in conflict with the body, whose basic needs, to say nothing of its lusts, are described as demeaning, unmanning, and swinish. Speaking more of himself than of other men, Emerson blames not inherent talents or excessive debauchery for shortcomings, but everyday activities needed to sustain the life of the body. In an earlier 1823 entry, he likewise spoke of his ambitions and personal faults in the familiar terms of the body, blaming indolence, sloth, and sensual indulgence for barring success from him. Moreover, like the advocates for moral self-cultivation, he holds the self accountable for the character he forms and hence for his fate:

> Every young man is prone to be misled by the suggestions of his own ill founded ambition which he mistakes for the promptings of a secret Genius, and thence dreams of an unrivaled greatness. More intercourse with the world and closer acquaintance with his own faults wipes out from his fancy every trace of this majestic dream. . . . Nev-

---

14. Taylor, for one, makes this point in *Character Essential* when he addresses the youth who thinks his success depends on talent: "But with all his ability, he will find, if he neglects character, no talents can bear him up for any continuance" (42).

ertheless it is not Time nor Fate nor the World that is half so much
his foe as the demon Indolence within him. . . . But if a man shall
diligently consider what it is which most forcibly impedes the natural
greatness of his mind, he will assuredly find that slothful sensual indulgence is the real unbroken barrier, and that when he has overleaped this, God has set no bounds to his progress. . . We boast of
our free agency. What is this but to say God has put into our hands
the elements of our character, . . . to choose & to fashion them as we
will. (*JMN* 2:112)

At once claiming for himself the ability to shape the self, Emerson also
plays out the dialectic of morality and power on the individual body
rather than on time or fate or the world, asserting his power to overcome the pull of the body and to fashion himself as a man of the mind.

Indeed, Emerson learned from experience that this confrontation
with the self is in large part enacted in, and on, the form of the individual, as he witnessed the ascendancy of the mind over the body in his
own fights with tuberculosis, lameness, and blindness in his early years.
In 1825 he suffered a rheumatic lameness in his hip, difficulties with
his lungs, and failing eyesight, and was forced to postpone his divinity
studies. Instead, he retreated to his Uncle Ladd's farm "to try the experiment of hard work for the benefit of my health."[15] Then in the autumn
of 1826, just when he had been approbated to preach, he had to postpone his ambition because of ill health. In fact, the situation was so
desperate that after experiencing "lung complaints" (*L* 1:176), he decided to spend the winter in the South, the usual treatment for tuberculosis during the nineteenth century, going first to Charleston and then
on to balmier St. Augustine when his health still did not improve. He
had to defer his plans to find a permanent church home until his lungs
could stand the strain of preaching. Indeed, he spent the better part of
the next year guarding his health, writing sermons, and filling tempo-
rarily vacant pulpits. He wrote his brother William in February 1828, a

15. Quoted in Gay Wilson Allen, *Waldo Emerson*, 84. For a more complete discussion of the nature of Emerson's illness, see Evelyn Barish, *Emerson: The Roots of
Prophesy,* where she lays to rest the notions that Emerson's bouts with illness were
merely psychosomatic, a case that Allen, for one, makes in *Waldo Emerson*. Barish
contends that Emerson suffered from an indolent form of tuberculosis.

little more than a year after his trip South, "I am writing sermons. I am living cautiously yea treading on eggs to strengthen my constitution. It is a long battle this of mine betwixt life & death & tis wholly uncertain to whom the game belongs" (*L* 1:227).

Face-to-face with the finitude of being, Emerson knew that a practiced self-discipline ensured success — and life — and that the weakness of the body must be overcome to live a life of the mind. Moreover, he learned philosophically and personally that there is a law of compensation: "What is taken from a man in one way is made up to him in another" (*CS* 1:78). He knew very well that the responsibility for maintaining his health and attaining position in the world lay solely with himself. Unlike his brothers Edward and Charles, who rushed headlong after ambition and ruined their health, sending themselves to early graves with their ambitions unmet, Waldo knew that to live "cautiously" would in the end secure his life. Living "productively most of his life with a body riddled by a frequently mortal disease," Emerson proved to himself the power of his will and the validity of self-denial.[16]

The Body in the Sermons

The lessons that he learned from his own life and from the public rhetoric, and that he inscribed in his personal journal, Emerson transcribes to his sermons. He preached much that was already familiar to his first congregations, and he often echoed conventional discussions and tropes pertaining to temptation, retribution, and manliness. As in his private documents, Emerson infuses his sermons with the rhetoric and image of the body, spelling out sin as a bodied intemperance and prescribing a morality of self-denial and control, a refashioning of the body through habit, industry, and temperance. As he warns of sin, he also warns of the consequences of sin. This he does in fairly materialistic terms at first, arguing a direct correlation between act and result, figuring a physical compensation of direct reward or punishment, and embodying compensation in the character that the individual forms. That

16. Barish, *Roots of Prophecy*, 184.

these solutions are not quite satisfactory to him is evidenced in the tentativeness of his discussions about compensation and the beginning of his move inward to the conscience, to finding compensation within, rather than only through external evidences of character, success, or otherworldly reward. In various ways the sermons demonstrate his increasing discomfort with not only the body but also the figure of the body, as Emerson disengages himself and his philosophy from the external and spirals inward to find meaning within.

Following the lead of his contemporaries, then, and echoing the personal humiliation and self-condemnation found in his private journals, the Reverend Emerson preached that "at our best estate we are imperfect and frail" (*CS* 1:70). Unlike his later essays and their "strangely limited" sense of evil,[17] Emerson's early sermons convincingly address the role of sin in human life and the need to form a saving character by resisting temptation. He warns his audience that we learn vice with a "fatal facility" beyond our capacity for learning good, for society teaches more readily the lessons of vice than those of moral behavior (*CS* 1:72). In Sermon No. XVII he warns his congregation, "Temptation never ceases. Our passions never relax their hold. Our appetites are never satisfied. Pleasure never forgets to swing her baits before our eyes."

Calling upon the Fast Day congregation of April 3, 1828, to repent and change their ways, Emerson nonetheless acknowledges that the basic nature of man has not changed over the centuries, that "here he stands, the same being God made in the garden; he has not lost one passion, nor parted with one frailty" (*CS* 1:169). Emerson clearly links human frailties with "human passions" (*CS* 1:169) and appetites, and advises a sublimation of the demands of the body through self-denial, of which fasting constitutes an important cultural example and experience. Finding that intemperance is "unmanning" and leaves the transgressor bloated and in a "swinish sleep," Emerson in Sermon No. XXIV preaches self-command and the practice of such habits as industry, humility, fortitude, and self-restraint "that we should have all our appetites and passions under controul" (*CS* 1:210). Like his fellow ministers and the promoters of the myth of success, he preaches complete control and

17. Quoted in Arvin, "House of Pain," 47.

abstinence, for he distrusts the individual's ability to indulge the body even moderately. He says:

> Passion takes us at unawares; carries us by surprize — in a moment, and then we sit hours and years deploring the consequences of obeying an extravagant impulse. Now herein consists the value of self command. Let us learn to master ourselves for that brief interval — to keep the rebel eye and hand and tongue, as under bars of steel for one important moment, till reason shall have time to decide. (*CS* 1:212)

This passage clearly demonstrates the war between the body and mind, and the necessity of a strict regimen of self-control to repress even the momentary impulses and moderate indulgences of the body. Indeed, Emerson likens the mind to a jailer who must forcibly restrain the unruly body. Implicit in the exhortation to exert self-control is a definition of manliness that locates power in the resistance to, and sublimation of, the demands or impulses of the body. Inherent also in this reading of mankind is the belief that the individual makes his own character just as he makes his own economic success. Spiritualizing the notion of the self-made man, Emerson states that "our character is in our own hands" and that, "What we are depends on what we do" (*CS* 1:211–12). Moreover, just as the individual is responsible for forming character, so too is he held accountable for it.[18]

But just how individuals are punished and rewarded for their actions and the mess they make of their lives is problematic for the young minister, and the sermons suggest that he tested various theories of compensation before he finally arrived at a settled definition with which he could feel comfortable. He knew that somehow, "All things are double one against another"; that a system of balances existed whereby the assets and debits of this world would be computed in a "balance of figures" in the "ledger" kept by God (*CS* 1:78–79).[19] But in the early

18. See Cayton, *Emerson's Emergence*, 44, for further discussion on accountability in Emerson's ethics.

19. Barish, *Roots of Prophesy*, points to Hume's *The Natural History of Religion* as an influence on Emerson's notions about compensation (156). The passage she quotes from Hume does have the ring of Emerson's articulations about balance: "a universal compensation prevails in all conditions of being and existence." But

years, his sense of the mechanisms for making just compensations fluctuated and shifted rather freely.

One way of addressing the dilemma of compensation is to claim that the deeds committed and decisions made in this world will effect results also of this world. In the myth of the self-made man, which looks to material and temporal success as a primary goal in life, the immediate link between deed and result seems to be a necessary corollary. As the promoters of the myth of success suggest, compensation is made in this world, for he who works hard and diligently and at the same time forms a good character will be rewarded with happiness, health, and monetary success. Echoing and secularizing a biblical passage used recurrently in Emerson's sermons, "whatsoever a man soweth, that shall he also reap" (Galatians 6:7), Daniel Wise in *The Young Man's Counsellor,* for instance, warns his young readers:

> Indulge your appetites, gratify your passions, neglect your intellect, foster wrong principles, cherish habits of idleness, vulgarity, dissipation, and in the after years of manhood you will reap a plentiful crop of corruption, shame, degradation, and remorse; . . . But if you control your appetites, subdue your passions, firmly adopt and rigidly practice right principles, form habits of purity, propriety, sobriety and diligence, your harvest will be one of honor, health[,] happiness."[20]

Emerson too finds a direct and temporal correlation between action and result when in his first sermon, "Pray without Ceasing," he asserts that all prayers will be answered. Inspired by discussions with a Methodist laborer on his Uncle Ladd's farm, Emerson suggests that in one way or another our "prayers are granted." To make this assertion, he expands the usual meaning of the term "prayer" to include "the daily, hourly, momentary desires" of the soul and assigns to man the power and ability to effect those prayers. Thus he says, "And will not the votary of other lusts, the lover of animal delight, . . . who loveth meats and drinks, soft raiment and the wine . . . surrender himself over to

---

while Emerson certainly did read Hume, I would suggest that the origins of Emerson's theory were more cultural than literary.

20. Daniel Wise, *The Young Man's Counsellor: or, Sketches and Illustrations of the Duties and Dangers of Young Men,* 16–17.

the last damning debauchery." Like the myth purveyors, he finds the individual accountable for his life, for "God so furnished us with powers of body and of mind that we can acquire whatsoever we seriously and unceasingly strive after" (*CS* 1:57–58). In other words, God grants us our secret wishes in that he has given us the power to achieve them. Compensations are the results of choices made and actions taken by humans and do not here involve a participant God who changes the course of history. Thus the person who lusts after wine will indeed get wine and its consequent moral and physical debilities, and he who strives after greatness will achieve it. But this is rather a simplistic and unsatisfying notion of compensation because it does not take into account the realities of life, that morality is not always a necessary requisite for success and that deeds and consequences are not always obviously and clearly linked. Indeed, as Emerson realized even in this first sermon, balances are not always figured in apparent ways. Struck by the seeming incongruities of life — "A being come from the author of all good with a machinery of faculties in him which, being put in operation, go in discord, and the result is unhappiness" (*CS* 1:63) and that often "poor struggling worth [is] rewarded only with worth" (*CS* 1:61) — Emerson attempts in Sermon No. I to reconcile these incongruities.

To make up for the shortfall in what seemed at first to be a psychologically sound argument, Emerson reverts to a more traditional rendition of compensation near the end of the sermon: rewards and punishments will be carried out in the afterlife. Thus he evidences a confusion apparent in other moral advisers about the time and location of compensation, looking both to this world and to the one to come for rewards and punishments. He articulates the very spirit of revenge that he would later criticize in "Compensation" (1841) and that Nietzsche would excoriate in *On the Genealogy of Morals* as the vengeance engendered by temporal impotence. Jonathan Bishop argues that in his later ideas on compensation, Emerson "dismisses the need for another world to make good the injustice of this"; but in this early sermon, Emerson nonetheless participates in a rather traditional Christian economy of power whereby the powerful but corrupt suffer eternal torment and the meek inherit the blessings of heaven. Whereas "Compensation" is a criticism of Christian compensation as, in David Jacobson's words, "no more than a reactionary revaluation of the real power of the world," Emerson the young minister sounds much like the minister parodied in the 1841 essay. In his first sermon he preaches that the evil-doers will finally be tormented by their own appetites and "gnawing lusts," which will have "coiled themselves with a serpent's trail" into their soul. That "great class of human beings who in every age turned aside from temptation to pursue the bent of moral nature shall now [in heaven] have *their* interests consulted" (*CS* 1:61). Emerson's articulation of otherworldly revenge as a mode of compensation may be due to the tentative nature of his definition of compensation in the first years of his ministry. But it is also surely indicative of the "condition of impotence" inherent in such a reading of compensation, for it indicates that one way to empower the self is to transfer power away from the powerful, even if to a location and time out of this world. That this answer, too, is not completely satisfying to Emerson is revealed in his later essay, which finds the fallacy of such a view of compensation to lie in its eventual gratification of worldly appetites and in its "deferring to the base estimate of the market of what constitutes a manly success."[21]

Actually, the difference between finding retribution either in a life of debauchery and financial ruin or in eternal torment is not as incongruous as it may at first appear, for both theories of compensation presuppose that polar universe, "All things are double one against another," in which balances exist and can be realized. Compensations *for* the type of character formed can be made materially or spiritually, now or in the eternal future. Hawes put the matter succinctly when he told the young men of Hartford and New Haven that character *"opens . . . a sure and easy way to wealth, to honor and happiness"* and that *"On the character you are now forming hangs your own eternal destiny."*[22] Emerson suggests not only that one's character determines the outcome of events but also that

21. Nietzsche "credits" the Jews with inverting the aristocratic value equation and asserting that the weak, rather than the powerful, are blessed in God's eyes in *On the Genealogy of Morals* in *Basic Writings of Nietzsche*, ed. Walter Kaufmann, 470. Jonathan Bishop, *Emerson on the Soul*, 73. David Jacobson, "'Compensation': Exteriority beyond the Spirit of Revenge," 110, 112. *Complete Works*, 2:95.

22. Hawes, *Lectures to Young Men*, 112, 116.

the compensation may *be* the character itself; the self becomes the prayer answered. Indeed, it is within the individual character that the material, spiritual, temporal, and eternal conditions of compensation are reconciled, and that the individual is held accountable for the created self.

Echoing a Lockean account of human nature as malleable and formed by experience, Emerson notes in Sermon No. XXIV that man is not born with character but builds it during his life: "What we are depends on what we do" (*CS* 1:211). Emerson knew that out of the choices made and wishes granted, each person forms his own character and that the character formed is a remuneration in and of itself. He preached that "every individual transgression has stamped its impress on your character" (*CS* 1:62) and stated, "We can, as we choose, be trained into angels or deformed into fiends" (*CS* 1:229). Implicit in this reading of the self-made man of morality is the dual notion that the individual has the freedom to form his life, to make decisions that shape not only immediate, mundane goals but also his eternal being, and that one's outcome and character are determined by habits of thought and living. Arguing that there is in nature a firm foundation for the doctrine of Election, that God does not love all but only some of his children, Emerson suggests in Sermon No. XXXV (May 3, 1829) that God's love is compensation for a lovely life and, further, that character, the result of choice and discipline, is also reward for a lovely life, since "if you love what is grand and pure, you also shall be raised and purified" (*CS* 1:276). While the formation of a perfect character is a daunting task, Emerson and the Unitarians argue that "things long reckoned impossible, a steady perseverance will perform" (*CS* 1:273).[23]

Like other Unitarians, Emerson understood that character is formed from the adversities of life, that "Trial is education. Pains are teachers" and that "Poverty is the blessed nurse who by hard habits braces the nerve of manhood to athletic strength" (*CS* 1:65, 69). He taught that life is a "state of discipline" (*CS* 1:214) imposed by God, the main object

23. Robinson makes clear the "paradox of achievement" inherent in Unitarian self-culture, which of course could never be completely attained (*Apostle of Culture*, 4.)

of which is the formation of character. Life is "our school," which through its lessons of prosperity, tragedy, and loss educates and prepares the soul for the greater adventure of being, eternity (CS 1:214). Yet even as he taught that life's hardships school the self in character development, he was also convinced that life is inevitably balanced: "Nothing is given or taken without an equivalent" (CS 1:78). This conviction of balance, that losses may actually be gains, enabled him to see through temporary adversity to the larger questions of character formation and compensation. For Emerson, lessons of character are learned from particular moments of adversity that contribute to making life lovely or degraded and to the regard or disregard for the individual by God, society, and the self.

Regardless of how the character is formed, whether through a self-imposed fate or as a result of the larger laws of Providence, the type of character that emerges from the choices and events of life is itself a heaven or hell on earth. Suggestive of his impulse to locate power within the mind or soul of the individual, Emerson hints as early as 1827 in Sermon No. IV that compensation is an internal and present force rather than one distanced by time or place. Already musing about the kingdom within the soul, Emerson preaches that "he that has committed a sin has done himself a fatal injury, and though the disorder that is in his soul may be concealed a moment, it will break out somewhere without delay" (CS 1:81). The result of sin is a perverted soul, one "stamped as with the curse of Cain" (CS 1:82). Although the outward circumstances of one's life may belie his wrongdoing, the sinner nonetheless smells of "corruption and folly and feel[s] the sad inefficacy of things without, to mend the error and deficiency within" (CS 1:82–83). Not only has the transgressor "ceased to be an honest man" (CS 1:81), but also, more seriously, he has loosed himself from the checks and restraints of religion and the spiritual healing inherent in religion.

Emerson explores the correlation between compensation and character development on a more positive note in Sermon No. LXXXVII (September 5, 1830), composed as he was beginning to develop the idea of self-trust, than he did in Sermon No. IV. In conjunction with his call for members of his congregation to improve themselves, he uses the same phrase — "All things are double one against another" — to exhort them to resist temptation and overcome evil impulses. As he had declared in No. IV, he reminds the congregation that the reward for resisting temptation is self-improvement and the formation of character. Echoing the "whatsoever a man soweth, that shall he reap" text, Emerson says, "A retribution, however imperfect it may be, does thus run into every moment of life, . . . It will not therefore do to neglect your soul a moment, lest you reap a harvest of thistles for a harvest of wheat" (*CS* 2:248). But while No. IV had warned of spiritual perversion, No. LXXXVII projects personal power as Emerson calls upon each member of his congregation to "live by design" and become the master of himself (*CS* 2:248). For Emerson, there is a double edge to correct living: by avoiding the horrible retributions of God or of the self, the individual gains power, in part through progressive self-improvement and in part through an emergent autonomy, of being master of the self. The compensation for life decisions, whether reward or punishment, helps to shape the self that the individual becomes, a being either progressively closer to God and hence to spirituality or one distanced from the love and benefaction of God and the institution of the church. While compensations may not always be externally apparent at the moment, they will show in the character that the individual forms of himself.

As Emerson develops a growing sense of the autonomy of the self in making his own character, he also sketches the parameters of a self-contained monitor and judge of right living. In doing so, he sketches a more disembodied, spiritual mechanism for compensation than the physicality of direct reward and punishment or even of character formation. These early discussions of compensation locate the arena of reward and retribution more and more consistently within the self rather than in the materialism of secular success or the revenge of eternity. Indeed, Emerson finds that it is the conscience or moral sentiment that distinguishes right from wrong and "points as with a silent finger" at temptation (*CS* 1:117). It is "that man within the breast" who commands "what *not* to do" (*CS* 1:192–93, emphasis added).

Emerson's strategy diverts power away from external reality and eternal distance to the interior reaches of the self, yet it is not without its problems. Through its emphasis on negativity and self-denial, Emerson's tactic still contains that pervasive dualistic habit of mind that splits the self from itself. Although one might contend that the conscience could exercise its power in positive ways, telling the self what *to* do, it is clear in Sermon No. XXI that Emerson transcribes the power of the conscience in negative terms. He uses the language of negativity, the "*hortatory* negative" of command. Kenneth Burke recognizes this negative as an element not only of theology but also of an ethics of polarity that presumes a moralistic prescription against the choices and activities of one-half of the unity of body and soul.[24] As Burke points out, this kind of negativity and polarity is indicative of a distrust of the body and a strategy for empowering the soul by means of self-condemnation and sublimation. While Emerson's attention on the conscience empowers the self by relocating powers usually ascribed to God within the self, his strategy also empowers the mind or conscience at the expense of the body, another evidence of his masculinist reading of human nature and power.

Nonetheless, locating powers of retribution in the conscience of the individual appears to be a viable way of answering the apparent dilemma of managing compensations in the real world of the here and now. Punishment can be handed out to wrongdoers in the temporal arena even if observers are not always aware of it. Emerson preaches that the conscience has the power to "punish human transgression" as it fastens its "fangs on the memory" of the sinner: "The accuser Conscience is curdling his blood here in these pleasant chambers. Which way soever he looks he is scared by grisly visions. The sleepless remembrance of his crime pursues him and all the medicines of the world will not soothe him to repose" (*CS* 1:193–94). Like his contemporaries, Emerson found the conscience to be the "tribunal" and "vicegerent" of "divine justice . . . from which it is impossible entirely to escape." Excerpted from Joseph Stevens Buckminster's sermon, "Evidence of Retribution for Sin," by the *Christian Examiner,* these comments stress the punitive qualities of the conscience: "the avenger, which waits only for a moment of solitude, . . . pursues [the guilty] even in his dreams, and terrifies him with visions of the night."[25] Likewise, Emerson ex-

24. Kenneth Burke, *The Rhetoric of Religion: Studies in Logology,* 20–24.
25. *Christian Examiner* New Series, 4 (1829): 45.

plains that the conscience is an "uneasy monitor that now burns and now whitens the cheek, against our will; that hinders a man of his sleep; takes away his appetite; unsettles his eye; fills his ear with ugly sounds; sits heavy at his heart, when he sits alone, and makes him afraid of others" (CS 1:194). As suggested by these descriptions, the duty of the conscience is to judge and punish the individual for his transgressions, whether in the secret recesses and private dreams of the soul or in more public, "divulgatory" ways (CS 1:201). Although Emerson remarks in Sermon No. XXI that the conscience rewards good, his attention, like Buckminster's, is on the retributive, negative qualities of not only the rhetoric of religion but also God himself, for as Emerson and Buckminster assert, the conscience is the agent of God and proof of his existence.

Yet even here Emerson's sense of the nature and duty of the conscience, and of compensation, remains tentative. In Sermon No. XXI, first preached on August 17, 1828, Emerson does more than describe the conscience as an instrument of retribution and punishment. Here he assigns power to it and to the individual who heeds it. As I have suggested, the theory of compensation is intertwined with a theory of power and Emerson's personal attempts to empower himself. Compensation, he has said, is God's economy by which deficiencies and excesses are balanced, whereby the weak are made strong and evil is punished. Haunted as he was during his early ministry with illness and an unmet ambition, he hoped to "exchange the rags of [his] nature for a portion of the majesty of [his] maker" (JMN 3:130). A theory of compensation, "What is taken from a man in one way is made up to him in another," provided one strategy for balancing and strengthening his own position in the universe. Even more, locating God's power to judge and punish within the self empowers the self by metaphorically linking the individual with God and his powers.[26]

Indeed, Emerson speaks of the conscience as being an intermediate link between man and God, beginning early on to sketch out the

---

26. In JMN 3:70, Emerson says that God "secured the execution of his everlasting laws by committing to every moral being the supervision of its own character[,] by making every moral being the unrelenting punisher of its own delinquency."

themes of attachment (to the spiritual) and detachment (from the physical) that run throughout his thought. In Sermon No. XXI he tells the story of Socrates, who was guided, even in his decision not to avoid his execution, by his conscience, or as Emerson puts it, by "an invisible Genius or Daemon" (*CS* 1:192). Emerson tells his audience that Socrates was accustomed to obey inner warnings "as if they were the voice of God" (*CS* 1:192). Clearly, Emerson is suggesting that the conscience, like the daemon, connects man to God and is a channel through which the direct word of God may be heard by the individual. In another example used in this sermon, that of Bessus, an inhabitant of Poeonia who was prompted by his conscience to divulge his secret murder of his father, Emerson describes the conscience as "the work and the power of God" (*CS* 1:195). Perhaps more telling is a journal passage in which he compares the conscience to an umbilical cord that unites humanity with God. Writing on July 30, 1828, when he was preparing Sermon No. XXI, Emerson mused, "a child is connected to the womb of its mother by a cord from the navel. So it seems to me is man connected to God by his conscience" (*JMN* 3:139). As with the fetus that receives physical nourishment directly from the mother, so the human receives spiritual nourishment from God. And like the prenascent child who is a separate being and yet still a part of the mother and contained in the universe of her womb, man is also a free agent who is nonetheless contained by the umbilical conscience within a moral universe and subjected to God's laws of compensation.

Yet Emerson also calls the conscience "that man within the breast," at once suggesting a further identification between man and God and transferring to man powers of the conscience and, therefore, of God. Perhaps the result of a democratizing impulse to make the conscience less a figure from Greek legend and to imbue it with characteristics more common to his nineteenth-century audience, his shift from "Daemon" to "man" has also the effect of equating daemon and "voice of God" with "man." Since he has correlated the conscience with the daemon and with God, to here also identify it with man is by association to suggest an identification between man and God. Indeed, if part of God's task is to monitor and punish transgression and if the conscience has also that duty, then the logical assumption is that the conscience is like God and its powers like God's. And if, as Emerson has consistently suggested, the control over temptation is manly and avoids effeminacy and corruption, the agent that controls temptation is also associated with manliness. In the moral equation that Emerson has constructed, the conscience as a tool of God connects man not only to the Supreme Being but also to his own powers and manhood. Both because it is a construct of his own making and because it aligns man with God, this equation also promotes Emerson's own bid for empowerment and autonomy.

Sermon No. XXXVII extends this schema as Emerson locates heaven and hell within the self, reading Luke 17:21, "The kingdom of God is within you," as further support for his discussions of compensation and the role of the conscience. But what is different here, as will be made more explicit in his later sermons, is that the self, through its powers of retribution, gains a kind of sufficiency apart from an external God. More than the earlier psychological perspicuity about the role of guilt or a bad conscience in the workings of retribution, this sermon moves the eternal realms of heaven and hell within the self, making the individual mind the arena of immortality. In the paragraph in which he introduces the line of Scripture from Luke, he explains, "Thou art made sufficient to thyself. Thy joy, and thy glory, and thy punishment, thy heaven, and thy hell are within thee. There is the heavenly host; there is the eye of God" (*CS* 1:287). Unlike the metaphor of the umbilical cord by which man is connected to God and contained within his space, this passage suggests an inversion whereby God is contained within the human space. In Sermon No. IX he had asked, "What is Man?" — and had answered his question with the question, "What is God?" — finding the identity of man "wholly dependent" on the being of God (*CS* 1:114). In No. IX Emerson finds man (his mind) to be made in God's image and thereby dependent on God for his identity. But Emerson's reading of Luke in No. XXXVII and in subsequent sermons expands in radical ways the meaning and power of the self. This is a very important text for Emerson, "the prime article of Emerson's faith," according to Wesley Mott, for he replaces the distant kingdom of God with an immediate kingdom of the self in which the "obstructions," "temptations," and "diseases" of the body "shall be dropt" and the mind can act with freedom and power (*CS* 1:289). When he says, "Heaven is not a place, but a state of the mind" (*CS* 1:287), he means more than a psychological or relativistic reading of human nature, for the mind that is uncontaminated with the impulses of the grosser self contains within it, as we have seen, powers of immortality. Indeed, the mind (though not the body) participates in the unity of God; it "beat[s] pulse for pulse in harmony with the universal whole" (*CS* 1:290). Although Porte argues that Emerson used the text from Luke in *Nature* to construct the "ultimate kingdom of integrated being," accommodating both mind and body,[27] Emerson's initial reading of the text unites man with God at the expense of a whole, integrated self. He attempts here to integrate only the mind of man with the Vast Mind that is God. As his sermons have consistently argued, to the extent that one controls his passions, he becomes manly, powerful, and more like God. Exercising and realizing the muscle of his thought, a confident Emerson who reaches beyond conventional discussions of compensation to construct an intimate, empowering relationship with God emerges in 1829.

Depression and the Social Body

In May 1829, when Emerson wrote No. XXXVII, his vocational life was fairly settled and secure. In June 1828, Henry Ware Jr., pastor of the Second Church of Boston, had become gravely ill, and Emerson was called to supply his pulpit. When Ware had attempted to resign in December 1828, the parish, reluctant to let him go, proposed a colleague "to assist him in the discharge of his duties." Emerson, who had been steadily engaged as supply minister since June, was chosen and was ordained on March 11, 1829, as junior pastor. Although he was worried about the health of Ellen, to whom he became engaged on December 17, 1828 (she had "raised blood" in January 1829 [*L* 1:259]), and although Emerson had some doubts about the capacity of his own health to meet the rigors of full-time pastoring, he nonetheless seems to have thrived intellectually during the years of his pastorate at Second

27. Mott, *"Strains of Eloquence,"* 108. Porte, *Representative Man,* 78.

Church. Indeed, before Ellen's death Emerson felt free to explore beyond the conventional readings of the Bible and man's relation to God, and the sermons of the middle period of his ministry, from 1829 to Ellen's decline in health during the autumn of 1830, are generally marked by an optimism about man's capacities.[28] There exists in Emerson's writing a consistent correlation between his attitude about his own life and the mood of the sermons. When Emerson feels himself to be weak morally and physically, he echoes the conventional messages of retribution and sin. And when he is unsettled vocationally, as he was until 1829, his interpretations of compensation have about them a tentativeness. But when, as is evidenced in No. XXXVII, he is secure in his profession and appears finally to be meeting his ambition, his thought is fresh and risky.

There is, then, a period of optimism marked by happiness and contentment in his life and writing, a period during which he made strides toward self-autonomy. Unfortunately, this period was short-lived, for it was interrupted by Ellen's degenerating health after their marriage on September 30, 1829. Unsurprisingly, the mood of the sermons during this crisis reflects his personal situation. Caught in the grips of depression, in a Melvillean "damp, drizzly November" of the soul, Emerson in the autumn of 1830 returned his focus to the primeval forest of the soul and the darkness of death. While the letters and journals do not demonstrate fear for Ellen's life, even though she was to die just one and one-half years after their marriage, his very real and heartfelt concern for her situation is evidenced in the abrupt shift in the sermons from topics of self-trust and self-culture to topics of death and sin and judgment. With Ellen's pending death, Emerson is reminded both of man's divinity and of his evil. He sees the possibilities of immortality in the angelic spirit of his wife, but when he compares himself to her and to the ideal of Christian deportment that she represents to him, he feels inferior and is conscious of his own weakness. Fear of annihilation turns his previous readings of unity to humility in the face of the greatness of the universe, and sounds its voice in Sermon No. LXXXII when Emerson says:

28. Quoted in Robinson's introduction, *CS* 1:13. See *CS* 1:13–16 for Robinson's quick account of Emerson's coming to Second Church.

I have nothing, I am nothing that is not his gift. All this world of sense and thoughts that have formed my history, are his teaching. I float on the tide of his beneficence. . . . And I, deformed with error, spotted with sin, not master of my will or my being for one moment beyond the present, and loaded all the time with a bounty whose worth I do not yet know. (*CS* 2:223–24)

In working out a theory of compensation that accounts for death and the immortality of the soul, Emerson seems to have looked alternately through a bright glass and a dark one. He saw that while there is a heaven within the human soul, there is also a hell. In Sermon No. XCIII, first delivered on October 31, 1830, a little more than three months before Ellen's death, Emerson's personal anxiety is translated in the tentativeness of the short-lived optimism found in sermons of just a month or so earlier and in the doubleness of his vision. Here he tells his audience: "There is no heaven so high and glorious as a mind dedicated without any reserve to the love of God — to all the truth which is his nature and all the goodness which he imparts. There is no hell so deep and dark as the misery of a human spirit which wholly hates what is good, which hates his brother, and hates God; a soul that is lost" (*CS* 3:27). Oddly enough, while Sermon No. XXXVII, written on the same theme, "The kingdom of God is within," presented man as an empowered participant in the immortality of God, No. XCIII speaks most tellingly of loss and unhappiness. Indeed, a note added in pencil, probably after Ellen's death (he gives a second date of delivery, April 22, 1832), articulates even more clearly the pervading mood of the sermon and a certain confusion about the definition of the kingdom of God — that it may, as tradition has taught, reside outside the mind of man and in a realm removed in time and space. In this note, Emerson seems to again participate in the "condition of impotence,"[29] which

29. Herman Melville, *Moby-Dick*, 12. Jacobson, "Compensation," 112. Barish, *Roots of Prophesy*, hypothesizes that Emerson "may have felt fear and anguish, but he appears to have used his sensitivity and skill as a writer to render his voice unequivocal" (229). Barish's contention is that while obsessed with death, Emerson generally repressed personal expressions of grief. What I attempt to demonstrate is that Emerson's anxiety and grief were channeled symbolically through the sermons in ways that at once gave voice to his personal mood and yet camouflaged it from himself and others.

looks outside of the self and beyond this world for actualization of desire, as he hopes to be "united to the society & restored to the blessed spirits of our friends departed from the earth" (MS).

His sermons during his depression indicate a renewed and intensified concern with the wrath of God and the judgment that is to come—themes of his first sermons. He enjoins his congregation in Sermon No. XCV, first delivered on November 14, 1830, to let "the great doctrines of the New Testament, of death, of judgement, of heaven and hell, be studied" (*CS* 3:35). Emerson not only describes Jesus as "*the judge of the world*" rather than as a model of human perfection and envisions the wrath soon to be incurred on the individual and the nation for their "share in the guilt with accumulated evil," but also reverts to an older reading of revenge whereby "The judgment of Christ . . . shall be fully carried out in the spiritual world upon the good and the evil" (*CS* 3:37–39). Feeling more intensely than before the presence of God in all things, Emerson felt an oppressive sense of humility and declared in Sermon No. XCVI, "Every crime is the fruit of this low detestable love of self. . . . All laws are directed to enforce God's will, and it is self that always breaks them. If self was permitted to seek and gain its ends, it would turn the world into a hell. The abasing of self, the seeking of God's will by all men, would constitute heaven" (*CS* 3:43). Here Emerson sounds an Edwardsian desire to lie low before God as he advocates the "renouncement of *my* will for *thine*" (*CS* 3:44). While he speaks of the "glory of a free agent to bring his will into a perfect sympathy and obedience to God's; it makes him divine," the mood of the sermon is not of man's power but of the negation of self in the face of the forces of the universe (*CS* 3:44). With Ellen's illness, he feels the powerlessness of his own will against the all-powerful machinery of God's law, speaking in Sermon No. XCIX of "the hand of the Adversary of God . . . beckoning us backward" into sin and pleasure (*CS* 3:58). And with the evident weakness of Ellen's body, he returns his gaze to the body, the individual body and the social body, working out his personal anxiety on this symbolic code.

In the jeremiads that mark this period of personal depression, Emerson speaks as he had not before of national sins. As Mary Douglas has suggested, the human body is always treated "as an image of society";

in Emerson's case, the social body also acts as an image of the human body, providing him with a code for articulating an unnarratable personal anguish. In his discussions of the American jeremiad, Sacvan Bercovitch also recognizes this correlation between the private and the public. Bercovitch notes that "the American jeremiad was a ritual designed to join social criticism to spiritual renewal, public to private identity, the shifting 'signs of the times' to certain traditional metaphors, themes, and symbols."[30] In traditional jeremiadic form, Emerson had sought a renewal of virtue and religious observance in his early sermons. In Sermon No. XVII (April 2, 1828), Emerson claimed, "The sins of the nation are *our* sins" (*CS* 1:171), but he also saw prosperity coming out of adversity and the real ability of community members to correct the sins of the nation. On July 15, 1827, he had reminded his congregation of the trials and triumphs of the Puritan forefathers and of the prosperity of the nation as he called for a more consistent observance of the Sabbath and warned against a "degenerate effeminacy." And in his next sermon he had predicted a personal and national millennium, an "approaching era of human bliss" marked by a religion that "is cheerful, social, masculine, generous" (*CS* 1:110, 112).

But in the sermons of 1830, Emerson's jeremiad had a more urgent tone; the assurance of the earlier jeremiads is replaced by a mood of desperation and impotence. As Bercovitch further notes, jeremiads "betray an underlying desperation — a refusal to confront the present, a fear of the future, an effort to translate 'America' into a vision that works in spirit because it can never be tested in fact." As such, the jeremiad is a construct of the authorial self who inscribes onto the national paradigm his own "moods and motivations." In Emerson's case, Ellen's disintegrating health and his corresponding depression and powerlessness to avert the disaster or find a satisfactory compensation for loss and separation expanded to the national arena, as he warned of the consequences of the national evil perpetrated against the weaker inhabitants of the nation, primarily the Indian, the slave, and the disempowered individual. As Wesley Mott has pointed out, "Emerson's political out-

30. Mary Douglas, *Natural Symbols: Explorations in Cosmology*, 70. Sacvan Bercovitch, *The American Jeremiad*, xi.

look . . . is closely related in the early years to his psychological landscape."[31] Indeed, evidence from newspapers and journals suggests that 1830 was probably no worse nor better than other years during Emerson's ministry. There was real concern about the plight of the Cherokee and Creek Indians, who were being pushed from their lands in Georgia. Emerson's brother Charles even participated in "this nefarious Indian Subject" (*L* 1:316). Yet public discussion of the problems of slavery and other social ills do not appear to have escalated in the autumn of 1830.

Although the popular literature of the period does evidence concern about the Indians, slavery, dueling, and other issues, this concern is often meliorated by a vision of progress and reform and does not seem to have been peculiarly insistent in late 1830. In the *Boston Evening Gazette* for January 2, 1830, the writer looking back on 1829 does indeed bemoan the victimization of the Cherokee Nation at the hands of "political intolerance of personal and local cupidity" and the perpetuation of slavery in the South, but he does so in an essay that looks more consistently at the progress of the nation and the liberating institutions of New England. If there are problems in America, this article suggests, they are distant from a progressive and enlightened New England. An article in the September 1830 issue of the *Christian Examiner* addresses the problem of the Cherokees and demonstrates that these Indians are not savage but are devoted to agriculture, education, and Christianity. While the author does plead for justice and the proper exercise of executive power by the president, his is the only piece in the 1830 *Christian Examiner* that notices the plight of the Indians.[32]

On July 3, 1831, in a speech that was an expanded version of the one he delivered from Emerson's pulpit on May 29, 1831, Samuel J. May indicted in stirring words the nation, the South, and New England for the injustice served the black man and the southern Indians. Although this particular speech was delivered months after the period in ques-

31. Bercovitch, *American Jeremiad*, xiv. Geertz, *Interpretation of Cultures*, 90. Mott, *"Strains of Eloquence,"* 114. See also Len Gougeon, *Virtue's Hero: Emerson, Antislavery, and Reform.*

32. *Boston Evening Gazette*, January 2, 1830, 2. *Christian Examiner* New Series, 10 (1830): 107.

tion, it can serve as a model for the antislavery rhetoric of the time and provides a means of contextualizing Emerson's own rare pronouncements on social issues. May speaks of the "great sins we have committed [and] the foul stains . . . upon our national character," of the "lust for wealth," "unprincipled speculations," and "arts of dishonest traffic" evident in a country that held *two millions* of our fellow men in the most abject servitude." His concern centers on the distortion of freedom, liberty, and the creed that all men are created equal, and he predicts, "Certain destruction will overtake us if we persist in our iniquity." Even so, May participates in the American ideological assumption that freedom and equality are human rights that will persevere, comparing the imminent struggle of blacks for freedom with the "power of oppressed humanity," which in Europe was upsetting "the thrones of tyrants." Unlike Emerson's indictments during the autumn of 1830, which echo May's rhetoric and yet are unrelieved by a vision of reform, May's jeremiad becomes a profession of faith that Americans can, if awakened, correct injustice and establish a union of harmony and equality. Indeed, the news from Europe, Mexico, and South America concerning the revolutions of 1830 affirmed the American belief that the desire for freedom and liberty was flourishing and that the revolts were a "splendid illustration of the inviolability of the rights of man."[33]

In the autumn of 1830 and into 1831, Emerson echoed the current worry about the state of the nation in his sermons. While concerns about the southern Indians, slavery, and other national ills were certainly in the air and were disturbing to one committed to moral reform, for Emerson these topics are suggestive also of personal ills. What I want to suggest is that while Emerson had solid ground for criticizing society and the politics that condoned injustice and that while his political vision throughout his life was characteristically "bifurcated, ambivalent,"[34] his outspokenness now and in only a handful of sermons, rather

33. Samuel J. May, *Discourse: Slavery in the United States,* 3, 4, 12, 16. May notes, "A part of the following discourse was first delivered in Boston on the evening of the 29th of May." Since he spoke from the Second Church pulpit on the twenty-ninth, we can assume a great similarity of remarks between the Boston and Brooklyn lectures (*Boston Evening Gazette,* November 20, 1830, 1).

34. Mott, *"Strains of Eloquence,"* 114.

than consistently and throughout his ministry, bespeaks something other than moral anger. To my mind it reveals a personal sense of impotence aggravated by the declining condition of Ellen's health and his own depression in the face of personal trauma. It appears that he transfers and transforms his personal tragedy in the sermons, giving vent symbolically to his own moods in publicly acceptable ways and at the same time disguising from himself and his audience a tale unnarratable because it is inappropriate and painful. In this way, the narrative of national sin and injustice serves as a cipher of his private narrative, for the larger story mirrors his private despair and impotence. Unable to control the real catastrophe of his life, he enacts it in the jeremiadic sermons, distancing and controlling it through language that metaphorizes his own situation.

It may be that Emerson was himself aware of this rhetorical stratagem, for he hints that he understood the correlation between the private self and the national scene. When he indicted New England for its economic condonation of slavery in a journal entry for November 10, 1830, he found fault with those who "with their sinful eyes can not see society without slaves," and he addressed the need for reform, for the "progress of every soul." In this passage, Emerson correlates personal sin with the perpetuation of slavery and personal reform with the reform of society (*JMN* 3:209). Yet he also seems to map out an interior landscape by means of the political terrain. The old concern for the potential usurpation of the mind by the untamed body is translated onto the body politic. This concern is represented in the sermons by his discussion of "the ferocious usages of savage nations, — War, Duelling, Assassination" (*CS* 3:37–38), of "nameless dens of intemperance and debauchery" that threaten the moral well-being and power of the nation as well as the individual (*CS* 3:59). Moreover, his political sermons have a sense of catastrophe about them, envisioning a civil war that breaks up the national family at a time when Ellen's illness threatens to break up his own family. In April 1831, a month before May's speech from the Second Church pulpit, Emerson declared that the evil "we discern impending over us" speaks of a change that may "blow the trumpet of civil war" (*CS* 3:140). Anticipating the pernicious change within his own household, Emerson finds in the images and rhetoric of antislavery propaganda a means for expressing the anxiety that he could not and did not make explicit. Painting a picture of a nation turned criminal and murderous, he claims:

> It needs only certain change in the speculative principles which we ourselves entertain. It needs a preponderance of passion over reason, a little more violent preference of selfish interest over honest shame than now we permit in ourselves, a little more casting off of the restraints of Puritan principles and Puritan manners, a little greater progress of unbelief which springs from a bad heart. (*CS* 3:141)[35]

As in his earlier diatribes against the self, he constructs a moral equation for the nation with the same factors — the war between the passions and self-control, between morality and sin, between impotence and power. The sign he sees of his nation's "bad heart," its "treatment of the Indian in one portion of the country, a barefaced trespass of power upon weakness, . . . and the general indifference with which this outrage passes before the eyes of the whole nation" (*CS* 3:141), indicates his concern with the dichotomy of power — with the impotence of the individual in the face of overwhelming and oppressive power held by the tyrant few, and of the tyrant universe whose power spelled out most agonizingly to him the word death.

Weighed down by the burden of personal anxiety (and national guilt), Emerson in 1830 saw little to hope for in the final judgment. His predictions are uncharacteristically gloomy and sound more like an Edwardsian prophesy than an Emersonian one. Emerson warns that to disobey God's principles is "to seal our doom . . . to incur the reproaches of our conscience . . . to ruin our peace of mind" (*CS* 3:38–39). Compensation is again synonymous with Calvinistic retribution — painful, hellish retribution — and Emerson again imagines the self to be weak, alone, at odds with the world and himself: "The consequences of sin in this world are painful thoughts, fear, further desire to sin, and a blindness which hides our interest and happiness from us, and,

---

35. See Cayton's discussion of this sermon in *Emerson's Emergence*, 51. Cayton's focus, unlike mine, is on the political corruptions of Jacksonian America.

beyond this, the disapprobation and united opposition of all the rest of mankind" (*CS* 3:39). As Hawthorne would in "Young Goodman Brown," Emerson describes those "representatives of savage life" who "in the face of the sun and nourished by the overflowing bounty of the benevolent Father, carry about a fire in their souls that seems to have been lighted from hell" and who "hide their thoughts from the day, and take a diabolical pleasure in brooding over the injuries they have received and rendered" (*CS* 3:53). The image of the sinner, the one fallen away from "the overflowing bounty of the benevolent Father" who carries about "a fire" in his soul, resonates with the personal anguish and pain of the young minister who too felt separated from happiness and whose future promised only doom and "painful thoughts." As Emerson's vision darkened, his forecasts sounded the same note that they had in his first sermons. Echoing the warnings of an earlier Calvinism and at the same time giving voice to his own mood, Emerson proclaims the operation of Satan in the world: "Thus out of the bosom of every good comes forth the hand of the Adversary of God and man beckoning us backward with pleasant invitations to give up the good we have so hardly bought" (*CS* 3:58). Like his image of the individual, Emerson's homiletic narrative again retreats back to the darkened wood, signaling his own psychic and intellectual retreat as he retells the old story of man's fall, itself a narrative mirror of Emerson's personal subtext.

Despite the tentative advances he had made in shaping a theory of compensation coincident with a godlike, self-sufficient self, at the close of 1830 Emerson's surest answer to the question of evil was that sin and temptation provide lessons of resistance and that "the soul is proved and sanctified by progressive and proportioned trials and increases her strength by the strength of her adversaries" (*CS* 3:60). He attempted to find the hand of Providence in the adversities of life, to find some rationale for suffering, and earlier that year had told his congregation that "nothing is uncertain in its infinite plan" and that "the seeming exceptions and violations of the general Order, are made to contribute to ultimate good" (*CS* 2:142). That the positive perspective of a universe informed by an "infinite plan" seemed untenable to Emerson at this point in his life and ministry is evidenced both by the pessimism of his rhetoric and by his regression to earlier, more conventional discussions of compensation and the nature of man. Depression and regression, both strategies of the mind to avoid the painful, mark the sermons at the end of this chapter of Emerson's homiletic narrative.

As life around him — at least the life that really counted — was falling apart and disintegrating, Emerson's "rage for order" found expression not in original, risky thought but in the safety of the widely accepted tradition of God's omnipotence and man's weakness. Although Emerson never mentions Ellen's situation in his sermons and refers to it only elliptically in his personal texts, Ellen's ill health nonetheless provides the "mood and motivation" for his philosophical position during the last months of her life.[36] As his version(s) of compensation in the first stages of the auto-biographical text are complicated by his passional life, so too is the more satisfactory meaning of compensation as correspondence that he finds near the end of his ministry. Where the text "All things are double one against another" at first suggests to him a paradigm of reward and punishment, it later represents the doubling and unity by which he compensates for the immediate loss of his wife. In either case, the language of attachment and detachment, of the body and of the spirit, provides a means for formulating his thought. Indeed, throughout his ministry, the problems of the body, spirituality, and selfhood continue to intersect in perplexing ways.

---

36. Barcus, "Structuring the Rage Within," 45–46. Geertz, *Interpretation of Cultures,* 90.

3

The Flames of Baptism: Grief and Consolation

"We are baptized into suffering." (*CS* 1:87)

"The universe is pervaded with myriads of secret analogies that tie together its remotest parts as the atmosphere of a summer morn[in]g is filled with innumerable gossamer threads running in every direction but revealed by the beams of the rising sun." (*JMN* 3:256)

Ralph Waldo Emerson's personal and philosophical epiphany in the year following the death of his first wife was not simply a recovery from grief. Rather, it was a change in perspective that allowed him to see the "myriads of secret analogies that tie together [the] remotest parts" of the universe, revealing to the "illuminated mind" a world that "burns & sparkles with light" (*JMN* 3:256, 255). Baptized by death and depression, Emerson emerged from his grief with a new insight, in which the primacy of personal vision was declared. With this new perspective in which he saw the correspondences and unity of being, Emerson saw also the light and wisdom and power not only of the universe but also of himself. Ironically engendered by the death of Ellen, this vision gave Emerson the freedom and power to form himself and his thought. While trying to "deprive death of its sting," he wrestled with the need both for spiritual assurance and for intellectual freedom and self-sufficiency. This he did by looking at ways to cheat death of its power, by negating the loss and saying in different ways that death is not the termination of being. Contrary to Harold Bloom's proclamation that Emerson had nothing to say about sex and death because "Emerson had no sexual problems, and was a Stoic about death,"[1] the reader of the sermons finds that Emerson did have something to say about these subjects. Indeed, his narrative tells of the strange, yet very human, alliance in his imagination between death and Eros, between loving and knowing, in the fictions he creates of the self's victory over the separation and negation of death.

During the crisis years of his youth, before he became the mature author of *Nature,* Emerson was confronted with the reality of death and the necessity to survive not only death's threatening hand but also the grief attendant with loss. Faced with loss and the potential of loss, the young Emerson constructed fictions of the self in an attempt to avert personal disaster by distancing it with words and by giving the raw, chaotic experience narrative order and structure. At the same time, his fictions represent and transform the imagining self, for as he acts out his own trauma through the play of the narrative, translating his experience into story, he converts it into a manageable text and himself into an author who controls and determines the fictive experience. In doing so, he affirms the power of language over death. But he also affirms his own power as an author and as an individual over negation, by means of the mirrored or replicated selves of his fictions and the progressively satisfactory resolutions to the trauma that the fictions achieve. During these early years, Emerson created three kinds of death stories that correspond to distinct moments in his psychic life and that demonstrate a self whose imagination was fired both by personal nightmare and by contemporary narratives of death and consolation. In all three story types — the Byronic death quests, the Christian version of immortality, and the Ellen Tucker story — Emerson represses the idea of death by inscribing his fears of negation and separation on mythic or salvific figures, imaginatively transferring their bravery, dignity, and power to himself. His personal trauma is both mirrored in and deflected by the heroes of legend and imagination, those larger-than-life

---

1. Harold Bloom, *Poetry and Repression: Revisionism from Blake to Stevens,* 257.

figures who act out our nightmares and fantasies and who convert the nightmare into a dream of paradise and the promise of mortal power.

The Youthful Death Quests

As a boy, Emerson faced the sudden and untimely death of his father, who died on May 12, 1811, at the age of forty-two. The Reverend William Emerson left his wife, Ruth Haskins Emerson, and his six children virtually penniless. He died without making future provision for the family, trusting in the power of Providence and his family's own pluck to see them through the economic and emotional crisis.[2] Waldo was a young boy, just days away from celebrating his eighth birthday, when his father died, and the burden of finding emotional resources to deal with the disaster was surely overwhelming for such a lad. Unable to work through the normal course of a father-son relationship and apparently unable to work through grief in more conventional and emotionally satisfying ways, Waldo at age sixteen turned to writing fantastic stories of magic, horror, and murder in his journal. The young Waldo was apparently obsessed with death, dedicating two volumes of his early journals to it; according to Evelyn Barish, this early obsession was linked to the unresolved grief caused by his father's untimely death. In the early texts Emerson describes life as "a few dark hours poisoned by evil, and clouded by anxiety" (*JMN* 1:107) and writes stories and poems peopled by dragons and hags who entangle young knights with their fiendish magic (*JMN* 1:104). He tells nightmarish stories of a lone, questing hero who must confront extraordinary dangers and use superhuman powers to subdue the forces that threaten to extinguish him. Like the young author who lacked the guidance and assistance of the older man in confronting the ordeals of life, the heroes of these tales must often face the enemy alone in dazzling defiance of the overwhelming odds against them. He writes of terrible superheroes, of a Scottish chief who, with "a giant form, with dazzling steel" and "A cry of fear, a dying yell," laid to rest the "best of Britain" (*JMN* 1:107). Even the

2. See John McAleer, *Ralph Waldo Emerson: Days of Encounter,* 23.

landscapes are eerie and foreboding, as when he writes of "A breathless solitude in a cottage in the woods" and of "Precipit<i>ous and shadowy mountains, thick forests and far-winding rivers," the silence of which is "broken only by the far cry of the night bird" and by a "voice of dying worlds" (*JMN* 1:99–100). In pseudo-Byronic fashion the young boy-poet defies the world and gladly seeks death:

> I stand amid the wilderness. Disdain
> Hath marked her victim; Hunger, Cold,
> Misfortune shake their shrivelled hands at me
> And gird me in their hideous company.
>
> . . . .
>
> Come! scatter ashes on my fragrant couch
> I will shake hands with Death and hug Despair
> So I may rid me of the iron fiends
> Who haunt & hiss me
>
> (*JMN* 1:82)

As Barish has noted, Emerson's first journal, written in 1820, "contains no fair maidens, no towers, no frog princes, and no happy endings." In the immature tales there appear to be only victims and no rescues, for "Death had swallowed up his father when Emerson was so young that to lose a parent was to lose some yet unformed part of himself."[3] Indeed, Barish contends, the death stories are populated by patriarchal figures who nonetheless do not effect the rescue of the young quester. In these tales, the young boy seems to play out his own grief, to supercharge the quotidian experiences of his own life with fantasy, giving his personal struggle a mythic quality and deflecting his own powerlessness on larger-than-life heroes who, though they may perish in the end, do so in grand and terrific ways. While these stories and poems attest to the young Waldo's unresolved grief and an obsession with death and decay, they attest also to the way that myth structures personal imagination, for his heroes and villains come out of the pages of history and

---

3. Barish, *Roots of Prophesy,* devotes a chapter to discussion of the young Waldo's obsession with death and the romances of his early journals (72–98). Cayton, *Emerson's Emergence,* also looks at the early dark romances and declares them to be evidence that young Emerson saw in nature a tendency to decay (64–65). Barish, *Roots of Prophesy,* 75, 82.

literature. In fact, the same sorts of tales and apparatuses, with updated modifications, continue to inform the imaginary adventures and fantasies of young boys today, who populate their tales with super- or extra-human heroes, swords, laser guns, and strange events in strange lands, always colored, it seems, with plenty of blood and gore. In both cases, these fantasies evidence an immature understanding of the ways of the world and of the death that claims all, often in unromantic and mundane ways. Nonetheless, they evidence the power of narrative to give structure to nightmare and to transform the "I" of the dreamer into the "I" of the tale, a being more able because of the fantasy to play out the struggle between the forces of life and death.

The Christian Story

The second narrative about death, the Christian version of immortality, is told in the early sermons, those written in the face of his own brush with death in the winter of 1826 to 1827. The hero of this story is, of course, Jesus Christ, who conquered death and promises immortality for those who follow him. At the same time that Emerson uses homiletic storytelling in the new fashion of Unitarian ministers, who were turning to more personal ways of preaching, he seems to have embedded in the very old story of Christian consolation his own story, inscribing in the figure of Jesus his own hopes for deliverance from the "death [that] pursues us always & intrudes on us suddenly" (*JMN* 3:91). Keenly aware of his own physical frailty and the likelihood of an early death, Emerson found in the person of Jesus both the historical example and the symbol of the individual's power over the negating forces of failure and death.

Having wrestled with the very real prospect of his own untimely death, the newly approbated minister returned from Charleston and St. Augustine in June of 1827, strengthened in body and in spirit. The possibility of succumbing to the disease that claimed so many young men and women of New England was quite real to Emerson. Indeed, the possibility of losing health and life seemed an occupational hazard. For ministers on the New England seaboard, one writer complained, "it is notorious that the health of a large proportion of clergymen has failed, or is failing them." Just a few months before departing for the healthier climate of the South, Emerson, aware of his own physical frailty, wrote lamenting his own loss of health and postulating a consolation for the waste of his talents and energy: "It would give me very great pleasure to be well. It is mournful the expectation of ceasing to be an object of hope that we may become objects of compassion, and then go gloomily to nothing ⬆in the eye of this world⬇ before we have had one opportunity of turning to the sun what we know is our best side." Before his journey he had only his will, the lesson of stoicism, to shake him from depression, and he ended this "consolatory soliloquy" with the challenge, "Die? pale face, lily liver! go about your business and when it comes to the point then die like a gentleman" (*JMN* 3:45–46).

But as he regained his health, measuring its tangible evidence by the gain in weight at 141 1/2 pounds in February and 152 pounds in March of 1827 (*JMN* 3:75, 77), he also confirmed the validity of Christianity and the example of Jesus against the skepticism and atheism of his friend Achille Murat. A "humble disciple in the school of truth" (*J* 2:185), Murat had befriended Emerson on the sea voyage homeward from St. Augustine to Charleston. In fact, the outcome of their extensive conversations was not Emerson's conversion to the skeptic's point of view, but Murat's acknowledgment to Emerson that "your system has acquired as much in proberbility as mine has lost in certainty" (*J* 2:187–91). Countering the skepticism of Murat's position and the vulnerability of his own body, Emerson discovers a new version of the death narrative, a narrative with a hero capable of rescuing the quester from despair.[4]

4. *Christian Examiner* 3:2 (1826): 96–97. The Murat passage is quoted in McAleer, *Days of Encounter*, 88–91. Robert Milder argues in "Emerson's Two Conversions," 21, that Emerson's first conversion, which occurred during his Southern journey and in the early months of 1827, was an intellectual transformation influenced by his reading, especially of Sampson Reed. He also suggests that "no sooner did Emerson set aside his hopes and ambitions than he began to recover from despair." Although Mott finds Emerson to have undergone a kind of saving identification with the person of Jesus, he would contest the use of the word *conversion* relative to Emerson's experience. Mott claims that Emerson was "a man who could

In "Christ Crucified" (Sermon No. V), Emerson taught that death leaves for the survivor valuable lessons that he would not otherwise learn. First drafted during his trip south, No. V features a hero and a moral that transform victim into victor and that provide possibilities for rewriting and reinterpreting the narrative of death. One possibility that Emerson discovers in the crucifixion story is the value of trial and loss in strengthening and educating the individual — both sufferer and survivor. Finding that "giddy prosperity" is only a delusion and that the real and valuable lessons of life derive from sorrow and suffering, Emerson also finds that life's losses could be turned to gain: "By these passions our attention is arrested, our faculties are startled from their sleep into strenuous exertion. Our pride is prostrate, and vanity is sick, and the love of pleasure sleeps, and anger dies, when God darkens the chambers of the soul with grievous affliction and the voice of Reason begins to be heard amid the silence of the passions" (*CS* 1:85). Emerson not only finds a kind of profit from suffering but also argues that suffering is necessary for ennobling the self; that since the emblem of Christianity is "not a crown but a cross," mankind finds glory and strength "in the dark soil of affliction" rather than in "luxury and gay prosperity" (*CS* 1:87). Having himself been plunged into a "moonless night" of illness and doubt, Emerson had awakened to the possibilities of life by the time he first drafted this sermon and surely by the time he delivered it on June 24, 1827. By that time, he had learned that his "business is with the living" (*JMN* 2:316), finding thus a compensation for his own suffering.

But "Christ Crucified" contains another possibility for interpretation in the drama of Jesus' crucifixion, for "that most affecting page of human history" (*CS* 1:86) not only teaches the value of suffering but also participates in transforming the self — the sufferer as well as the witness to suffering. As a dramatic story, Jesus' crucifixion has the elements of pity and terror that Aristotle recognized to have cathartic value for the spectator. Quoting Aristotle's declaration, "We are purified by pity and terror," Emerson suggests that while Jesus was himself ennobled by his

---

never claim a single moment of Christian conversion," for he was always involved in an ongoing process of character development ("*Strains of Eloquence,*" 15).

"sublime" death, the spectators of his suffering, at Calvary and in Boston, are also purified by it if the example of Jesus' sacrifice and heroism are the catalysts for a personal conversion experience (*CS* 1:85–86). The image of the cross both symbolizes and can become the vehicle for spiritual change that rescues the individual from loneliness and spiritual barrenness. The person of Jesus enacts a "sublime sympathy" that "invites" and "implores" the spectators of his death "to love yourselves as he has loved you" and, like him, to "despise the sufferings of the body" in the quest for "the welfare of the soul" (*CS* 1:91, 90).[5] In this early sermon, Emerson preaches that death startles the survivor into reexamining himself and his relation to God and into reinventing the self through a spiritual baptism. He also preaches what he would learn even more intimately: "We are baptized into suffering."

Having faced personally the truth that change rather than permanence is the rule of the natural world, and having stood "tottering upon the brink of everlasting annihilation" (*CS* 1:269–70), Emerson returned from his confrontation with ill health and the possibility of mortality strengthened by adversity and convinced of the permanence of God's law. Keenly aware of the weakness of the body, Emerson sought to empower the self against the laws of nature by assimilating the power of God through the person of Jesus and by identifying the self with God, at first in fairly conventional terms. Indeed, the personal and the conventional intersect in the early sermons about death. At the same time that he was recording in his journal the mutability of his own body, noting changes in his weight, he was drafting key passages for Sermon Nos. V and VI, which deal with trial, death, and decay (*JMN* 3:72–75; 62–64). As he was writing, "Decay, decay is written on every leaf of the forest," first in his journal and then in No. VI, he had only to consider his own emaciated body and weak lungs for confirmation (*CS* 1:93). And as he assured his congregation, and himself, of the permanence of the soul, he was reiterating a message already familiar to his audience and to himself: "Man's conscience . . . will survive death" and "our character . . . will endure."[6]

5. Wesley Mott, "'Christ Crucified': Christology, Identity, and Emerson's Sermon No. 5," 23.

6. *Christian Examiner* New Series, 9 (1830): 280–81.

Like "Christ Crucified," Sermon No. VI was drafted during the southern journey and first delivered upon his return home. Like No. V, it sketches vivid scenes of death abundant in the natural world and seeks compensation for man's mortality.[7] Impressed with the mutability of the natural world, Emerson constructs the sermon around description of the decay of natural forms and of members of the congregation. As he does in several other sermons, Emerson predicts the death rate of his congregation, saying, "Twenty years, my brethren, will carry many of us, — it may be, the most, — very possibly, all of us into the world of souls" (*CS* 1:95). He tells his congregation:

> The world that looks so fair and substantial to the eye is found to be unsubstantial. The ground on which we stand is passing away under our feet. Decay, decay is written on every leaf of the forest, on every mountain, on every monument of art. Every wind that passes is loaded with the solemn sound. All things perish, — all are the partakers of this general doom — but man is the chief victim. (*CS* 1:93)

He does not portray change and decay objectively as components of the laws of nature. Rather, because they have been so personally proximate, he finds them to partake in a "progressive ruin" (*CS* 1:96) and death to be a marauder and enemy against which the individual must battle and attempt to assert himself. Against this universal fate, natural man and the particular beings of nature are powerless.

Despite these "melancholy images" of human powerlessness and destruction, Emerson posits a victory and a consolation. He finds that humans hope for something beyond the vicissitudes set upon them by "Pain and Death, our ghastly enemies" (*CS* 1:96, 94). He also finds that the idea that God's "sovereign will" controls the "commotion" and force of nature keeps man from "growing giddy whilst he gazes on these turning wheels of nature" (*CS* 1:96). Furthermore, as he had done in his discussions of compensation, Emerson figures the universal "commotion" in terms of a mirrored struggle between the body and

7. Wider, "What Did the Minister Mean," examines the notes of Anne Tilden, a young woman of Boston, who often listened to Emerson's sermons and recorded them in her journal. Wider makes the point that Tilden's notes disarm Emerson's images and substitute more usual Unitarian interpretations of death that entreated congregations to trust in God.

the mind of the individual: "Our bodies were made of the dust of the ground, but our minds were made in the likeness of God" (*CS* 1:97). In language that speaks both of the universal and of the personal, he suggests that the mind or conscience maintains a kind of eternal vigilance and superiority over the "mortal part." He predicts that after the release of "the spirit from its prison of clay," the individual in godlike fashion "shall . . . look down from a serene height on the storm and commotion of the world below; with pity, on men in the bondage of passion; with courage, on the changes which menace your mortal part" (*CS* 1:98). By thus identifying the mind with God and by asserting the agelessness of the moral nature of man, Emerson hopes to undermine the power of death and empower the self that is the mind.

This strategy is not, however, original with Emerson; other Unitarians preached man's likeness to God, finding the similarity between man and God to reside not in the physical nature of man but in his spirit. In his 1828 sermon, "Likeness to God," William Ellery Channing preached that "man has a kindred nature with God" that is derived "from our own souls." He also preached that religious instruction should be aimed at the "perfection of the soul, which constitutes it a bright image of God," and at subduing the animal side of man through "habitual watchfulness and prayer." Similarly, Unitarians, as well as more orthodox Christians, encouraged the battle between the material and the spiritual self, proclaiming for the soul or conscience ascendancy over the body and death. A reviewer for the *Christian Examiner* declared, "It is not death . . . that we should fear, but the eternal retribution of conscience." Hoping to inspire right living and character development, he urged his readers to break the spell of the grave and to view it as "the place where man lays down his weakness, his infirmity, his diseases and sorrows, that he may have a new and glorious life."[8]

While Emerson's early discussions of death confront personal finitude with a kind of moral and physical courage forged by experience, they do so more with rhetorical freshness and vigor than with intellectual originality. It may be that his reiteration of conventional attitudes

8. Channing, *Selected Writing,* 150, 146, 162. *Christian Examiner* New Series, 11 (1830): 176, 182.

about death and the spirit, and his presentation of Christ crucified, represents his emotional investment in the kind of assurance that accepted doctrine can provide the individual by explaining and "processing" the unknowable and distressful. While these two sermons record Emerson's own victory over the "abysses of night" (*CS* 1:96), they also evidence his alignment with Christian/Unitarian thought rather than the freedom of intellectual adventure of his final narrative of death, the narrative of his affective baptism into suffering. While Emerson's return to health and to New England mark what Robert Milder calls an intellectual conversion,[9] it was not until his heart had been seared by the suffering and loss of Ellen that Emerson underwent a transfiguration of vision and power.

The Ellen Tucker Story

On December 25, 1827, Waldo Emerson met sixteen-year-old Ellen Tucker while he was preaching in her hometown of Concord, New Hampshire. During this period of his career, when he had no home church, he had gone to Concord to minister to the new Unitarian parish being organized by Colonel William Austin Kent. The day after Christmas, he was introduced to Ellen, stepdaughter of the wealthy and influential Kent.[10] Surprisingly yet characteristically, Emerson had little to say about her in his private papers. The letter marking the occasion of his visit to New Hampshire was directed to his stepgrandfather, Ezra Ripley, and is concerned with family matters and the kinds of things a young, aspiring preacher would discuss with the seasoned pas-

9. Geertz, *Interpretation of Cultures,* 81. Geertz maintains that the "cultural concept" of religion "denotes an historically transmitted pattern of meanings embodied in symbols, a system of inherited conceptions expressed in symbolic forms by means of which men communicate, perpetuate, and develop their knowledge about and attitudes toward life" (89). Milder, "Emerson's Two Conversions," guesses that Emerson's second conversion occurred in mid-1830, but I will argue for a slightly later period, more closely aligned with Ellen Tucker Emerson's death. Indeed, in the autumn of 1830, Emerson sank into a depression that predated his conversion.

10. See McAleer, *Days of Encounter,* 102–3, for an account of Emerson's first visit to Concord, New Hampshire.

tor of the Concord, Massachusetts, church. Emerson mentions the "large & respectable" Kent family who were instrumental in his appointment to fill the empty pulpit, but says nothing about Ellen (*L* 1:222). He returned to New Hampshire in May and June 1828, but it was not until December 21, 1828, when he was again in Concord, New Hampshire, that he mentions her in his journal — and that was on the occasion of his engagement to her. Evidently ready to propose to her without preliminary outpourings to his journal, he arrived bearing a gift book, *Forget me not,* inscribed with her initials. Even then his journal entry is terse and to the point: "I have now been four days engaged to Ellen Louisa Tucker" (*JMN* 3:148–49). The silence in the private papers at this juncture may suggest that he was a long time coming to know his own heart or that he was reticent to commit to paper his emotions, which he had consistently thought to be "cold" (*JMN* 3:72).

But his love for Ellen was complicated from the beginning by her physical frailty and by the consumption that would too soon claim her. Emerson could not help but know that Ellen was doomed, that she was "too lovely to live long" (*L* 1:259 n 3). Almost immediately after their engagement, he had to face the fact of her illness and the real possibility of her death. He wrote to William on January 28, 1829, "my beautiful friend has made me very sorry by being very ill & with that dangerous complaint which so often attacks the fairest in our stern climate" (*L* 1:259). And so it may be that his silence and emotional distance regarding Ellen and her illness disguised the fear from himself and from others, for Emerson's "private" texts were never completely private and were shared and read by a number of family members. Instead, the public texts, the sermons, become the arena for his personal and philosophical struggle with mortality and loss, particularly in the months prior to Ellen's death. The sermons provide Emerson a way of abstracting personal pain, as in the jeremiads of 1830, through symbols, those already formulated by Christian tradition and those he would compose himself. Symbols, religious symbols particularly, provide a way of coping with personal pain and distress in ways accepted by the larger culture and in ways that provide a buffer between the self and the object symbolized.[11] In Emerson's case, he needed that kind of buffer to distance himself from heartache that was intense, for he not only loved the beautiful Ellen but also identified himself and his regeneration with her.

In the entry in which he announced to his journal his engagement to Ellen, he also wrote a prayer to God "to strengthen & purify & prosper & eternize our affection!" He regards Ellen as a "gift of [God's] mercy" and identifies her with the religious purity of which he hopes to be worthy: "She has the purity & confiding religion of an angel. Are the words common? the words are true. Will God forgive me my sins & aid me to deserve this gift of his mercy." Emerson's language here betrays that he regarded Ellen from the beginning with the kind of awe usually reserved for deific figures and that he saw in her an agency of his transformation. By metaphorizing Ellen into "an angel," Emerson abstracts the real Ellen and inscribes his own desire for spirituality and salvation on her fictionalized figure. She had already transformed him from a "cold" man to one warm with affection. But the religious language in his prayer hints also of a spiritual transformation (*JMN* 3:149). In fact, this passage of January 17, 1829, is sandwiched between his engagement announcement and a paragraph that considers the salvific quality of the phrase "Forgive our Sins." Echoing or foretelling the January 17 section, which is clearly in reference to Ellen, the December 30, 1828, entry again suggests that Ellen had more than a lover's mission: "Were it not desireable that we should have a guardian angel that should go on our errands between heaven & earth, that should tell us how God receives our actions; when he smiles & when he frowns; what petitions he hears with favour, & what he rejects?" The language is too similar not to suggest that Emerson regards Ellen as more than human and their love as more than mortal, that she represents an intermediary

---

11. Geertz, *Interpretation of Cultures,* explains that "human thought is basically both social and public" and that "[t]hinking consists not of 'happenings in the head' . . . but of a traffic in . . . significant symbols" that are "disengaged from . . . mere actuality and used to impose meaning upon experience" (45). He suggests also that organized systems of thought bridge "the emotional gap between things as they are and as one would have them be" (204–5).

between him and God, and that she participates in his spiritual reformation (*JMN* 3:148–49). From the beginning he identified not only his "Beauty" with spirituality and mortality but also himself with her, writing himself on the fictionalized and disembodied figure of his "angel" and "Beauty." In the letter to William in which he wrote of Ellen's "dangerous complaint," he also wrote, "Beauty has got better & so I am better" (*L* 1:259). As this passage also indicates, Emerson was able to identify with Ellen because, through the agency of metaphor and allegory, he had converted her into an idea and had begun already to erase her real, physical presence from his texts. Perhaps by making Ellen an abstraction, he could more easily cope with the real deterioration of her physical self. Perhaps by metaphorically erasing her corporeality, he could more easily find in her an emblem of spirituality and purity. Whatever the case, she becomes under his hand a cipher of his own desire, a text of his own making — of his own invention and self-generation.[12]

That Emerson should turn outside himself for regeneration is not surprising or new. In April 1824, when he dedicated himself to the Church and was on the verge of being "legally a man," he had written: "My trust is that my profession shall be my regeneration of mind, manners, inward & outward estate; or rather my starting point, for I have hoped to put on eloquence as a robe, and by goodness and zeal and the awfulness of virtue to press & prevail over the false judgments, the rebel passions & corrupt habits of men" (*JMN* 2:237, 242). As with his regard for Ellen, here he seeks more than external changes. Indeed, he seeks a complete regeneration of self, his "inward" as well as his "outward" estate, a transformation of emotion, morality, vision, and power, through the agency of an external other. As the sermons demonstrate, he received more from Ellen than a monetary legacy

12. Of parallel interest is Helena Michie's discussion of Dante Gabriel Rossetti's poem "Jenny," and how the sleeping prostitute is "transformed from a complex individual into a system of signs" and a "cipher of male lust" (61). Though Emerson is not transforming the figure of Ellen into a cipher of his sexual lust, through his textualizing she does become a cipher of his lust for spirituality. See Helena Michie, *The Flesh Made Word: Female Figures and Women's Bodies.*

from her estate;[13] he received a spiritual legacy by which to invent and write himself.

Sermon No. XXVI, written just prior to his engagement announcement and preached during his stay in New Hampshire, echoes some of the themes evident in the private texts written at this same period. Part of a series of three sermons organized around the biblical verse "We should live soberly, righteously, and godly in the present world" (Titus 2:12), No. XXVI speaks of godliness and the cultivation of the affections, particularly of the affection toward God. His purpose in the sermon is to bring the congregation into relationship with God. But when we set the homiletic discussion of affection in proximity to Emerson's growing love for Ellen, we hear a personal voice that tells of the beauty, the "life, interest, and grandeur," and power that derive from affection for a "friend," of the power of sympathy in transforming a life (CS 1:220).

Yet in concert with what might be called confessions of love appear also the anticipation of death and the formulation of a compensation by which the future mourner would be strengthened and guided by the angelic dead. The logic of No. XXVI suggests the doubleness of his attention, not only in its biographical connection to Ellen but also in Emerson's anticipation of death at the same time that he celebrates this new friendship and his imaginary conflation of the human Ellen with an angelic intermediary who leads the lover to God. Moreover, the sermon itself represents a doubling and perplexing of discourse aims; Emerson manipulates the religious text to underwrite his own story at the same time that his personal story is manipulated and disguised by the form and function of the public sermon. Yet the very complexity and

13. Too often, I think, scholars get caught up in the circumstances of Ellen's will and Emerson's legal disagreements with her family. See Henry F. Pommer, *Emerson's First Marriage*. Indeed, Porte, *Representative Man,* complains that "it does seem nevertheless odd that her death could be so easily and quickly assimilated into Emerson's calculations of thrift" (8). The real legacy, I argue, is the conversion derived from real suffering and his efforts to construct a consolatory version of the universe. That, as well as his personal discomfort with his ministerial duties, is what compelled him to leave Second Church, rather than the promise of money from Ellen's estate.

fusion of aims and discourse types mirrors his larger, philosophical project, to find a law of compensation that depends from the connections between the human and the divine. In this sermon, the figure of the "friend" hints at that connection. Emerson suggests that human love seeks a "perfect character" and that by loving one another we become "acquainted with this perfect character, in parcels" (*CS* 1:223). As in the private texts in which he speaks of his "guardian angel" who goes on "errands between heaven & earth" (*JMN* 3:149), Emerson suggests in the sermon that the link between man and God resides in love and the object of love: "Consider that every good man, every good thing, every good action, word, and thought that you love, is only a fragment of the divine Nature" (*CS* 1:223). And as in the private texts, love and death, attachment and loss, are topics that seem inextricably linked in Emerson's thought: "Every one of us is joined to some others whose society we seek with unconquerable desire: whose loss, by the stroke of death, is contemplated as making a chasm in our happiness which nothing but the Christian hope that they are only removed and have not perished, and that we shall see them again, saves from being remediless" (*CS* 1:221). Already, from the moment of his engagement, he anticipates Ellen's death and the need for consolation. Yet he is also determined to love Ellen despite the obvious, against all odds, for he immediately rejoins, "We *must* love" (*CS* 1:221).

Early Versions of Consolation

Although the Reverend Emerson remained always a private man to his congregation, avoiding explicit references to his personal life in the sermons, the mood and tenor of the theme of death beginning with No. XXVI are marked and motivated most tellingly by Ellen's suffering and his own subsequent need to confront human impotency against physical annihilation. As death became increasingly personal for Emerson, the ready answers of Christian doctrine gave way to his search for strategies by which to sublimate the transience of the body and find permanence in the soul. Aware of the potency of death, Emerson nonetheless sought ways to defeat death, to assert the power of the human will against all odds. As he wrestled with the meaning of death, he also grappled with the meaning of compensation and consolation. The seemingly ready answers of Sermon No. CVII (the sermon that marks Ellen's death) give testimony not to his indifference but to the long foreground in which he tested versions of consolation for the mourner and of the meaning of death.

Just more than a month after his ordination on March 11, 1829, as junior pastor of Second Church, Emerson, voicing perhaps his own anxiety that his ill health or early death might prevent him from reaching the greatness that he hoped to be his, told his congregation: "You will think of young men who set out in life with the reputation of excellent habits or of great acquirements or of fine genius, who deceived this expectation by an ill life or by an early death" (*CS* 1:266). He may be echoing what John Frost warned of, the pernicious phenomenon that "at least one-fourth of those who pass through a course of education for the learned professions, sink into a premature grave, or drag out a miserable and comparatively useless life, under a broken existence." He may also be referring to his own career, for almost simultaneous to his finally finding a church home, and a good one at that, he was struck in the summer and fall of 1829 with the arthritic pain in his knee, tubercular in origin, which had become chronic.[14] He wrote to William on October 21 that he was so lame he was not "able to walk a step without a cane — & Sundays I preach, *sitting*" (*L* 1:285). But Ellen's health was even more precarious, for in January she had "raised blood," one of the most serious danger signs of tuberculosis. Out of his fears, out of the fears of death that all men have, of "a grief sitting heavy at the heart of each of us . . . that darkens all our hopes" (*CS* 1:267), Emerson seeks consolation in a belief in immortality. Going beyond a doctrine of formless immortality, he describes a resurrection in which the spirit has some form that the living can perceive and with which the living can communicate. Such a belief would rob death of its power, for the life of the soul would continue beyond the grave. Such a belief represses

---

14. John Frost, *An Oration, Delivered at Middlebury, before the Associated Alumni of the College, on the Evening of Commencement. August 19th, 1829,* 7–8. Barish, *Roots of Prophesy,* 213.

and denies the separation caused by death by positing a parallel existence in which the dead retain their form and the mourner retains contact with the departed one.

In a sermon, No. XXXIV, that lacks his usual control of language and logic, Emerson presents an unorthodox kind of evidence of resurrection. Although he borrows a Platonic reading of the existence of ideas and although he argues the need for faith to hold society together ("Take out of man the hope and the belief of everlasting life and the world would run riot with strange excess" [*CS* 1:270]), it is personal experience — or the report of personal experience — that constitutes the persuasive evidence of his sermon. Rather than turn to Scripture or religious history to support his thesis of the individual's immortality, Emerson turns to common tales for proof that the dead continue to interact in human affairs in tangible ways. He says, "It was for ages believed that the souls of departed men revisited the earth in frightful forms, and even now I do not know that all its superstition has departed from the shroud." He continues by observing that it is strange "that ever this belief was entertained with fear and horror/strong repugnance of its objects, — that it should have been so universally connected with low and disagreeable images. One would think it should have been in the highest degree grateful" (*CS* 1:267, 382).

Here Emerson is calling up the belief, superstition, or hope that beings have form, movement, and presence beyond the grave. He may be thinking of some of the popular reports of sightings, but he seems also to be reaching beyond more orthodox definitions of resurrection to posit that more than the spirit is eternal and that the dead are not really dead. Certainly ghost stories have always played a role in folk literature, but it appears that belief in ghosts was reputable enough in Emerson's day to allow stories about communications with the dead to find their way into respectable newspapers and journals. For instance, an article appearing in the *Boston Evening Gazette* on May 1, 1830, recounts the sighting by a Mr. John Jerningham of the ghost of his deceased father and Jerningham's subsequent death a year later, apparently caused by the trauma of his experience. Presented in the form and language of a news report, "The Haunted Mansion" is a confusing blend of fiction and journalism, but the subject matter seems not to have automatically consigned the piece to the fiction column. In fact, a similar kind of experience appears in an 1831 book by James Thacher, *An Essay on Demonology, Ghosts, and Apparitions, and Popular Superstitions,* which relates the stories of "Mrs. B's" having heard and seen apparitions. Dr. Thacher's purpose seems not merely to tell amusing ghost stories but also to seriously explore ideas and possibilities relevant to the afterlife. Indeed, the reviewer of the book for the *Christian Examiner* enumerates with Thacher some of the notions held by people about what to expect after death: "The opinion of others is, that the soul after the decease of the body continues still in action in another sphere; that death, in short, is a mere change of state." The reviewer suggests that the most commonly held view is that the dead "are still interested in the weal or woe of those whom they have left behind them." These speculations do not represent an oddity, for the September 1829 issue of the *Christian Examiner* contained a long piece, "Future State of the Just," which asserts that in the afterlife we will know each other: "But there are beings, we may hope, who could not fail of finding each other again." Moreover, a "cult of mourning" with its own consolation literature that focused more on mourning than on death itself, and that included death poetry, funeral sermons, consolation essays, and mourning manuals, was just beginning to emerge in the early decades of the nineteenth century, demonstrating the period's almost obsessive interest in death.[15]

The stories about apparitions also formed a part of the Emerson family legends. Emerson's aunt Mary Moody Emerson, always fascinated with death to the extent that she rode about in her shroud and had her bed shaped like a coffin, told the story about the angel of death who appeared at her grandfather's deathbed.[16] Emerson relates the story in his journal: "I heard with awe her tales of the pale stranger who at the time her grandfather lay on his death bed tapped at the window &

15. *Boston Evening Gazette,* May 1, 1830, 1–2. James Thacher, *An Essay on Demonology, Ghosts and Apparitions, and Popular Superstitions. Also, an Account of the Witchcraft Delusion at Salem, in 1692* and *Christian Examiner* New Series, 7 (1832): 106–11 and 4 (1829): 48. Karen Halttunen, *Confidence Men and Painted Women: A Study of Middle-class Culture in America, 1830–1870,* 127–28.

16. See Barish, *Roots of Prophesy,* 136–37, 141 for discussion of Mary Moody Emerson's obsession with death.

asked to come in. The dying man said, 'Open the door;' but the timid family did not; & immediately he breathed his last, & they said one to another It was the angel of death" (*JMN* 5:323). Indeed, Mary Emerson often discussed and looked forward to her own death. In 1827 she wrote Waldo of her own desire to imagine her existence into "never, never, never," into an eternal nothingness, a feat that Waldo never attempted, preferring, instead, to stretch his imagination to construct eternal be-ingness (*JMN* 2:392).

All of this popular literature of death, ghosts, and consolation must have lent a degree of popular veracity to Emerson's Sermon No. XXXIV, but more important, it offered a kind of historical precedence to his statement that "the souls of departed men revisited the earth." The stories buoyed his hope that the doomed Ellen might not be lost to him entirely or forever and that he could "communicat[e] with the soul of a departed friend" (*CS* 1:268). Through the imaginative render-ing of departed friends visiting and communicating with mourners, Emerson tests the viability of a social afterlife as a means of consolation, suggesting in the sermon that such visitations assure one of one's "own eternal nature," which survives that "dark and noisome mansion — the body" (*CS* 1:268). In doing so, the sermon finds a clue to the "secret analogies" of the universe, peering as it were with the departed through heaven's gates into the unknowable.

When he wrote No. XXXIV in April 1829, Emerson probably had no personal experience with visitations from the dead; at least, his journals and letters do not record such an experience. But at some point after he had written the draft, he penciled the letter W twice and over that "Ellen L. Tucker" at the end of the paragraph previously cited: "One would think it ["reappearance of the departed"] should have been in the highest degree grateful ↑to the mind W W Ellen L. Tucker↓" (*CS* 1:267, 382). The preaching record indicates that the sermon was preached four times, the last time on June 30, 1830, approximately eight months before Ellen's death. That the emendation was made prior to June 30, 1830, makes sense in terms of the preaching record, though it is possible that Emerson made the addition after her death and declined to deliver the sermon again. Nonetheless, the sermon suggests that be-fore her death he had a belief or hope in the return of the dead to the living. Moreover, at some point, probably after her death, he had an experience that he believed to be a visit from her or he at least hoped for a visit from her to assure him that she lived on beyond the grave, that death does not terminate life. Indeed, the poems that fill his journal after her death call out to Ellen, entreating her to visit him:

> Ellen can we not yet meet on
> the midnight <dr> wing of dreams
> In the firmament of thought
> Sails thy fervent s<p>oul
> As on solar beams
> I see I know that in the deep
> Of new power & the realms of truth
> Thine affections do not sleep
> Thou canst love the friend of youth
> (*JMN* 3:230)

Another entry in his journal gives further evidence of his hope, albeit disappointed, for communications from the dead Ellen: "O suggest, coming from God's throne, suggest to this lone heart some hint of him. O forget me not, think with me[,] pray with me" (*JMN* 3:240). Emerson's cries to the dead Ellen attest to the force of his will to imagine a figure that retains the form, voice, and affection of the bodied woman. Having abstracted or textualized the living Ellen, he attempts now to reembody the figure of his poem with his own desire for consolation. Quite obviously, visitations from the dead Ellen would provide a kind of compensation for losing her physical presence, for he would be assured of the cohesiveness of experience, of the web of the universe.

But this kind of unearthly compensation puts the power of consolation in the gauzy hands of the dead, who could choose when or whether to visit the mourner, rather than in the brawny hands of the living. While he exultingly proclaims that these visits from the dead would confirm the belief in the immortality of the soul, he places the living man in the position of spectator rather than participant, displacing the individual's facility for self-determination. In No. XXXIV he wavers, then, for he desires both the confirmation of eternal life already given and the active participation by the individual in deciding his own destiny: "My fate is in my own hands. Let me carry up my actions to the high level of my destiny" (*CS* 1:271). While he seeks evidence that "this poor clay, suffering from its low necessities and its unclean diseases, would come forth to take the free air, to be a citizen of the Universe, to grow up in its powers to the colossal measure of its desires and its virtues," he also wants the individual to be responsible for his own life (*CS* 1:268). The compensation for death is consolation, assurance that beyond this earthly life of pain and powerlessness there is an eternal life of power and virtue. But the compensation comes from the example of the dead and not from the living who must work for their virtue. Thus, there is a disjunction in Emerson's thinking at this point, for he cannot yet reconcile fate with freedom, cannot yet find a reconciliation between his needs for both consolation and self-reliance. And so he continued to search for ways to cheat fate and empower the self.

A few months later, after a relapse in Ellen's always precarious health, Emerson wrote Sermon No. XLI. In a letter to Charles on June 19, he wrote, "Yesterday Ellen was taken sick in the old way," suffering much and raising blood. And he tells his brother that with the change in her health his mood has changed: "I was perfectly happy now I am watching & fearing & pitied." At the same time that he attempts to remedy her situation, summoning Dr. Jackson to the case, he translates her (and his) experience into the sermons. In the letter he wrote, "Ellen has an angel's soul & tho very skeptical about the length of her own life hath a faith as clear & strong as those do that have Gods kingdom within them" (*L* 1:271–72). Looking from Ellen and her Christian faith and vision of the afterlife, Emerson writes in No. XLI of the immortality of the soul. While he had written in No. XXXVII that the kingdom of God resides within the human heart, a phrase echoed in the letter, his concern had been with an eternal system of retribution and reward. Indeed, he had very early linked compensation with immortality, telling his journal in January 1823, "Upon the foundation of my moral sense, I ground my faith in the immortality of the soul" (*JMN* 2:83). Then, he had declared the conscience, that which survives death, to be the judge and executor of sin and temptation. But the point of No. XLI is not to locate retribution; rather, it is to seek consolation for death. Pivoting on the axis of the verse from Luke 17:21, which proclaimed the

God within, is his imaginative association of Ellen with God(liness) and of himself with her. On this verse rest Emerson's notions of both authority and correspondence, that there is a correlation between like beings and between the God within and the God without. From these explorations of the God within, Emerson would find consolation for personal loss and establish a philosophy of cosmic interrelatedness. And as his line to Charles demonstrates, the movement of his logic proceeds from Ellen to himself as the "pitied" mourner-to-be, from the prospect of death to the mourner's need for consolation, and finally from the personal to the universal. It is a movement that also participates in (and depends upon) the erasure of the real (dying) Ellen as he inscribes his own needs for spirituality and consolation on the figure that she represents.

Searching, then, for definitions of life and a strategy for coping with loss as he anticipates the inevitable, Emerson tests the viability of the Christian response to death. In No. XLI he proposes that Christianity is the consolation for death, that the Christian "becomes reconciled to death as a process of nature as essential as birth, and indeed as it is a second birth the separation of the spirit from the body as the first was a separation of the body from its parent body" (*CS* 1:310). Here Emerson seems to be suggesting what Richard Grusin calls "the procreative function of death," whereby death becomes "a constitutive element of moral improvement." Indeed, Karen Halttunen notes that in popular consolation literature mourning is likened to a conversion experience by which the mourner is brought closer to God.[17] But Emerson's atten-

---

17. Grusin, *Transcendentalist Hermeneutics,* 42, 41. Grusin here centers his discussion of Emerson's views about death around the Lord's Supper tradition. Grusin makes the analogy that "it was necessary for Jesus to die so that his followers could reinterpret the Passover as a new covenant with God, or for Ellen to die so that Emerson could reinterpret his commitment to the ministry of the Second Church" (42). Grusin's comment simplifies, I think, the trial and anguish that Emerson underwent before he could reassess his pastoral commitments. Halttunen, *Confidence Men and Painted Women,* 129. Halttunen lists four stages of the mourning-to-conversion experience: (1) the mourner realizes a sense of spiritual insufficiency; (2) becomes aware of the vanity of earthly happiness; (3) is reminded that the mourner's death is to come; and (4) is brought to a realization of the need to resign him/herself to God.

tion in No. XLI on the improving, progressive nature of death falters, and he is drawn back and forth between proclamations of reconciliation and descriptions of the horrors of death and decay. Even though he states that "this world is only a porch and a threshold and not itself the temple of the divine glory" (*CS* 1:309), much of the emotional power of the sermon resides in his descriptions of the death of the body, indicating his anxiety about illness, especially Ellen's. Rather gruesomely he spells out the particulars of illness and death:

> We are each of us to be sick. Fever or Consumption or palsy will come in turn to each. Cold shaking rheumatism or frightful convulsions, and a bed will be made for each in the bosom of the ground. . . . the dismembering clay will have lost its form and long ere that, most of us shall be gathered in dust. Soon the eye shall lose its nimble expression, and the porches of the ear shall be stopped to the voice of reproof and the sound of flattery. The worm already reckons on his banquet. (*CS* 1:308–9)

Riveted still to the scene of death, he describes the period of mourning: "We put on black garments and encourage each other in the indulgence of the most miserable sorrow" (*CS* 1:309).

As if shaking himself awake from a trancelike fascination with the scenes of death and mourning, he counters his fear by looking to the eternal world beyond in which the individual will exist "with new and infinite powers." Imaginatively projecting a future state of eternal society in which his mind can have "an uninterrupted intercourse with the majestic society of all souls," the minister looks forward to "the event that releases [him] from the prison" of the flesh and sends him "to the presence of all that is holy and ravishing in moral beauty" (*CS* 1:310–11). While No. XLI identifies that "presence" as Christ and uses language traditionally used to refer to Christ, the words "holy," "ravishing," "moral," and "beauty" echo Emerson's descriptions of Ellen, eroticizing the biblical text and death. Of his "Beauty" (*L* 1:259) he wrote, "She has the purity & confiding religion of an angel" (*JMN* 3:149), that she is "the fairest & best of her kind," that "Her feelings are exceedingly delicate & noble" (*L* 1:256), and that "she is fairest, virtuousest, discreetest best" (*L* 1:270). Thus the "presence" to which the minister refers may be either or both Christ and Ellen, for both have the qualities of moral beauty. Moreover, the language of the passage calls to mind the marriage motif that is represented in the Song of Solomon and becomes a key image of the apocalyptic marriage mentioned in Revelation. As Alan Hodder has suggested about Emerson's use of apocalyptic imagery in *Nature,* so too here we find Emerson calling to mind the marriage motif to imagine the relationship between the soul and Christ. As Hodder points out, "Christian mystics of the Middle Ages and afterwards conceived the relationship between the soul and Christ along the lines of the erotic union between bride and bridegroom." Emerson extends this trope in *Nature,* again as Hodder observes, to reinvoke "the image of the divine marriage as a way of imaginatively overcoming the separation between Nature and Spirit."[18]

At the same time that the metaphorical language of No. XLI and the marriage trope suggest the relationship between the soul and Christ and the merging of the individual's interests with the will of God, they suggest also the kind of communion between husband and wife by which individual interests merge. Just as the biblical marriage trope operated to image forth the saving union between the worshiper and Christ, so it represents for Emerson a means of overcoming the separation humans are fated to endure. The metaphor suggests to Emerson a way to bridge separation and to build a correspondence between this existence and the next. His vision of immortality, then, extends beyond Christian piety and conventional consolation formulas to a private, emotive evocation of correspondence and transformation. When Emerson reminds his audience of Jesus' victory over death, he may again be merging the figure of Ellen, whom he will soon marry, with the figure of Jesus as one who too "shall never die" (*CS* 1:311). As the marriage motif and the example of Jesus' resurrection provide for him images by which to counter the nullifying quality of death, he moves in

18. Alan D. Hodder, *Emerson's Rhetoric of Revelation: Nature, the Reader, and the Apocalypse Within,* 25, 27–28. Hodder points to the texts in Revelation 19:7 ("for the marriage of the Lamb is come, and his wife hath made herself ready") and Revelation 21 ("And I, John, saw the holy city, new Jerusalem, coming down from God out of heaven, prepared as a bride adorned for her husband"), which coincide with the new creation, the new heaven and new earth, and the eternal covenant between God and his people (25).

this sermon beyond discussion of eternal retribution to a projection of the eternal being of the self.

The sermons of 1827 to 1829 provide a preview of Emerson's depression in the last year of Ellen's life. They sketch out the confused way in which Emerson confronts death, at one moment overwhelmed by the decay he sees about him and at the next trying to find consolation through Christian doctrine. As with the sermons that explore the meaning of compensation, the sermons with death as their topic also have a tentativeness about them as the minister explores the viability of various perspectives, exploring first traditional and conventional definitions and moving later toward more original and radical pronouncements. As with the compensation sermons, the sermons about death and immortality demonstrate Emerson's descent into depression in the autumn of 1830, the baptism of suffering from which he will emerge a new man with a new vision.[19]

Although Emerson believed that God ordered the universe and that all that happened in it was part of God's master plan to educate man to moral goodness, his beliefs were tested by his own experiences. On February 13, 1830, a year before his wife's death, Emerson wrote, with some difficulty, a sermon, No. LXVI, on "Providence." Looking at his subject from a distance, from the perspective of God and from the scope of geology, Emerson told his congregation that "nothing is uncertain in its infinite plan" and that "the seeming exceptions and violations of the general Order, are made to contribute to ultimate good" (*CS* 2:142). Recalling his brother Edward's bout with temporary insanity in 1828, Waldo wrote that even "madness hath its uses" in God's plan for the instruction of man (*CS* 2:332). The "disorders of nature"

19. Although scholars have sensed Ellen's role in Emerson's resignation, none have yet traced just how her experience informed and participated in his conversion. Grusin, *Transcendentalist Hermeneutics,* 161n, notes that Loving calls "Ellen's death and her husband's reflection on it . . . the catalyst and not the cause of Emerson's resignation" and that Whicher suggests that Ellen's "death helped to further" both a "revolution in his way of life and wonted occupation" and the development of Emerson's "own hard-tested secret of insulation from calamity: Live in the Soul."

and adversity teach "that God interests himself in the education of the race of man, in their progressive improvements; — and so I get a nearer view of his Providence" (CS 2:141). This "nearer view," which is really a further, distancing view, shows Emerson that "sorrow and success" are to be seen as "trial, as discipline, as reward, or as prophesy" (CS 2:142). At the same time that Emerson is reminding his congregation of the universal economy of morals by which sorrow and loss are converted into character, he seeks to diminish for himself the immediacy of pain and loss by projecting his vision to the distant and timeless future, to a time and place, as he wrote in a poem about Ellen, "When all but Love itself is dead, / And all but deathless Reason gone" (JMN 3:182). By denying the power of the physical world over him and by seeing real power residing within the soul, Emerson attempts to compensate for his own sense of powerlessness and for the loss of the wife he loved "too deeply"[20] by sublimating his experiences and by recasting his vision.

Indeed, in a note added after the text of Sermon No. LXXIV, written while Ellen was in Philadelphia trying to recuperate from her "red wheezers" (L 1:296), Emerson wrote to himself more than to anyone else, "The true effect I believe which a good life produces is to satisfy the mind that there is a part of it which is permanent that there are objects which are permanent & that the temper in which death is to be regarded is that of absolute resignation" (CS 2:354).[21] At a period when any previous optimism about Ellen's health must have been shattered by the necessity of moving her to the warmer climate of Philadelphia, Emerson turned in Sermon Nos. LXXIII and LXXIV to the subject of death, rehearsing again the prospects for the dead and consolation for the mourner.

By October 1830, Ellen's health had again worsened, and Emerson

20. Loving, *American Muse*, 14.

21. The editors of the *Complete Sermons* suggest that the emendation may have been made after Ellen's death and may belong to the January 15, 1832, delivery of the sermon (CS 2:352). Whether written before or after Ellen's death, the note nonetheless attests to Emerson's ability to cast his vision on the permanent rather than the mutable and suggests that this focus derives from his need to assert human potency in the face of loss.

was in the depths of a depression that expressed itself in sermons dark with the images of sin and death. He argues, of course, for the consolation of Christianity, but the language and some of the changes in the text of the sermons of this period suggest not only that the topic was deeply personal but also that he was exploring strategies that would lead him away from the conventional and traditional sources of consolation.

When he asks his congregation in Sermon No. XCI about the means of consolation, we hear in the slowed pacing and darkened images the resonance of his own suffering: "Then death comes and all mortal hopes are defeated and the house full of social comfort and hope is lonely and the rooms are darkened and the face and the heart are yet darker. How shall they be comforted?" (*CS* 3:14). When he answers, we catch the swing of the argument that will direct him away from previous definitions of death and consolation; we hear, still tentatively, what he whispered in No. XLI, that consolation resides in the idea of connections or correspondences between the realms of experience:

> Nor have you learned to regard those whom you love, husband, wife, children, father, mother, with the highest kind of love if their death will destroy your peace. The love of them must combine with the love of God; they must be to you in all the comfort they give you here the tokens only of God's kindness, their graces and virtues the faint types of God's perfections that the faith may grow into your souls[,] that when the earth shall claim its dust, the connexions of affection and virtue shall not cease, but shall revive and strengthen and be glorified — in <heaven> the presence of God. (*CS* 3:17 and 273)

At the same time that Emerson sounds as if he turns to the greater glory of God for consolation and meaning, a penciled addition between the lines betrays that his consolation lies in the belief that the dead remain present to the living, for "when they depart you may feel they are not wholly gone." Although he has been speaking in the sermons and journals of the permanence of the mind, of the greater importance of virtue over "bare existence" (*CS* 3:34), he yet envisions that there will be a place for the dead to reside, that as a reviewer for the *Christian Examiner* noted, "the future state will be a social state."[22] In a penciled

22. *Christian Examiner* New Series, 14 (1829): 48.

addition to Sermon No. XCIII he writes, "Then when thy corruptible puts on incorruption, when not only we are fitted for the society of the good but united to the society and restored to the blessed spirits of our friends departed from the earth, shall we ask any other good than the indulgence of our affections and the use of our immortal faculties" (*CS* 3:28). Unwilling to let go of the belief or superstition that the dead retain a form by which they can be identified, he writes in No. XCIV that in the future state we shall know each other, "that is, Abraham as Abraham, and Isaac as Isaac" (*CS* 3:33).

Willing himself into a belief in the correspondences between this world and the next, he finds hope in the "connexions" that the dead represent. The dead in the passage in Sermon No. XCI are not just the "husband, wife, children, father, mother" lost through death, but "tokens only of God's kindness" and "faint types of God's perfections" and of the "connexions" between earth and heaven (*CS* 3:17). As with the marriage metaphor in No. XLI, he finds hope in the "marriage" or "connexion" between the human and the eternal, between the worshiper and the object of worship. The metaphor of correspondence eases Emerson's pain by providing a construct for continued companionship with Ellen and by embedding the lived experience in symbol. At the same time, then, that the experience of death is real and personal, prompting him to scribble in pencil, "If you love them you cannot spare them without pain" (*CS* 3:273), it also becomes for Emerson a symbolic event, transforming experience into idea and validating the power of the symbol maker over experience.[23] Emerson's text readily illustrates the power of language to transform the subject — death or Ellen — into constructs of the mind, as well as to transform the signifier as one able to overcome or manage alienation and separation.

The conflict between his emotional impulse and the direction of his thought is demonstrated in the sermons written during the autumn of 1830. Consistent with the mood of depression, answers to difficult problems such as death and immortality did not come easily nor did they come readily for a young man once convinced of his coldness who

23. Langer argues in the second chapter of *Philosophy in a New Key* that symbolization is a primary need in humans, that it is the essential act of mind, and that it transforms experience into meaning of one's own making (33–54).

had at last learned he could love. If Emerson had not been a thoughtful person, he could have been emotionally and intellectually supported by church doctrine or by contemporary wisdom and habit. But Emerson was not prone to blindly accepting another's thinking, and at the period marked by his ministry and the death of Ellen, his ideas were in process, neither already formed by him nor mere reiterations of accepted philosophy. They were a little of both. And they were tinged with the emotion of his personal anxiety.

Death

Then on February 8, 1831, Ellen Tucker Emerson died. The descriptions of the death scene by Waldo and Charles preview the direction of Emerson's thinking after her death, for not only did Emerson make of the event a symbolic experience but also he objectified Ellen, transforming her from a frail human to an angel, a saint, a romanticized and mythical creature who would have powers akin to other mythic figures of intercession and salvation. With Ellen's death, Emerson's erasure of her figure in his text intensifies as he metaphorizes and abstracts her into an idea. At once transforming her figure along conventional, sentimentalized versions of consolation that depicted the dead as angels as a way "to stop raw emotion from pouring out onto the page,"[24] Emerson also invests in her idealized form his own version of consolation. He inscribes on her the text of his own need, making of her angelic purity a sign for the erasure of fearsome corporeality — of decay and temptation — reading into her figure a symbol of spirituality, immortality, and purity. This he does by means of conventional consolation rhetoric.

A few hours after Ellen's death, Waldo wrote to Aunt Mary to tell her of the passing of his "angel": "My angel is gone to heaven this morning & I am alone in the world & strangely happy" (*L* 1:318). The descriptions of her death by both Waldo and Charles stress the spiritu-

---

24. Lensink, *"A Secret to Be Buried,"* 381. See Susan Sontag, *Illness as Metaphor,* for a discussion of the romanticization of tuberculosis.

ality of the occasion, finding Ellen to be "saint like" (*L* 1:318n) and a "blessed Spirit" (*JMN* 3:227) and noting the prayers not only for Ellen but by Ellen: "And truly & sweetly did she pray for herself & for us & infused such comfort into my soul as never entered it before" (*JMN* 3:227). The descriptions of Ellen's death appear to be consistent with the kind of romanticization of death current in early nineteenth-century consolation literature, in which the dead are described as angelic and the mourners find a consoling piety in the sublime experience of death. Halttunen notes that in the early decades of the nineteenth century, mourning was viewed as a Christian response to death: "In weeping over the dead, the mourner was thus performing an act of Christian piety." Reminded of his own mortality, the mourner would flee "to Him . . . who is rich in mercies and mighty to save."[25] According to the rhetoric of consolation, mourning is like a conversion experience that brings the mourner closer to God. While the Emerson depictions omit scenes of weeping, standard fare in consolation literature, they do include the sentimentalized piety that celebrates the prayers, the "blessed" last words of the dying woman who looks forward to, and perhaps from, the ethereal realm: "Take me o God to thyself . . . I have not forgot the peace & joy" (*JMN* 3:227).

But whereas the conventional mourner is brought closer to God, Emerson objectifies and sanctifies Ellen, finding his consolation not so much in Christian piety as in the belief that she has not really left him, that her spirit is ever-present, and that she will be his guide to purity and his intercessor with the "Father of our Spirits" (*JMN* 3:227). And whereas the mourner in consolation literature experiences a conversion, finding God to be the "one 'True Consoler' and Christianity the 'religion of consolations,'"[26] Emerson undergoes a conversion away from conventional Christianity, for the dead and angelic Ellen not only comforts him in his grief but also directs his transformation of Christian compensation into idealistic correspondence. At the same time that he turns to her to "comfort . . . my soul," he asks her, "Pray for me Ellen & raise the friend you so truly loved, to be what you thought him."

25. Halttunen, *Confidence Men and Painted Women,* 129–30.
26. Ibid., 130.

He prays to her, asking her not only to comfort his grieving heart but also to "suggest good thoughts as you promised me, & show me truth. . . . [to] stay by me & lead me upward." Echoing the language often used to describe beings more divine than human, Emerson fashions out of language an Ellen who, like divine beings, is not conquered by the death of the flesh and whose task will be "to see, to know, to worship, to love, to intercede," to "go first & explore the way" to heaven and to truth (*JMN* 3:226–27). The metaphorized Ellen is to effect a transformation of spirit and insight in the heart and soul of her more human companion. The figure Emerson makes of her is doubly transformative, for as he transforms her into metaphor, Ellen as symbolic representation of death and immortality effects an emotive and intellectual transformation in her author/husband. When Waldo writes that her death has left him "strangely happy" (*L* 1:318) and that "There is one birth & one baptism & one first love" (*JMN* 3:227), he may be giving voice to the baptism of suffering and conversion of spirit so closely connected with the figure of Ellen and her saintly death.

Had Emerson spoken of Ellen in these terms only in his private papers and only on the occasion of the trauma of her death, we would find his prayers to her a passing whim of his grief. Yet his sermons prior to her death were not the only ones to effect the metaphorical transfiguration of Ellen. In the sermons following her death — and not just those about death — Emerson translates the experience and the being of Ellen, making her a symbol of and means to his own turn in thought. This conversion of insight would eventually enable him to declare himself a self-reliant, genuine man, a New Man baptized by suffering.

In Sermon No. CVII, "Consolation for the Mourner," commemorating Ellen's death, Emerson transcribes his earlier description of the death scene and seeks ways of "depriving death of its sting." This he does by citing Christian doctrine and echoing the rhetoric of consolation, showing how pious faith overcomes the fear of death and sees beyond the grave to a "natural reward of goodness and wisdom, in the removal of all doubt as to the course and the end of their secret journey" (*CS* 3:103). Although the language of the sermon suggests emotional distance from the trauma of death and although the argument of the sermon suggests an easy assurance about the future state, the sermon is nonetheless intensely personal, its images corresponding to the private texts and its argument the result of a long foreground that had tested various consolations for the mourner. When he writes, without specific reference to his own "incalculable loss" (*L* 1:318n), of the death of the pious, he translates the private experience into the general, gaining power over the immediacy of experience through the vehicle of language: "Yes they teach us better — the pious dead — whose hope in God grew stronger as the heart it agitated, was ceasing to beat. They went down to the tomb with prayer and praise on their lips, and the thoughts of heaven found their way in to the convulsions of death" (*CS* 3:103). Whereas Sermon No. V, "Christ Crucified," celebrated the example of Jesus' victory over death, here Ellen is the central figure: she is the "pious dead" whose example frees Emerson from fear of death and teaches him the continuity of being. From her he learns that death is "a change and not a termination of our being," for by gazing upon her face he sees the "secret journey" beyond the here and now (*CS* 3:101, 103). Like Dante's Beatrice, who teaches the poet "life's itinerary" and Poe's Helen, whose eyes "illuminate and enkindle,"[27] Ellen's face mirrors a life beyond the physical one and suggests the "secret analogies" that link the here and now with the hereafter (*JMN* 3:256).

While Sermon No. CVII celebrates the survival of the soul, making the doctrinal distinction between it and the body, proclaiming that "All that part of man which we call the character, survives and ascends" (*CS* 3:103), Emerson's grief is not assuaged by the mere faith that the soul lives on in some amorphous state. He wants continued communion with his "angel," for he believes that there is a "conviction on the mind of the mourner that the dead are present. They speak to him out of the darkness words of comfort which the living could never utter. He is assured of their sympathy, of their prayer, and of whatsoever aid the spirit out of the body can give to the spirit in the body" (*CS* 3:104). Since the spring of 1829, when he wrote of the visitation of the dead to the living, he has hoped for and believed in a communion with the dead. Now, Ellen is to be his "holy society" and through her "personal

27. Dante, *The Divine Comedy,* 722 (10.1.132). Edgar Allan Poe, "To Helen," 950.

interest of love," to intercede for him in heaven: "The soul that has thought with us, and preferred our interest to its own, and known well what was in our heart, is now only a step removed from us, and, we believe, looks back with more than earthly love, mixing the recent knowledge of human wants, with the newness of the revelations now made to it by change of state" (*CS* 3:104). Although he has cited Christian texts and referred to Christian faith, it is this belief in the perpetual society of the dead — of Ellen — to the mourner that provides the real consolation for Emerson. He has not so much lost a wife as gained a heavenly intercessor, a personal correspondent to the unknowable and ethereal truths. At the same time, then, that he deifies Ellen, giving her powers and virtue usually ascribed to divine beings, he also objectifies her, making her an instrument in his search for consolation and knowledge. Indeed, during the winter and spring of 1831, his journal is sprinkled with supplications to his dead wife to become the liaison between himself and God: "O suggest, coming from God's throne, suggest to this lone heart some hint of him. O forget me not, think with me[,] pray with me" (*JMN* 3:240). Like the poet in T. S. Eliot's *Ash Wednesday* who prays to the "Blessed sister, holy mother" to "Teach us to sit still," Emerson prays to the spirit of his wife. And as the *Ash Wednesday* poet asks the "veiled sister"[28] to pray for him, Emerson asks for Ellen's prayers, and her tomb, both figuratively and literally, becomes a religious shrine: "we return with an eagerness to the tomb, as the only place of healing and peace" (*CS* 3:104).

What is evident is that Emerson not only fuses sex, death, and psychic if not spiritual renewal in the figure of Ellen, but also transforms her into a private symbol ("My holy wife" [*JMN* 3:234]) that assimilates qualities usually ascribed to holy personages, particularly Jesus Christ and the Virgin Mary, man's special (female) intercessor. As the example of Jesus provides for the believer a symbolic bridge over the emotional chasm of loss, fear, and finitude, so too does the example of Ellen. And as the example of Jesus proclaims the infinitude of the self, so too does the example of Ellen for Emerson. For not only does Emerson believe that her being continues to be present to him, but also through the

28. T. S. Eliot, *Ash Wednesday,* in *T. S. Eliot: Collected Poems, 1909–1962,* 95, 92.

symbol that she becomes, he can proclaim his own infinitude and deny the finitude of (his) spirit and vision. Like Jesus, she is a symbol that saves and empowers and is the means toward a transformation of self.

What is also evident about the meaning of Ellen's death for Emerson is his realization that correspondences exist between Nature and Spirit that serve not only to unite opposite poles of being but also to illustrate the unity of all being. Prompted by his emotional need to retain contact with Ellen, to convince himself that death is "a change and not a termination of our being" (*CS* 3:101), Emerson began to develop a new meaning for compensation, one that emphasized not reward and punishment but the connections and analogies between states of being. When he wrote in August 1831, "That word *Compensations* is one of the watchwords of my spiritual world" (*L* 1:330), he had discovered the natural meaning of compensation that taught the magnetic interconnectedness of life, the web of life, that linked not only like to like but all being together.

"Like Must Know Like"

"Like must know like" became for Emerson the key that unlocked the lesson of nature that "Every chip & sea weed contributes its part to the gravity of the system & every object in the universe[,] every truth bears testimony to God" (*JMN* 3:235, 254). An ancient phrase, credited variously to Heraclitus, Xenophanes, Parmenides, and Plotinus, its meaning was made pertinent as it became personal to Emerson. It is a phrase that occurs and recurs in his journal in conjunction with his confrontation with death. He wrote on December 10, 1830, "It is one of the oldest principles of philosophy that like must beget like, & that only like can know like" (*JMN* 3:213). Just ten days later he wrote, "The first difficulty is that the like must be known by the like" (*JMN* 3:217). On February 23, 1831, he wrote, "It is worth recording that Plotinus said, 'Of the Unity of God, Nothing can be predicated, neither being, nor essence, nor life, for it is above all these'. . . . Thus 'Design proves a designer', 'Like must know like'" (*JMN* 3:235). On July 15, 1831, he again wrote, "Like must be joined to like" (*JMN* 3:273). And in his blotting book for 1830, apparently fresh from reading Gérando's discussion of Xenophanes, Emerson summed up "Ex nihilo nil fit" to mean "Like must produce like" (*JMN* 3:368). That this phrase recurs in Emerson's private journal during this period indicates its importance in Emerson's developing theory of correspondence as well as his effort in "depriving death of its sting." For Emerson there exists a connection between the experience of Ellen's illness and death and the idea of the cosmos. Indeed, the meaning Emerson derived from the phrase suggests not only that he identified himself with Ellen, finding in her a kindred spirit, but also that the personal relationship suggested to him a universal interpretation, that man and God are kindred spirits and that the identity of either party is intertwined with the other. Like the marriage motif that images the union of man and woman as well as of man and God, so too this phrase has human as well as universal implications.

In a poem written to Ellen shortly after her death in which he beseeches her to remember him, to heed his call and listen to his prayer, he identifies his well-being on earth with her continued favor:

> Teach me I am forgotten by the dead
> And that the dead is by herself forgot
> And I no longer would keep terms with me.
> I would not murder, steal, or fornicate,
> Nor with ambition break the peace of towns
> But I would bury my ambition
> The hope & action of my sovereign soul
> In miserable ruin.

Linking his purpose in life with the continued presence and love of the dead Ellen, he also writes of the interchangeable quality of their beings:

> But the spirit that dwelt in mine
> The spirit wherein mine dwelt. (*JMN* 3:228–29)

What makes Ellen special to Emerson is not so much her beauty or virtue, though he often praised them, but the "sympathy" that existed between them, the "common thought" that tied them. Echoing the passage about likeness, he wrote on June 25, 1831, "No love without sympathy. Minds must be alike. All love a seeking in another what is like self. . . . If we both love God we shall be wholly alike & wholly love each other" (*JMN* 3:260–61). Indeed, the true friend is one whose being is preternaturally receptive because sympathetic to the "subtle electricity" of the other's thoughts. And this receptivity, like true love, derives from union with God and the union made by God, "Heaven's Matches" (*JMN* 3:273).

While the idea of correspondence is grounded in Emerson's emotional need to compensate for Ellen's death, his thought did not remain at the personal but instead extended beyond the moment and the particular to consider the wider scheme of the cosmos. Indeed, the paradigm of reciprocity suggested by his relationship with Ellen becomes just that, a paradigm for interpreting the more universal relationship between man and God. In Sermon No. CXI, Emerson borrows the terms of his relationship to Ellen to describe the individual's relationship to Jesus. In both cases, he stresses the role of sympathy in bringing the two friends together and the importance of likeness for love, since "all love is likeness" (*CS* 3:130). In fact, he argues that the individual's love for others prepares him to love Jesus, to establish a personal relationship with God based on love and sympathy. Here, he writes as he had in his journal, "You find sympathy, that is, you find something of yourself in your friend and so you seek his society" (*CS* 3:130). Clearly, for young Emerson the philosophical and the personal are intertwined, with the need for personal resolution driving him toward a metaphysics.

Thus on July 15, 1831, the day after he had written about friendship and "Heaven's Matches," he wrote again, "Like must be joined to like," but this time in the context first of the intellectual receptivity of "[t]he chemist's secrets," and then of the spiritual receptivity of the truth of God, that "God in us worships God" (*JMN* 3:273). Looking for the secret of the universe in the word *likeness,* Emerson translated the private musings into a sermon in which he argues, "The way to perceive a spirit is to become like it" (*CS* 3:190). Demonstrating that a "bad man," one who is given over to a life of sensuality, "loses the evidence of God's being" and that "a good man," one who has "uniformly a strong conviction of God's being," draws closer to God, Sermon No. CXXI argues that men become like that which they practice (*CS* 3:189).

The lesson of the two types of men is of the reciprocity of action: "By keeping the commandments [the good man] learns them better" (*CS* 3:190). And it is a lesson of evidence, for the "bad man" knows only of the sensual, material world and of the "total annihilation" of death, while the "good man" knows because he has faith in the spiritual existence of being. Indeed, Emerson argues, "By drawing nigh to God, God draws nigh" to the faithful, and as the self becomes more godlike, the evidence of God's being resides within the human soul. Having discovered the key to the secret of the cosmos "in one word, Likeness" (*CS* 3:190), Emerson explored the ramifications of the idea of correspondence in the sermons of the last year or so of his ministry.

When Emerson wrote in Sermon No. CXXVII of the "unity of God" and the "harmony and relation" of all the parts of nature, he seemed to be echoing intellectual and cultural influences that could confirm his developing notion of the "secret analogies" of the universe (*CS* 3:221, *JMN* 3:256). When he wrote in this September 1831 sermon of the "strict correspondence of the outward to the intellectual world" (*CS* 3:221), he may have echoed the proposition of phrenology concerning the correlation between mind and matter, "that the mind . . . operates through the agency of . . . material organs," "protuberances on [the] Skull." Even though the reviewer for the *Edinburgh Review* of George Combe's *A System of Phrenology* (1825) discredited the phrenological proposition, he did concede that "in our present state of existence, the mind is united, in some mysterious way, to a living and organized body."[29] The notion that palpable connections exist between mind and matter apparently encouraged Emerson in his own theory of correspondences, for he told his brother William that Combe's 1829 publication, *Constitution of Man,* is "the best Sermon I have read for some time" (*L* 1:291). As a means of reading character from configurations on the skull, phrenology analogously suggests that connections between physical, material reality and a reality more ineffable exist that are real, pervasive, and knowable to the alert reader.

So too must the translation of the Egyptian hieroglyphics and the

29. *Edinburgh Review* 44 (1826): 255–57. One might also make a corollary case for the influence of science on Emerson's emergent theory of reciprocity. In Sermon

revelation of previously unknown secrets have confirmed Emerson's vision of the web of connectedness between the material and the spiritual, between that which is known and that which is hidden, between art and science. In Sermon No. CXXVII Emerson speaks of the "common bond betwixt the sciences and betwixt the arts; and . . . betwixt spiritual truths and betwixt the virtues" (CS 3:221). Similarly, an article in the Edinburgh Review claims that "the Hieroglyphical Inscriptions on its public monuments contain a summary of the most important mysteries of nature, and the most sublime inventions of man," which had been "so studiously concealed by the priests from the knowledge of the vulgar."[30] As the translations of the hieroglyphics demonstrate, there are both direct and symbolic correspondences between the characters and the ideas they represent. Indeed, the hieroglyph later becomes a significant trope by which Emerson figures the relatedness of "all truth" (CS 3:221) as well as the problems of interpretation. Although Emerson's explicit use of the trope in the sermons is rare, he does use it to suggest the interrelatedness between man and nature. In an early sermon (No. XXXIX) he says, "There is nothing in external nature but is an emblem, a hieroglyphic, of some thing in us" (CS 1:299). He repeats the notion in No. CLV (May 1832) when he says that the "works of nature . . . seem all to be hieroglyphicks containing a meaning which only [man's moral nature] can decipher" (CS 4:144). In both passages, he sketches the premises he will develop in Nature, using the "hieroglyphick" trope to figure both the correspondences between the physical and the spiritual and the mind's role as the "key" for deciphering "the works of nature" (CS 4:144).

Certainly the ideas and images of Sampson Reed are evident in Em-

---

No. 5, he used the example of the loadstone to suggest, "All nature is full of symbols of its author." See note 5, CS 2:20.

30. Edinburgh Review 45 (1827): 98. Edward Everett wrote an essay for the North American Review in 1831 on "the Hieroglyphic System of M. Champollion" and J. G. H. Grappo's book on hieroglyphics. See also John Irwin, American Hieroglyphics: The Symbol of the Egyptian Hieroglyphics in the American Renaissance, for more complete discussion of hieroglyphics and phrenology and how they figured in the American imagination. Irwin's discussion of Emerson and the hieroglyphic trope, of course, looks only at the post-ministerial work and how it figures in his mature, rather than emergent, thought.

erson's sermon. Emerson had heard Reed's "Oration on Genius" in 1821 and had read *Observations on the Growth of the Mind* when it appeared in 1826, noting in his journal the ideas of unity and harmony that he would sound in his own work: "It has to my mind the aspect of a revelation, such is the wealth & such is the novelty of the truth unfolded in it. It is remarkable for the unity into which it has resolved the various powers, feelings & vocations of men, suggesting to the mind that harmony which it has always a propensity to seek of action & design in the order of Providence in the world" (*JMN* 3:45). When Emerson turns to the idea of unity as he does in Sermon No. CXXVII, the influence of Reed and consequently of Swedenborg lies below the surface of the text, providing a kind of linguistic and philosophical foundation upon which he builds his own ideas and images. When Emerson declares, "The unity of God has always been taught by the unity of design that reigns in all nature" (*CS* 3:221), he may be echoing a phrase of Reed's extracted in an 1826 review in the *Christian Examiner:* "When there shall be a religion which shall see God in every thing, and at all times; and the natural sciences not less than nature itself." The eye metaphor, so important for Emerson's later works, appears in this sermon and echoes Reed's metaphor in the "Oration." Emerson wrote: "It is because the author [of nature] is one that every eye sees and every heart feels the harmony and relation of all the parts, of each to the other and of the mind of man to all" (*CS* 3:221). Reed's passage reads: "The intellectual eye of man is formed to see the light, not to make it, and it is time that, when the causes that cloud the spiritual world are removed, man should rejoice in the truth itself, and not that he has found it."[31]

The point here is not to collate the works of Emerson and Reed, or for that matter of any of the other intellectual influences on what was to become Emerson's mature thought (Coleridge, Cousin, deGérando, the German philosophers) line for line, and image for image, but to suggest that in September 1831, when Emerson composed Sermon No. CXXVII, he borrowed from, was influenced by, and echoed the intellectual work and images of Reed and others whose thinking intersected

---

31. *Christian Examiner* 3:5 (1826): 423. Sampson Reed, "Oration on Genius," 51.

with his own emergent thought. Furthermore, the evidence of the sermons indicates that while Emerson responded favorably to Reed's work as early as 1821 and 1826 and to that of Combe, Coleridge, and deGérando in January 1830, he did not begin to incorporate their lessons and images in significant and consistent ways until after Ellen's death and his own attempts to find consolation through a personal vision of correspondence, reciprocity, and unity. The direction of his logic imitates the direction of his life, for, as Emerson knew from experience, the heart teaches the mind. In the summer of 1831, a time when he was pondering the "word Compensation" (*JMN* 3:266), he broke off thought about moral progress to muse, "But this came from heart — not head. This union & this liberty were not dictated so much by reason as by feeling" (*JMN* 3:270). Emerson knew full well what his journals and sermons demonstrate, that his thought was directed by his grief, that musings about Ellen and about correspondence and unity are inextricably and necessarily bound. Contrary to James Cox's contention that "Emerson literally feeds off the death of those around him" in almost piranha-like fashion, Ellen's death catapulted Emerson into what William James calls a "forced option" predicated by his will to deprive "death of its sting" and to retain connection with her. James too understood that our "passional nature" influences in "inevitable" and necessary ways our opinions and options, particularly those "genuine," "living," "momentous," and "forced" (inescapable) options that involve our personal and religious lives.[32] At this crucial period in Emerson's personal life and in his intellectual work, the matters of the heart inform the life of the mind. The cultural and intellectual debts are not so much influences on thought as they are verifications of strategies formulated from the heart.

Indeed, he knew that the desires of the heart inform the cosmic communications between man and God and that there is an unrelenting reciprocity between thought and action. When he preached in his first sermon that all thoughts are prayers and that all prayers are answered, he assumed the existence of a God "out there" who meted out rewards

32. James M. Cox, "Ralph Waldo Emerson: The Circles of the Eye," 71–72. William James, "The Will to Believe," 718, 728, 718.

and punishments in a Calvinistic scheme of compensation. Echoing the
text suggested to him by a Methodist laborer on his Uncle Ladd's farm
(1 Thess. 5:17), Emerson stated that "every desire of the human mind,
is a prayer uttered to God . . . [and that] our prayers are granted" (*CS*
1:57). But he knew also the role of the individual in the causal opera-
tions of the moral universe, for he found that "the true prayers are the
daily, hourly, momentary desires," which individuals by their "unceasing endeavours" bring to fulfillment (*CS* 1:57, 59). While this sermon
suggests a reciprocity between thought and action, between the physical and spiritual realms, it is informed by a Calvinistic understanding
of retribution and reward as well as by a democratic psychology that
finds individuals capable of attaining their goals and responsible for
their actions. As he wrote in Sermon No. LXVII, "There is nothing
done for nothing. You cannot have honor without being honor-
able. . . . You cannot be loved without becoming lovely. You cannot
receive without asking; nor seek without finding; nor be happy without
deserving" (*CS* 2:148–49).

But when he returned to the topic of prayer after Ellen's death, he
had located God within the soul, and the lines of communication between man and God were fused together into a harmonic circuit within
the self. Although he continued to echo his earlier thought, "that God
makes us the answerers of our own prayers" (*JMN* 3:268) and that
"what we love that shall we seek" (*JMN* 3:301), he had focused his
attention on the harmony and unity between soul and body and between God and man. William Ellery Channing taught, "The idea of
God, sublime and awful as it is, is the idea of our own spiritual nature,
purified and enlarged to infinity." Emerson repeated Channing's notion
in Sermon No. LXXXVI when he declared that one grows "godlike"
through prayer (*JMN* 3:183), for man discovers that the idea of God is
"our own soul stripped of all inferiority and carried out to perfection"
(*CS* 2:243). But having convinced himself of the harmony and unity of
all being, Emerson in the spring of 1832 tentatively located God, and
not just the idea of God, within the self. Having looked inward into
the heart of man, Emerson discovered not only God but also the evidence for religious and moral truths, evidence internal and fueled by a

"direct revelation which I have from God" (*JMN* 3:312).[33] In No. CLI, echoing Neoplatonic images, Emerson told his listeners, "It is because our fountains drink of the Sea. It is because we feel and know that somehow we are connected with God; that his life flows into us; that the expression current in every age of the world, 'God in us,' has real meaning" (*CS* 4:121). In No. CLV he suggests a reciprocity between mind and matter that is better imaged by metaphors of containment and circulation than by the traditional images of asking, seeking, and knocking (Matt. 7:7–8). Finding that which resides within the mind to be more real than matter, Emerson declares that the moral nature of man, like the "hieroglyphicks," is the "key by which the works of nature are to be read" (*CS* 4:144). Not only does truth flow outward from the mind of man to physical reality, but "in your conscious self are contained the Heaven, in you are the objects of love and of desire, the images of your friends . . . and more than all, God dwells in you—the Father with the child" (*CS* 4:143).

While these passages foreground the idealism of *Nature,* they also indicate new possibilities for prayer. Moving the focus of prayer away from its practicality for Christians concerned with doing their religious duty and with cultivating the self, Emerson suggests that prayer is a state of mind made possible by the oneness (not just the likeness) between God and man. "Prayer," he wrote in his journal, "does not at all consist in words but wholly is a state of mind. Consider it also in connexion with the doctrine that God is in the Soul of man" (*JMN* 3:308). His discussions of prayer indicate that the shift in the direction of his thinking coincides with the trauma of Ellen's death and his subsequent fashioning of a philosophy by which he could meet the crisis and psychically survive the baptism of suffering. Having formed a philosophy that subscribes to the oneness of the physical and spiritual realms and at the same time denies the absolute reality of the physical realm, the grieving Emerson found a consolation of his own making, a new way

---

33. Quoted in *CS* 2:243n. In *"Strains of Eloquence,"* Mott argues that "The 'God within,' Emerson's version of the Christian evidence, is the definitive theme of the sermons" (69) and "the prime article of Emerson's faith" (108).

of perceiving the universe by which like spirits are forever linked in the mind. Intriguingly, these sermons prove his own theory about prayer, "that God makes us the answerers of our own prayers" (*JMN* 3:268).

Ellen, Once More

This willed version of the cosmos lies behind Emerson's advice to Edward, who was attempting to recover his health in Puerto Rico. Encouraging the tubercular Edward, who would die in 1834, with the idea of the deathlessness of the soul and of the unity of all beings, he seems to be instructing him as to how the soul overcomes the weakness of the body: "High over all calamities, high over all fears, let the constant soul linked by philosophy & faith to the First Cause, calmly pursue her own appointed & glorious path careless of the moment when she passes the confines of matter to keep that identical path in other states" (*L* 1:331). Here he suggests not only that a purpose exists beyond the particulars of life but also that a vision which sees unity behind the details and commotions of the physical, superficial life is a bridge to overcoming fear. Rather than indicating Emerson's "cold" nature (*JMN* 3:72) or inability to cope with death,[34] this passage demonstrates his affection for his brother, with whom he shares the strategy for meeting death derived from his own hard-won vision of the power of thought over the exigencies of life. This note demonstrates as well the personal anguish that lies behind Emerson's high-minded philosophical pronouncements about unity and "the First Cause" as he reminds Edward and himself of the human element of beingness: "Friends warm & true there are to beckon & welcome us there" (*L* 1:331).

Emerson's willed vision of the cosmos also lies behind his experiment to meet with Ellen on the planes of the mind. Having resolved that the God within the self corresponds to the God within other selves, and

---

34. Barish, *Roots of Prophesy*, explains that Emerson's lack of emotion or self-deprecation in the face of death, particularly of those he loved immensely, Ellen and later his son Waldo, is the result of "prior scarring"; indeed, she argues, "it was precisely the extremity of his loss that led to such inappropriate and clearly neurotic reactions" (96).

having been convinced since childhood of the need to temper the bodily appetites as an avenue to spirituality, Emerson engaged in a bizarre but short-lived experiment to make himself more soul than body and to test the bonds of sympathy. With Ellen totally spirit, Emerson in the spring of 1832 attempted an experiment in physical deprivation, cutting his food intake, to make himself more spirit and thereby more like the pure and metaphorized being of his dead wife. Attempting in this odd way to "try to angel it thro' the world" (*JMN* 3:243), to erase his own physical self, he began in his journal an account of his diet:

> 28 March my food per diem weighed 14 1/2 oz
> 29---   ---13   oz
>   2 April   12 1/2   oz
>   (*JMN* 4:6)

As ever for Emerson, measurements of body weight provide tangible evidence of the self's viability. While his weight gains of 1827 attest to the body's recuperation, the deliberate fasting of 1832 attests to the force of the soul or will to fashion the self. The sermon written during his experiment (No. CXLIX) urges self-cultivation, "that we can be what we would be," and independence from the "common views and acts [that] are really such as we have never settled for ourselves" (*CS* 4:103, 105). It also finds the self to be a construct enhanced and made possible by the sympathy and love of others — Jesus, God, family — those who have "the liveliest interest in your welfare" (*CS* 4:109). The point of this sermon as well as of the Fast Day sermon (No. CL) preached a few days later is the "subjection of the body to the soul," the creation of a self more mind than body (*CS* 4:111).

Coincident with this period of fasting and of self-fashioning, of making real the meaning of likeness and sympathy, of proving the power of the mind over the body, Emerson "visited Ellen's tomb & opened the coffin" (*JMN* 4:7). Of what he saw or how he reacted, Emerson leaves no word. But the act of writing for himself the terse reminder of an event no doubt significant may indicate an attempt to undo the ties of association to her physical person. Ellen's body as symbol no longer can have the same resonance it had before he peeked at her desiccated corpse. Instead, Emerson is reconfirmed in his valuation of the spirit and of a correspondence that transcends any sort of physical or temporal condition. As a result of his opening the coffin, Emerson is able to open himself to new possibilities, to reinvest his energy in working through grief to recovery, in creating a new self and a more cosmic version of sympathy. Acting out, rather than talking or writing out, his mourning for and identification with Ellen in ways justified by the morality of temperance and tested against the reality of what he found in the coffin, Emerson arrived at the point of being able to transform mourning into "morning or dawning,"[35] to transform himself from the mourner seeking consolation to a new man, his "loins girt about with truth" (*CS* 4:410).

The lessons of his twin experiments are born out in the sermons of April and May 1832. What he learned when he looked into Ellen's coffin is articulated in sermons that dance around the themes of consolation, correspondence, and self-cultivation. In the same sermon in which he tells his congregation that "no sorrow is without its alleviation," he also declares that "God hath set the world in man's heart" (*CS* 4:120). He suggests to his audience "that the outward world and all that it contains, was designed in God's plan only as a shadow or type of the world within" (*CS* 4:120). Here he draws consolation from a cosmic design that imitates and proves his own construct of sublimation and the superiority of the mind over the body. In his next sermon he preaches, "The natural remedy for this overestimate of private griefs is in the contemplation of the Universal Providence of God" and the recognition of God's "beneficent design" (*CS* 4:122–23). Again, in the sermon of May 6, he looks for consolation in a vision of immortal unity that reaches beyond and defies the particulars of this life. Duty he finds to be just such an eternal verity, a truth that affirms for him the immutability of the spirit, consoling his loss and pointing the direction for his own life. "Amidst all changes, this [duty] is the same," he writes; it is "not only a rest and a solace, but . . . also a principle of improvement" (*CS* 4:137,

---

35. Stanley Cavell, *This New Yet Unapproachable America: Lectures after Emerson after Wittgenstein*, 84.

139). In the sermon that follows, No. CLV, he tells of the power of the mind to contain reality: "in your conscious self are contained . . . the objects of love & of desire, the images of your friends." And he tells of the power of the mind over reality: "There is no form in nature but seems to be the expression of something in mind" (*CS* 4:144). The sermons of this period are about attachments, connections between entities of like mind and connections within the mind, the individual mind and the Vast Mind. Indeed, Emerson not only articulates consolation in the language of attachment, union, connection, but also works out the terms of self-reliance and selfhood in the same terms, finding himself and his possibilities through "intimate union" and "wonderful connexion and unity" (*CS* 3:222–23). The sermons at the end of his ministry, then, indicate the possibility for an Emerson secure in attachment to test his own muscle, to move beyond a "servile" dependence (*CS* 4:131) and toward a more thorough self-reliance.

Announcing his aversion to "the great mass of our common views and acts [that] are really such as we have never settled for ourselves" (*CS* 4:105), Emerson also announces his transformation or conversion into a being with "a new life" and "a new hold on existence" (*CS* 4:127). Convinced of the individual's ability to "be what we would be" (*CS* 4:127), Emerson fashions more than his religious character. He finds and discovers himself, uncovering the possibilities of a new self and shaping that new self from the flames of baptism. "Born again" (*CS* 4:127) in a conversion prompted by Ellen's death and his effort to find consolation, Emerson emerges from his crisis a new man, a man like the genuine man he will posit in Sermon No. CLXIV. Ever seeking the meaning of "That word *Compensations*," Emerson learned in the crucible of suffering the power of his own will to forge a philosophy that refashions and redefines for him the order of the universe, and at the same time redefines the self and the powers of the self.

4

The Myth of Success and the Man-Made Self

"A country, like an individual, has dignity and power, only in proportion as it is self-formed." (*Christian Examiner* New Series, 6 [January 1830]: 282)

"And that ye put on the new man, which after God is created in righteousness and true holiness." Eph. 4:24

The deaths of Thomas Jefferson and John Adams on July 4, 1826, marked a turning point in American history and American identity. With the fervor of the Revolution replaced by Jacksonian politics and the idyllic agrarianism of the federal period supplanted by a booming industrialization, America stood poised at the threshold of the modern era. What Americans would make of their new nation was up to them, for the territory was unmarked and the risk of political, economic, and moral failure was vividly present to them. The generation of Americans coming of age in the early decades of the nineteenth century, who rolled up their sleeves and set about the arduous task of shaping the identity and direction of the nation, knew that the opportunity and responsibility for forming this new giant lay with them. And thus they found their mission and their identity in this task of self-formation, making a myth out of a necessity and declaring themselves a nation of self-made men. "Ours is a country," wrote Calvin Colton, "where men start from an humble origin . . . and where they can attain to the most elevated positions, or acquire a large amount of wealth, according to the pursuits they elect for themselves. . . . This is a country of self-made men, than which nothing better could be said of any state of society." Converting the task of self-formation into an ideal, one writer representative of the era's popular literature proclaimed, "A country, like an individual, has dignity and power, only in proportion as it is self-formed." Authors of the popular literature set about the business of turning self-cultivation into a moral and practical enterprise for aspiring go-getters.[1]

At the same time that Emerson was confronting issues of autonomy, manhood, and the body, working through his own anxieties about physical frailty, the nation was confronting similar issues about the social body. And at the same time that Emerson was finding a solution to his anxiety and grief by fashioning a new self, the nation's anxiety about its emergence from an idyllic agrarianism was being voiced in a discourse of self-formation. Promoted by a flurry of sacred and secular texts about conduct, self-formation, and self-cultivation, the public discussion fashioned a discourse, a code, and an ideology that set the perimeters both for national definitions and for individual self-interpretation. On various levels, national and individual, secular and sacred, the ideal of self-formation, of being a self-made man, was pervasive and was supported in a wide range of public and private texts. So pervasive was the ideal of self-formation that it outlined individual choice and self- interpretation, as it did in Emerson's case. Basil Bernstein tells us, "We see and hear and otherwise experience very largely as we do because the language habits of our community predispose certain choices of interpretation."[2] Thus language, or particular discourse codes like the myth of self-formation, mirrors social attitudes and contributes to the construction of those attitudes and the shape of individual identity. It is not surprising, then, to see that Emerson's personal language about the self echoes that of the national discourse. It also should not be surprising that even Emerson's project of self-fashioning mirrors the political project of self-formation. In this way, we can see

1. Quoted in John G. Cawelti, *Apostles of the Self-Made Man*, 39. *Christian Examiner* New Series, 5 (1830): 282.
2. Quoted in Douglas, *Natural Symbols*, 20–21.

that Emerson's valuation of manliness and his project of self-formation intersect with and are informed by the ideology of his time.

Just as this discussion of self-formation takes place in the bodies of texts, it also takes place in the body as text. Emerson's persistent discussion in his journals and sermons about the temptations, appetites, and frailty of the body echoes cultural discussions of temptation and the body. Moreover, his working out a sense of identity on the body of Ellen, finding himself to be a man of the mind as he erases and witnesses the erasure of Ellen's body, speaks of more than a perverse, idiosyncratic vampirism. For as Mary Douglas suggests, social discussions of behavior and self-identity take place in and through the symbolic language of the body. Indeed, Douglas contends that "the human body is always treated as an image of society" and operates as a metaphor or code for regulating the social body. Smith-Rosenberg demonstrates the validity of Douglas's contention by showing its applicability to Emerson's era: "The nineteenth century's obsession with categorizing the physical, and especially the sexual, with describing the abnormal, and with defining the legitimate must be seen first as an effort to impose order upon the chaos of the nonsexual world." At a time when the nation stood "poised between the traditional agrarian and mercantile social order and the new ways of commercial and industrial capitalism,"[3] attention in the discourse of self-formation and autonomy was focused on self-control, behavior, and temperance; on control of the external self — the body. As with Emerson's own equations of selfhood, manliness is equated with control over the body, its temptations and its temporality. In similar ways, public discussions of self-formation were carried out through the metaphor of the body, of self-control, behavior, and habits, all of which are concerned with the external self, the bodied self.

Yet as Emerson's example will demonstrate, there is something uneasy and unsatisfying about using the body to talk about self-formation. Part of the difficulty is that the myth of the self-made man was constructed from two competing rhetorics, the regressive rhetoric of reform that celebrated self-denial and work and the progressive rhetoric

3. Douglas, *Natural Symbols,* 70. Smith-Rosenberg, *Disorderly Conduct,* 91, 99.

of freedom and individuality. The myth is also complicated by conflict between the codes for each rhetoric — the body, which represents consensus and the wider society, and the spirit, which represents personal liberty. What becomes evident is that while Emerson's use of the cultural code, like his discussions of compensation, remained fairly conventional in the early years of his ministry, with his discovery and refiguration of himself and his subsequent aversion to ready-made institutions, he refigures the self through the metaphoric code of the spirit, the inner self. How Emerson manages his own self-fashioning and creates a philosophy of self-reliance from the cultural materials is the story of this chapter. The task now is to flesh out the conventional descriptions and prescriptions of the self and self-formation, and to see how Emerson incorporated them in his personal and public texts.

The Self-Made Man

Like his contemporaries, the young Reverend Emerson participated in the celebration of the American way, like them troubling his discussions of transformation with a discourse that used the rhetoric of reform, of self-denial and work, of the external or bodily self, to speak about progress, transformation, and freedom. Employing the physical body of the landscape to talk about the social body, Emerson calls attention in an early sermon (No. III) to the external proofs of the nation's ability to reshape the raw materials of the landscape into an entity with meaning and purpose. In the 1827 sermon, he asked his congregation:

> What is it that has sprinkled [America's] hills and valleys with towns; what is it that has felled its forests, that has chalked the continent with roads and furrowed it with canals and reduced its noble streams into the servitude of man, that has filled its enormous regions with rejoicing nations, subdued them with laws, enriched them with arts, and consecrated them with temples to the living God, and multiplied innumerable blessings for which the voice of thanksgiving ascends from them all this day in a mingled incense to heaven? What is it under God but the joint human exertion; the cooperation of men in society? (CS 1:72)

The view of America this passage illustrates is of a civilized body, one whose wild(er)ness has been tamed by social institutions and by the hand of the common man skilled in the mechanical arts of building and invention. Implicit in Emerson's picture of the tamed landscape is a larger paradigm of reform for the nation and the individual that connects the transformation of the external surface (the felling of trees and the building of towns and canals) with an internal transformation of being, from wild and savage to civilized and godly. It is also a paradigm that both mirrors the physical evidence of the landscape and promotes transformation as an external, bodily phenomenon.

In similar ways, discussions about individual reform and progress, articulated in numerous advice manuals and represented by the fictive character, the self-made man, promoted the idea that self-formation was a task of external control or refiguration. Because the individual task also promoted the political project of national progress and self-sufficiency, it was validated and popularized by national spokesmen. With the future of the nation at stake, dependent on a corps of young, hardworking men for the corporate success, the promoters of a bourgeois version of America held out the promise of money, power, character, and morality to young men who would endeavor to shape the plastic self into something of value, the self-made man. In Boston, a series of lectures, the Franklin Lectures, were begun in 1831 to inspire young men to make the most of their opportunities. In the inaugural lecture, Edward Everett declared, "Our whole country is a great and speaking illustration of what may be done by native force of mind, uneducated, without advantages, but starting up under strong excitement, into new and successful action." Like Emerson's depiction of the landscape, Everett's description of the nation and its people ascribes change and identity to external conditions, to hard work, industry, and perseverance. Casting his gaze on the physical, embodied, masculine self, Everett and other advisers describe and shape the identity of Americans as "working being[s]" who are "eager, restless, and powerful," and who are to establish "habits of industry" and to "earnestly persist in [their] toil, adding little by little to [their] capital stock of ideas[,] influence or wealth."[4]

4. Edward Everett, *Orations and Speeches on Various Occasions,* 305, 265. John Todd, *The Young Man. Hints Addressed to the Young Men of the United States,* 2d ed., 27.

In congress with the idea that the nation's success was due in large part to individual projects of self-improvement and self-formation, manuals and guidebooks for young men became a regular feature of the popular literature. Although Benjamin Franklin's *Way to Wealth* was written in 1757, the literature of success really began to take off in the 1820s and 1830s. Beginning in the 1820s, a burgeoning number of youth's periodicals appeared whose aim was to prepare youngsters to be successful in life. Works such as the *Young Man's Own Book,* William Alcott's *The Young Man's Guide,* Joel Hawes's *Lectures to Young Men on the Formation of Character,* William Sprague's *Lectures to Young People,* and Isaac Taylor's *Character Essential to Success in Life, Addressed to those Who Are Approaching Manhood* were all published in the 1820s and 1830s. More were to follow as the years progressed. Advocating a self-reliance of economy, the reality and the dream of the self-made man appeared even before the term itself was coined. According to Rex Burns's findings, the term first appeared in print in an 1827 article in the *Companion,* "A Self Made Man," which told the story of an ex-yeoman mechanic who made his success and then retired to serve his fellowmen in Congress. Quite naturally, the meaning of the term evolved through time, and when Henry Clay used it five years later, he referred to a group of manufacturers who had amassed riches rather than virtuously accumulating and using wealth.[5] However the term was used, Americans seemed convinced of the ideal of the man who formed his own success.

Similarly, America's religious leaders, particularly Unitarian ministers, preached self-cultivation and character formation as religious goals. As David Robinson puts it, "the sermon was an ideally suited mode of expression for the philosophy of self-culture. The immediacy of its oral presentation, the authority of its homiletic context, and most importantly, the tradition of moral persuasion that it embodied made the sermon an essential tool for a movement whose touchstone was moral perfection." Like their secular counterparts, Unitarians looked to

---

William A. Alcott, *The Young Man's Guide,* 2d ed., 28. Wise, *Young Man's Counsellor,* 110.

5. Rex Burns, *Success in America: The Yeoman Dream and the Industrial Revolution,* 18, 63.

the self-made man as exemplary and found the direction of life to lie on the path toward moral perfection. Just as success is (theoretically, at least) the result of relentless labor, so too salvation is figured in terms of "right and vigorous exertion." William Ellery Channing preached that "true religion consists in proposing, as our great end, a growing likeness to the Supreme Being," the means for which lay organically within the self, "in our essential faculties, unfolded by vigorous and conscientious exertion in the ordinary circumstances assigned by God." Rather than preaching a religion of emotional conversion, Unitarians believed that salvation entailed a process of developing and unfolding the godlike potential of the individual. Salvation, like success, derived from the development of resources within the self by the self rather than by outside forces such as miracles, "supernatural additions," or "any thing foreign to our original constitution." Yet Unitarians, the young Emerson among them, advocated a program of reform of the external person, marked by habit and moderation, as a way of transforming the inner self. Indeed, a reviewer of Marie Joseph deGérando's *Self-Education, of the Means and Art of Moral Progress* suggests that the similarity between secular and moral improvement lies in a program of self-education: "The life of man, is, in reality, but one continued education, the end of which is, to make himself perfect." As with the secular version of success, the Unitarian doctrine found measurable and real rewards for self-formation, for as hard work bought money and power, character formation bought salvation and spiritual power. There is, then, a ringing similarity between the secular and spiritual versions of the self-made man. The goals, methods, and rhetoric of both versions parallel each other and at the same time intersect, often conflating the secular with the spiritual.[6]

Advocates of secular self-improvement and moral self-cultivation recognized a similar set of basic conditions upon which they built their

6. Robinson, *Apostle of Culture*, 48. Channing, *Selected Writing*, 146, 157. Robinson argues that Unitarian salvation entailed the process of "developing and unfolding of potential inner virtue" rather than an emotional conversion (*Apostle of Culture*, 13–14). Channing, *Selected Writing*, 157. *Christian Examiner* New Series,

recommendations for living. The first was freedom — political and economic freedom from the constraints of European traditions of entailment, privilege, and statutory subservience. Americans preached the freedom of opportunity, for this new nation provided an arena in which men could have a second chance and could escape the confining definitions of self inherent in a hierarchical society. Just as social position was theoretically fluid, so too was personality. Borrowing from Locke's psychology, self-help advisers like William Alcott and Joel Hawes preached that personality is malleable and dynamic, chameleonlike, subject to external events and circumstances that young men were urged to manage with habit and morally informed choices. Each person then had the freedom to make of himself "whatsoever [he] will resolve to be." Just as well, the individual had the responsibility to assure that the being etched on the psychic clean slate was moral and energetic. Freedom to form character carried with it the responsibility to use that freedom wisely to enlarge "a people's energy, intellect, and virtues." As Emerson put it, "liberty does not consist in doing what you please but in pleasing to do right" (*CS* 3:208). Raw freedom, then, is not the goal of these moral advisers, but rather a controlled freedom used for the formation of moral and useful lives. Even though the wild savages may boast of freedom, Channing argued that they are constrained by their ignorance and comfortless life, since true freedom finds expression only in a civilizing progress. Finally, without freedom of choice, moral decisions would be invalid, for they would not carry with them the weight of responsibility or compensation; as Horace Mann put it, "Free agency necessitates the possibility of perdition; moral compulsion, indeed, may save from ruin; but compulsion abolishes freedom."[7] Without freedom, whatever degree of success, material or moral, one happened to attain would be bogus, for it would derive not from the self but from privilege or compulsion.

The second basic requisite for self-formation is what Alexis de

---

10 (1830): 77. See my discussion of nineteenth-century self-improvement manuals, "Advice to Young Men in Ante-bellum Nineteenth-Century America."

7. Alcott, *Young Man's Guide*, 25. Channing, *Selected Writing*, 169. Horace Mann, *A Few Thoughts for a Young Man: A Lecture delivered before the Boston Mercantile Library Association on its 29th Anniversary*, 45.

Tocqueville called the "principle of equality." At the same time leveling all men to a common denominator by denying the value of inherent inequality, the advocates of the American way promoted the virtues of hard work and self-cultivation as causes for success rather than "luck, fortune, or even talent." Hawes, both a lecturer on self-improvement and a Calvinist minister, found the American character distinctive in that "All are born equal, and are alike left to make their way in the world by their own exertions." Of the great men of science, Newton, Franklin, and Fulton, Edward Everett proclaimed that "It was the patient, judicious, long-continued cultivation of powers of the understanding, eminent, no doubt, in degree, but not different in kind, from those which are possessed by every individual" to which they owed their eminent discoveries. Some religious advisers went so far as to declare that "the theory of Christianity is essentially republican," that the condition of equality requires virtue and hard work, duty and forbearance, in order that the political (or moral) state survive.[8] While surely these writers recognized that some people are born with more gifts than others, and that some people, even in America, inherit wealth, they downplayed inherited gifts of position or talent and promoted the *principle* of equality and the more utilitarian qualities of industry, character formation, and will. Their interest was in identifying and shaping America as a nation of moral workers, a people who accomplish national and personal goals without the ready assets of wealth or privilege (but with the advice they were selling).

Building on these ideological assumptions about the American character, the advisers of success and character formation advocated a hands-on, tangible, democratic version of success and human nature that empowered the individual to make what he will of his life. In a review, "State of Literature," the reviewer noted that in America "we are morally, as intellectually, the makers of ourselves": "All that [a man] learns is effected by self-discipline, and self-discipline is the mind's own work. We all are, under God, intellectually, the makers of ourselves.

8. Alexis de Tocqueville, *Democracy in America*, 289. Taylor, *Character Essential*, 36. Hawes, *Lectures to Young Men*, 44. Everett, *Orations and Speeches*, 285. *Christian Examiner* New Series, 15 (1831): 338–39.

Virtue, religion, as well as knowledge, must also be, mainly, the mind's own work." Americans represented themselves, then, as craftsmen of the self, fashioning and shaping a self to meet the other selves formulated by the ideology of self-culture. Moreover, advocates of self-formation figured self-culture as an organically unfolding, revelatory process, "the care which every man owes to himself, to the unfolding and perfecting of his nature." Using a common metaphor for the self, John Todd wrote that character "is a plant which every one may cultivate; but it is of slow growth and requires great pains-taking."[9] But the idea of organicism and the metaphor of the self as a plant is complicated by attention on the outer self rather than on the inner germ or seed of the self. Instead, inspirationalists pointed to various principles of life as ways of shaping and pruning the growth of the individual.

Given the democratic foundations for a reading of human nature—that man is born free and equal and apparently with little on his psychic slate—advocates of success and salvation found in habits the key that could make the difference between success and failure. Habits or right principles of living as methods of character formation had distinct advantages for an American audience interested in self-improvement and morality. First, because habits are so much the stuff of everyday living, anyone, regardless of inherited talent or position, can and does form habits. Many like George Burnap advised young go-getters that the difference between individuals resides not so much in inherited talent as it does in the early establishment of habits: "What usually passes for genius is the result of early intellectual habits, and still more often, of thorough and careful preparation for every individual effort." Second, cultivating good habits is practical advice appealing to a manipulative, mechanical people who are not much given to speculative thought. Authors of inspirational literature passed useful advice to young men who hoped to improve themselves, advising them to form "habits of industry, frugality, and benevolence," of reading, cleanliness, humility, punctuality, and temperance. Third, habit formation stresses self-reliant individualism, for although one may be influenced or tempted by the

9. *Christian Examiner* New Series, 6 (1832): 299–300. Channing, *Selected Writing,* 226. Todd, *The Young Man,* 57–58.

examples of others, the decision to adopt one set of habits or principles over another is personal. Indeed, the individual forms himself with the adoption of habits, and is thereby self-sufficient, relying on no one but himself for the outcome of his character or life. In addition, habits are obvious, evident, and measurable; one can assess his own as well as others' character by the kinds of habits demonstrated. A writer for the *Christian Examiner* prescribed the development of the "habits of religious thinking and feeling" as the means for forming a Christian character. Readily visible, habits both "constitute the character" and can be formed by "voluntary, persevering, prayerful exertions" that the individual and his fellows can witness. Further, much of the advice about habits clearly feeds into the Calvinistic distrust of the body, warning young men to "control your appetites, subdue your passions, firmly adopt and rigidly practice right principles, form habits of purity, propriety, sobriety and diligence." But finally the appeal of the idea of habit formation is that it makes the individual self-made and participates in the democratic version of the self, for one forms his character and hence his success from the habits established in life. The author of *Young Man's Own Book* told his readers, "Success in life depends in a great measure on the early formation of our habits," for habit "will render us much assistance, in forming a character useful, estimable, and efficient."[10]

Writers and moral advisers of the early nineteenth century seem to agree on some basic premises about human nature and about the specific ways that human nature is formed and transformed. Overwhelmingly, they see personal identity as the product of external circumstance (habit) and the responsibility of the individual. Just as they found that the landscape changes its identity with superficial modifications, such as roads and canals that transform a wild spot into a town, they found the identity of the self to be transformed by manners, habits, and duties. In both cases, the desired landscape is the civilized or tamed one — one in which raw physicality is transformed by the mind's will.

10. George W. Burnap, *Lectures to Young Men, on the Cultivation of the Mind, the formation of Character, and the Conduct of Life*, 63. Winslow, *Young Man's Aid to Knowledge*, 92. *Christian Examiner* 3:6 (1826): 454–56. Wise, *Young Man's Counsellor*, 17. *Young Man's Own Book*, 50–51.

Emerson and the Ideology of Self-Formation

Like the other moralists, Emerson in the early years of his ministry preached the external transformation of manners as a method for attaining an internal transformation of self. Although he would later subvert the ideology of success and would rebel against external forms of ritual, the work of his era remained with him, for he never doubted the role of self-control in the formation of self. Early in his ministry, then, Emerson declares, "What we are depends on what we do," that "our character is in our own hands" (*CS* 1:211–12), and that the habits the individual develops in life are more telling than any inherent intellectual or personality traits. Like his contemporaries, he stresses a democratic psychology of the self, which teaches that all are born with fairly equal talents and that the outcome of an individual's life is the result of his own actions. As he declared in Sermon No. XVII, "It is we ourselves and we alone who can cure that evil which we bewail," for our "whole duty lies in a narrow compass — is one practicable thing — that is to reform yourself, to bring up to the perfect mark of Christian perfection, one single man" (*CS* 1:171–72). While he was very much aware of the dangers and pitfalls of life, of the daily temptations that confront humans, he participated in the Unitarian and American vision of progress, enjoining his listeners to carry "all [your] powers to the highest perfection those powers can reach" (*CS* 1:209). Like his contemporaries, the young Emerson stressed the need to form habits both to meet the temptations of indulgence, sloth, and indolence and to shape the individual character. In Sermon No. XIX, in which he preaches the cultivation of the self — "The whole object of the moral and material creation to you is the formation of your character" — Emerson looks to "principles" or habits of charity, honesty, and temperance as virtues that "we are commanded to cultivate" and that in turn cultivate the self (*CS* 1:180). Concerned with the formation of a moral being rather than with acts of social benevolence, Emerson argues that although the beggar may be comforted and fed for one day because of an act of charity, "To him, your kindness has done little; it is to yourself the good was done. . . . The performance of that action has given a portion of strength to the noblest fibre in your moral frame; has done something to increase a disposition that is essential to your eternal well being" (*CS*

1:180). What is at stake for Emerson here is the cultivation of the habit of charity for the samaritan and his moral salvation. In Sermon No. XXIV he stresses the law of sobriety, or temperance, which "frowns upon all sensual indulgence, that interferes with your progress in goodness. It frowns upon sloth. Diligence is the first of its precepts, for this soberness, whilst it is a cheerful, is a laborious spirit. It keeps good hours" (CS 1:209). Temperance, self-restraint, industry, humility, fortitude, charity, and honesty mark the habits in the American ideology of self that will engender a being of morality, success, and strength, a being who is "master" of himself (CS 1:212).

Like his fellow moral advisers, then, Emerson participated in an American eschatology of progress that was articulated by the rhetoric of reform and self-control and embodied on and through a corporeal, physical presence. Mirroring the political task of taming the physical landscape and bringing into being a self-sufficient nation, Emerson and other advisers set for the individual the task of taming the wildness of the body and bringing into being a new self. Enchanted by the "man-making" power of self-mastery in the early years of his ministry, when his own career and self-identity remained liminal, Emerson borrowed the terms of the body/the social body by which to write versions of the self/himself (JMN 8:148). As he used different narratives to work through grief to an identity of the self as mind or spirit, so too Emerson uses different narratives of self-cultivation to find the terms of his individuality and manhood. Moreover, these two strands of thought intersect, reinforcing the problematics of the body in reading and fashioning the self.

The Christian Gentleman

The hero of the first narrative of self-cultivation is the kind of master of the self that sacred and secular texts described and prescribed for America: the Christian gentleman whose victory in life is the conquest of temptation, sloth, and indolence. Like the heroes of his father's generation, who exhibited the traditional values of duty, order, social obligation, and virtue, Emerson's hero in the first years of his ministry is a man who lives "soberly, righteously, and godly, in this present world" (Titus 2:12). The sober man, the topic of Sermon No. XXIV, directs his own life through "action, enterprize, industry," and he commands his life by abstinence and vigilance from an "unmanning intemperance" (*CS* 1:209–10). The righteous man conforms to and sustains the social order, for he does not "violate the rights of others" (*CS* 1:214). He "will not only give to the poor but he will freely contribute his part to keep up the good action and enterprize of society; will feel the claim of useful and of elegant institutions upon his countenance and aid" (*CS* 1:217). He "lives for friends, for society, for country, for man" (*CS* 1:217). And the godly man gives his "affections to God" (*CS* 1:220). While sober and righteous living may become "mere forms of service" derived from motives of self-interest, godliness derives from the heart and soul of man and seeks "always entire goodness and truth" (*CS* 1:219, 222). Clearly extending the parameters of right living beyond mere external forms of behavior to the ineffable regions of the heart, Emerson nonetheless tells his congregation that the "affections can be cultivated" (*CS* 1:223). In other words, just as one can make himself sober and righteous by practicing temperance and forbearance, so a person can make himself godly by exercising the affections. This is practical advice, and Emerson means it to be, for as popular advisers offered guidelines for self-improvement, so Emerson offers practical and tangible guidelines for forming a "perfect character" (*CS* 1:223).

Finally, the hero of the early sermons, like the hero of the last sermon, is a self-reliant man. Although Emerson uses the same biblical text for No. XXII and No. CLXIV ("Stand therefore, having your loins girt about with truth," Eph. 7:14) and in both sermons celebrates self-reliance as heroic, the early sermon articulates conventional attitudes about independence and manliness that are strikingly redefined in the later sermon. In No. XXII, Emerson praises as rare the man "whose mind is poised on itself" and who "appeals to his own eye, and his own conscience" rather than to "the great names" for truth. This hero knows of his God-ordained purpose and follows it responsibly, understanding "that no actions are without consequences." He sees through the superficialities of action and judges men not by their fortunes but by their truths. He is courageous, meek, "loved and honoured" (*CS* 1:200). The hero of No. XXII best exemplifies the Christian gentleman, the "perfect character," for he is sober, righteous, godly, and self-reliant—self-made and "sufficient unto himself" (*CS* 1:212).

Moreover, the Christian gentleman, as well as his secular counterpart, the self-made man, is just that, a man. Directing their gaze on the masculine self, advisers complicated issues of selfhood, morality, and power/empowerment with issues of masculinity. Indeed, discussions of power and character seem to take place primarily within the rhetoric of masculinity, a rhetoric that defined the self against the body. For nineteenth-century opinion setters, the struggle for morality, wealth, and power is also a struggle against the "unmanning" impulses of the self—the appetites and temptations of the body that were persistently labeled as feminine or effeminate (*CS* 1:210). By insisting on definitions of the self that excluded the feminine, that insisted on resistance to and control of the body, men attempted to ensure and justify their own power base by constructing a version of the self that seemed to contribute best to the bourgeois urge to accomplish, to bring order to life, to discover success in tangible, material, masculine terms. A quick sampling of definitions demonstrates how nineteenth-century male advisers complicated readings of selfhood, morality, and power with gender. Joel Hawes told young men intent on forming their character that pleasure "is utterly inconsistent with all manliness of thought and action" and "forms a character of effeminacy and feebleness . . . contempt . . . shame . . . self-reproach." Hubbard Winslow told his readers that "your piety must be thoroughly sound, enlightened, firm, manly, self-denying and efficient." Joseph Allen warned that where "regular habits of industry and thrift" do not thrive, then "effeminacy and corruption of morals prevail to an alarming extent." Daniel Wise called on his audience to develop a "manly strength of purpose" in combating temptation and forming a successful and virtuous character. Even when the attributes of success are not explicitly labeled masculine or manly, they are associated with definitions of the masculine. The OED lists as synonyms of *masculine* "relative superiority, strength, activity, . . . virile, vigorous, powerful," words that form a rhetoric of masculinity and power that runs throughout the literature of self-culture. The person who forms his own character does so through "energy of will," through "action

[that] forms his intellectual constitution to robustness, energy, and strength," and through "force." Further, the moralists' devaluing of the feminine is even more pernicious than is suggested by their masculinizing of virtue or their trivializing of the feminine as "miscellaneous, luxurious, impatient of immediate distinction, covetous of present excitement, and careless of real development of mind." Many of these authors described woman as the seductress who tempted man away from his nobler ideals. Indeed, what they often warned of the prostitute—"Her house is the way to hell, going down to the chambers of death"[11]—may serve as a cipher of the larger dangers posed by moral and physical temptations to men and a nation still in the process of becoming. By using long-standing representations of the feminine, the male writers both participated in culturally accepted metaphors and, by distancing themselves from the negative and weak, employed a strategy for asserting and justifying a masculine politics of power and spirituality.

In similar ways, Emerson incorporates the rhetoric of masculinity to support a masculinist reading of the self. In Sermon No. II, Emerson sneers at "effeminate repining" against the hardships of life, finding poverty "by hard habits" to brace "the nerve of manhood to athletic strength" (CS 1:69). In No. V, he derides those who, pampered in the "lap of grandeur," grow to an "effeminate manhood" (CS 1:87). And Emerson figures virtue as an "athletic," masculine event "that grows up nursed by temptation, self existent, self consulting, a tower of strength equal to the shock of great emergences" (CS 2:74). At the end of his ministry, when he is reformulating his own thought and the perfect character as one who thinks for himself, one who finds his interest "in manfully . . . opening the unfathomable mines of our own thoughts" (CS 4:106), Emerson nonetheless retains the language of masculinity, shifting only the parameters of manliness and not its power core. While it may have been convenient for the young minister to use language already so much a part of the cultural consciousness, it was also person-

11. Hawes, *Lectures to Young Men*, 69. Winslow, *Young Man's Aid to Knowledge*, 30. Joseph Allen, *Sources of Public Prosperity*, 10. Wise, *Young Man's Counsellor*, 73. Burnap, *Lectures . . . on the Cultivation of the Mind*, 65, 22. Channing, *Selected Writing*, 224. *Boston Evening Gazette* August 28, 1830, 1. *Young Man's Own Book*, 302.

ally pertinent to him, for at stake was his own identity as manly and powerful, an identity that Eric Cheyfitz suggests was tenuous for Emerson at this time.[12]

Given Emerson's and his contemporaries' persistent figuration of the body as unmanning, effeminate, and dangerous, it is curious, then, that he refigures himself on and through the body of a woman, discovering and uncovering himself by plunging beyond the corporeal self to the spiritual self that remains. Perhaps he was able to do so because this particular woman represented to him only purity, sanctity, and spirituality and because her physicality was erased both by Emerson's metaphoric handling of her figure and by her death. Certainly, his discovery of himself through Ellen coincides with his discovery of new terms for power, selfhood, and self-reliance and with his subversion of conventional rhetorics of the self.

The Anxiety of Self-Formation

Although the gendered reading of the self was intended to bolster men's position and importance in the emerging nation, it also imposed demands that constrained individuality and contributed a sense of anxiety, setting the young men on an emotional precipice. Urged to form themselves and to make their own fortune in ways prescribed by their culture, young men were also confronted with the possibility of failure. At a time when both the nation and its young men were liminal, caught between times in a period of intense transition, "Themes of doom and decline and vivid rhetorical images of a violent breakdown of social order began to dominate discussions of the state of the republic." It is no wonder that the young men coming of age in the early nineteenth century suffered psychic strain and felt as if they "were born with knives in their brains." The ideology of work and the cult of masculinity told

12. Eric Cheyfitz, *The Trans-Parent: Sexual Politics in the Language of Emerson,* 105. Cheyfitz contends that Emerson's descriptions of himself at this period portray him lacking "power of face" and as womanly, especially when contrasted with his descriptions of William or Edward. See *JMN* 3:137. Cheyfitz further argues that "what constitutes identity for Emerson is power" (15).

them not only to risk their health and happiness in the pursuit of success but also that their very identities were both at stake and prescribed for them. Indeed, the costs of becoming a self-made man were measured in psychic strain, "a state of personal tension and . . . a condition of societal dislocation" marked by self-doubt, anxiety, vertigo, and ill health as well as by exaggerated self-control and willpower. Even as the emphases on character formation and success contributed to individual psychic strain, they also countered national and nationwide anxiety and self-doubt. Indeed, Smith-Rosenberg argues, "The ocean of sexual words [words about bodily control] that rhythmically beats against the nineteenth century's awareness initially came into being not so much to control the behavior of others as to control that which was perceived as uncontrollable, the process of change itself."[13] By exaggerating the power of the will over the body, young men and their older advisers were participating in the "condition of societal dislocation" and at the same time combating it. Burdened by the very myth of success that they had formulated and by the fear of failure complicit in it, they attempted to bolster and secure their position with a rhetoric of masculinity, a philosophy of power, and a rigid psychology of sublimation.

Tortured by a sense of his own inadequacy, the young minister Ezra Stiles Gannett wrote, "I am very well in body, but am ready to scream, who is sufficient for these things? I am sufficient in no way. What shall I do? When I have neither talents nor virtues proper for such a place, ought I not quit it directly?" Gannett's cry iterates the desperation that informs the dialectic of many private and public texts of vocation and morality — the compulsion to succeed coupled with anxiety and self-doubt. Perhaps the experience of Channing represents the mix of relentless work and self-doubt that apparently stabbed at the health and

---

13. Halttunen, *Confidence Men and Painted Women*, 10. *Complete Works*, 10:329. Geertz, *Interpretation of Cultures*, 203–4. Geertz finds an interconnection between social and personal anxieties: "What is viewed collectively as structural inconsistency is felt individually as personal insecurity, for it is in the experience of the social actor that the imperfections of society and contradictions of character meet and exacerbate one another" (204). In *From Office to Profession*, Scott finds the generation coming of age after 1815 to be "a dislocated generation" whose journals and letters refer to life as "a scramble, a treacherous maze, a whirlwind" (79). Smith-Rosenberg, *Disorderly Conduct*, 90.

minds of many young men striving earnestly to make something of themselves. He wrote of his early experience with the Randolphs of Virginia:

> There I toiled as I have never done since, for gradually my constitution sank under the unremitting exertion. With not a human being to whom I could communicate my deepest thoughts and feelings, and shrinking from common society, I passed through intellectual and moral conflicts, through excitements of heart and mind, so absorbing as often to banish sleep, and to destroy almost wholly the power of digestion. I was worn well-nigh to a skeleton . . . If I ever struggled with my whole soul for purity, truth, and goodness, it was there. There, amidst sore trials, the great question, I trust, was settled within me, whether I would obey the higher or lower principles of my nature, — whether I would be the victim of passion, the world, or the free child and servant of God.[14]

Channing's letter tells the story of a vocational crisis complicated by spiritual wrestling, relentless toil, failing health, and aloneness. Like Gannett, Channing had to decide on his worthiness to pursue a ministerial career and in so doing discovered personal identity vis-à-vis a conquest of the weaker self. Like so many young men of his era, he framed his life story with the dualistic paradigm of human nature and power, posing the "higher" against the "lower principles of [his] nature."

Similarly, Emerson wrestled with self-doubt and battled the impulses of weakness as he attempted to form an identity of power in a demanding vocation that he hoped would facilitate his own manliness of character. Throughout his personal documents, affirmation and doubt forge a dialectic of the self that is informed by cultural and personal expectations and that informs Emerson's own identity as well as his assessments of mankind in general. No doubt urged by the peculiar circumstances of his own life — the early poverty brought on by his father's untimely death, familial expectations, and his own poor health — the young Emerson was compelled nonetheless to pursue a success and an identity largely defined for him by his culture. Indeed,

14. Quoted in Cayton, *Emerson's Emergence*, 125. Channing, *Selected Writing*, 9–10.

his personal doubts and ambitions are framed by language and ideology consistent with the cult of manhood. In his journal for September 1823, for instance, he evaluated his lack of vocational success, blaming his failure on the conventional bogies: indolence, sloth, and a swinish indulgence of the appetites. Complaining of the unsteadiness of his thought and writing, he lamented: "The dreams of my childhood are all fading away & giving place to some very sober & very disgusting views of a quiet mediocrity of talents & condition—nor does it appear to me that any application of which I am capable, any efforts, any sacrifices could at this moment restore any reasonableness to the familiar expectations of my earlier youth" (*JMN* 2:153). Pursuing the goal of great success rather than a middling competence, Emerson is disgusted with what he perceives to be personal weakness of thought and energy. He continues the lamentation by blaming "the ordinary temptations of indolence, of sensual gratification" and accusing those who "eat & . . . drink & . . . lie down in sleep" of leading lives more worthy of swine than of men who have purpose and meaning in life (*JMN* 2:154). Yet at the same time that he finds fault with his inability to make his mark, he questions that very ambition and begins to assert his voice against a universal and cultural fate that chains man to the fetters of ambition: "Man is a foolish slave who is busy in forging his own fetters" (*JMN* 2:154). In his journal, Emerson repeatedly pours out his fear of failure and his guilt, blaming ever a "want of sufficient bottom in my nature" (*JMN* 2:240), excoriating himself for being "a lover of indolence, & of the belly" (*JMN* 2:241), and turning to the ministry as his "regeneration of mind, manners, inward & outward estate" (*JMN* 2:242).

Emerson also repeatedly fights the impulse that sees the frailty of self, exerting his will to power as he cultivates a new being, a man resilient to societal and universal forces, a self that participates in the American myth of success at the same time that it rebels against the chains of material ambition. Beside the Emerson who bewails his mediocrity is another Emerson who shakes his fist at the universe and calls out, "Who is he that shall controul me? Why may not I act & speak & write & think with entire freedom? . . . Who hath forged the chains of Wrong & Right, of Opinion & Custom?" (*JMN* 2:189–90). Beginning already in 1823 to spell out the conditions of the "genuine man" who "speaks what he thinks, [who] acts his thought" (*CS* 4:206), Emerson tentatively sketches the form of a new being, a man-made self, whose identity is informed by cultural definitions of manhood and yet is not contained by usual notions of success.

The Double Vision

As in the impulses of his own imagination, a "double consciousness" (*CS* 4:215) runs throughout Emerson's sermons, observant of his own and others' frailty and freedom. Forming a dialectic of the self, this twin vision creates a tension in Emerson's thought as he bewails his and mankind's weakness and seeks to empower the self by locating authority within it. While his early sermons are more often informed by a vision of human frailty and by the need to conquer weakness with the help of society and its institutions, he speaks more consistently in his later sermons of the individual's power and inherent authority, finding strength to reside within the soul rather than in society. Thus the movement of the sermons is toward freedom, power, and individuality. Like his contemporaries, Emerson sought to overcome what he regarded as weakness and to empower the self as a condition of success or salvation. Like his contemporaries, Emerson was concerned with "man-making" (*JMN* 8:148), at first attempting to create the genuine man by conventional means, by preaching the self-cultivation of the individual and the formation of habits. But as he began to see the superficiality of such a scheme, he turned his vision to the inner self, finding there the strength and power he sought. Yet even though the direction of his sermons was toward freedom and self-reliance, the doubleness of his consciousness continued to shape a dialectic, an ebb and flow of confidence and self-condemnation.

In Sermon No. III, Emerson describes a self who, like himself, is "imperfect and frail," tempted more easily to evil and sin than to good. An inhabitant of the world, his "dependence on God is too lofty" to sustain him in the "daily warfare of the world," and he must depend on the more practical experiences and influences of life to guide him (*CS* 1:70). Not an independent being, he is dependent upon both God and society. And his powers of perception are weak; he cannot always hear the oracle or see the vision of God, for his eye is "clouded" to the presence of God and to the finer influences of the soul (*CS* 1:70). As Emerson complained of the ebb and flow of his own thought and visitations from the muse, "The worst is, that the ebb is certain, long & frequent, while the flow comes transiently & seldom" (*JMN* 2:153). Because the flow is so uncertain and because it is seen with clouded eyes, the individual cannot rely on his own intuitions but turns instead to the concrete experiences of life and society to guide and teach him. In fact, Emerson declares in this very early sermon, "In solitude [man] is weak; in society he is strong. In solitude his mind and body decay; his mind languishes in stupid ignorance; . . . In society, his mind is expanded in its efforts to accommodate itself to the large minds which every hour brings before him" (*CS* 1:72).

But as Emerson begins to discover the meaning of the text from Luke, "The kingdom of God is within you," he begins to locate power and reality in the human conscience and to move toward an original doctrine of self-reliance and self-determination. In Sermon No. XXI he claims for the conscience the power of authority as the "eldest revelation" of God, for it is "an overpowering proof of the Being and government of God"; it is the voice that "alway utters, 'There is a God'" (*CS* 1:195–96). And in No. XXIII he looks to personal faith instead of evidences found by "painful study," telling his congregation and himself, "It is the heart, which is the seat of the evidence. The kingdom of God is within you. And there its evidence is best explored" (*CS* 1:206). Looking for ways by which to conquer the ebb of his thought and confidence, Emerson begins to look beyond the conventional definitions of success and beyond Unitarian hermeneutics to find clues for constructing the self and a religion of the self based on freedom. Subverting both the secular and spiritual versions of the ideology of self-cultivation, Emerson, discontented with mere outward forms of improvement — "success in tying a neckcloth aright & making a fashionable bow" (*JMN* 2:258) — looks inward to the individual soul for empowering resources.

A telling clue of his change in perspective away from conventional ideology occurred in May 1829 in Sermon No. XXXVII, when he wrote, "Thou are made sufficient to thyself. Thy joy, and thy glory, and thy punishment, thy heaven, and thy hell are within thee" (*CS* 1:287). Written just months after his ordination at Second Church and just months before his marriage to Ellen, this sermon reveals Emerson's confidence and willingness to take risks, to explore beyond the conventional. Coincident with a redefinition of compensation based on the passage from Luke is a redefinition of human self-determination. Although he will continue to preach the denial of pleasure, extolling those who "have manfully given up . . . pleasure," Emerson hints in No. XXXVII that self-sufficiency also means independence from societal institutions (*CS* 1:288). Having glimpsed the "intimate connexion" between the self and God, suggested no doubt by his own "intimate connexion," Emerson tentatively posits that the truly powerful soul "beat[s] pulse for pulse in harmony with the universal whole" (*CS* 1:290).

Though he begins making steps toward reconsiderations of authority and self-sufficiency, Emerson remains pulled by nagging self-doubt. Indeed, a being "made sufficent unto [it]self" may also flounder and fail to meet the soul's potential. The emancipated individual risks himself and his future, for he must ultimately rely on his own will and not on the prescriptions and dictates of the larger, social will. As Emerson knew, it is often easier for most people to choose not to exercise individual rights and to have their fate determined for them, to be "led as a flock of sheep to the slaughter" by society. Too often, Emerson laments, the anticipated progress or perfection is rarely seen, for "We are slovens on Providence." Our sin is that "we are living without sufficient elevation of purpose" and that by following society rather than ourselves we commit "spiritual suicide" (*CS* 1:292–93). Determined to have his own way and to overcome a submissive powerlessness, Emerson exhorts his congregation and himself to act for themselves, to strive for perfection, to live a free and solitary life: "Every such action . . . elevates, ennobles the doer, makes you a more powerful being" (*CS* 1:294). But his determination to gain power betrays his fears of powerlessness, betrays the "paradox of achievement" with which he struggled. As David Robinson points out, the germs of both optimism and pessimism are inherent in a doctrine of self-culture that looks to an impossible goal of perfection. Indeed, this kind of dialectical reading of human nature seems to be a condition both of Unitarian salvation schemes and of a destabilized, liminal society, which intersected and aggravated each other in the 1820s and 1830s.[15] Given the control for forming character and hence for gaining personal salvation, the American Unitarian was thrown against himself and was forced to read his own as well as mankind's situation from a state of psychic vertigo. Similarly, Emerson is caught in a dialectic that causes him to fluctuate between aggrandizement and condemnation in his personal and public texts. And in No. XXXVIII, dissatisfaction with his and his congregation's abilities to live to their fullest potential urges Emerson on in his pursuit of perfection, a pursuit of that heaven within the mind; yet his pursuit also opens to him visions of failure and of "spiritual suicide."

This dialectic of the self is also evident in Sermon No. XLIX, in which Emerson describes both the religious character who strives to perfect himself and to become a heroic philosopher in the face of life's temptations, and the "moral sluggard" who merely adheres to religious rituals or turns to religion only when ill or dying (*CS* 2:55). The description of the "sluggard" is more vivid than that of the "hero," for at this point in his intellectual career what he would *not* be is clearer to him than what he could be. Indeed, the manuscript evinces this uncertainty. Emerson's heavily revised, nearly illegible exhortations to his congregation — "Cultivate this . . . confidence in your powers and opportunities" and "Let not the sense of present deficiency or the memory of

15. Robinson, *Apostle of Culture*, 4. Robinson uses the phrase to refer to the paradox that Unitarians pursued a goal, perfection, that they could never attain. I use Robinson's phrase to suggest the paradox that to attain power or achievement, one must subdue one's own (lower) nature. Again, Robinson turns his argument in a slightly different direction. On page 16 he says, "Although a philosophy that insists on a human capacity for betterment is optimistic, one which tinges that betterment with a recognition of ultimate frustration has its edge of pessimism." Halttunen, *Confidence Men and Painted Women*, notes that advice manuals were addressed to young men "who have just left home and now stood poised on the threshold of a new life in the city" (1). She contends that the fundamental assumption of the cult of self-made men "was that all Americans were liminal men, in passage from a lower to a higher social status" (29). Instructed on methods for attaining success, the young men were simultaneously warned of the dangers and temptations of city life.

past failure operate to discourage you"—parallel many of his private musings about his own potential (*CS* 2:55).

Emerson's thinking on the role of free choice in the determination of character is more fully articulated here than in his earlier sermons and indicates a turn in the direction of his thinking about self-reliance. Discussing the improvement of man, Emerson begins to articulate the theme of genuineness that reappears in later sermons and eventually in "Self-Reliance." But the sentence in which he asserts the doctrine of free will was not easily written; it required two attempts of a full paragraph each. He originally wrote that the religious life

> is designed to show us practically & every moment that we are not creatures of necessity but creatures of free will, improvable beings not moving like the silent orb<s of heaven> ↑we tread upon↓ in an inextricable circle but going backward or going forward in <the spiritual world which is our home> ↑our moral career↓ at our own free choice, & just as far & as fast as we will. (*CS* 2:287)

Some of the revisions to this sentence replace the Latinate or ornate with epigrammatic and vernacular phrasing, as when he changed "inextricable circle" to the simpler and homier "eternal round." But the revised sentence indicates more than cosmetic concerns, for Emerson was beginning to compose and realize his own self-reliance. The new sentence reads:

> All these things speak to each of us—and command us every moment to feel that we are not creatures of necessity, but creatures of free will,—improvable beings—not moving like the silent orb we tread upon, in one eternal round,—but going backward or going forward in our moral career, at our own free choice, and just as far and as fast as we will. (*CS* 2:52)

The dash-streaked revision emphasizes key points in Emerson's concept of self-reliance that may have been lost in the overcrowded first version: that man has the free will to choose his character and that the things of the world speak eternal truths to each person. Thus as Emerson empowers his rhetoric, he also empowers his theology—a process that parallels his efforts to achieve genuine "manliness" despite his self-doubt and hesitation.

In another canceled passage, Emerson first wrote three short lines, two of which are indented to indicate, I think, a new start at what he is trying to say:

> <The vegetable is formed of the <same> particles of a decaying vegetable & grows up & decays & its particles are ↑only↓ reproduced in a new form.>
> For this [the improvement of man] we are introduced to all this variety of character taught the elements of so many arts & the idioms of so many languages for this we are introduced to all this variety of character. (*CS* 2:287)

From these three false starts, he developed a paragraph that lists things in the universe that tell man he is an improvable being:

> For this [the improvement of man] suns rise, and seasons change; for this, the earth is stored with good; for this we are sent into the earth naked, and feeble and poor; and every good is held out to our labour; for this our fate is entrusted to our own keeping. For this the world is filled with wisdom, which comes to our minds by ten thousand avenues; for this are set before us the elements of so many arts, the idioms of so many languages; for this we are introduced to all this variety of character, and the solemn array of moral influence encompasses us; for this prophets spoke, and good men acted; and for this Christ died. For this, finally, came all the passages of our personal history, — for this sometimes we are put into society, and sometimes we are put apart, sometimes afflicted, and sometimes rejoiced. (*CS* 2:51–52)

While the first version is abstract, the new paragraph substantiates Emerson's vision of the correspondence between man and Providence with a catalog of specific examples of variety, indicating his developing sense of the "underlying identity of all things in the universe as manifestation of the divine plenitude" that Lawrence Buell identifies as a Transcendentalist impulse.[16]

Moreover, the first draft of this passage is negative, emphasizing the process of decay rather than of becoming in the dynamic changes in

16. Lawrence Buell, *Literary Transcendentalism: Style and Vision in the American Renaissance*, 169.

the universe. Evolutionary or geological decay is no new analogue for Emerson; he had used a similar illustration in Sermon No. VI ("Decay, decay is written on every leaf of the forest, on every mountain, on every monument of art" and a "universal fate . . . sweeps us on — day by day and hour by hour into the land of silence") when his own mortality was painfully evident to him. In Sermon No. XLIX, he again struggles against fate and determination as he wills for the individual a freedom from necessity. The revised sentence emphasizes becoming, as "suns rise and seasons change; for this the earth is stored with good" (*CS* 2:51). In the change from decay to becoming, he battles a preoccupation with death that is both personal and metaphorical as he deliberately wills himself to a more positive outlook.

Throughout his ministerial career, Emerson sought a religion characterized by industry and vigor, one that would attract virile men, not the effete who turn to religion only occasionally. He believed that "the only Religion is a progressive religion, a religion of every moment, not an occasional rule, for sick days or Sabbaths, but a religion that opens upon the heart as the faculties unfold, and lasts as long as life lasts in this world, or in all worlds" (*CS* 2:52). The true Christian would "comprehend the praise of heroism and philosophy" (*CS* 2:54). Emerson's call to his congregation and to himself to become heroic Christians is clouded, nonetheless, by his vision of man's failure to realize his potential and by his own preoccupation with death and decay in No. XLIX, delivered just ten days before his marriage to Ellen:

> When a <mortal> ↑severe↓ disease confines us in our house; <when we lie down without hope in our bed> when the physician shakes his head at our low & declining pulse; when the whole head is disordered, & the powers of attention well nigh gone; when the lessons of the school of life are done for us, & the God of nature gives us this signal to put up our tasks & come away — then <for the first> men take down from the shelf their religious books, then they go to prayer & try to give to these devout exercises the bewildered attention of a broken mind & ↑now yt [that] life is just coming to its end,↓ set their hearts to the question, *What is the object of life,* & how has it been answered by <me> ↑us↓? (*CS* 2:52–53, 287 and MS)

Emerson's illustration of the hypocritical Christian manifests not only his brooding on death and the annihilation of the self but also his will to overcome the powerlessness suggested by death in the changes from "mortal" to "severe." Indicative also of his brooding about personal impotence is the pronoun shift in the last sentence. Although the change from "me" to "us" may simply be a grammatical correction, it may also indicate his identification with the unmanly Christian he criticizes. Later in the sermon Emerson says, "The revelation [from God] proceeds on the assumption that man is sinful, and may become good" (*CS* 2:53). Similarly, he began his draft with the assumption of death — perhaps symbolizing his fear of the impotency of his intellectual imagination — and wills the birth of power, for men and for himself. More likely, his preoccupation with death at the beginning of his marriage indicates the threat posed by the consumption that held Ellen in its grip. In a sense, this sermon foreshadows not only Emerson's "incalculable loss" but also the way loss led him to finding himself and his vision (*L* 1:318n). It indicates as well how two threads of thought, about death and self-reliance, intersect and lead Emerson toward the construction of a heroically self-reliant being, a being that is both a fiction of his texts and a refiguration of his own being.

The "Perfect Character"

Much of the energy of the sermons written during the quiet time before the catastrophe of Ellen's death is invested in the construction of a self — one who can become the hero of Emerson's text and a model for his own refiguration. By sketching out different poses for the hero, whom he calls at this juncture the "perfect character," Emerson is able to test possibilities for his own auto-creation. It is not surprising, then, that this hero is fashioned from Emerson's own psychic struggles, from his worry about Ellen and his attempts to find consolation. It is also not surprising that this fictive hero reifies the turn in Emerson's thinking about morality, authority, and vocation. Yet the arch of this curve of thought was interrupted by the gloom of Ellen's physical debility and by his own depression. Not until after Ellen's death would he return to stretch the boundaries of the self, and by then his thought and vision had been seared in the flames of baptism.

Emerson's notions about freedom and self-improvement, still tentative before Ellen's death, suggest an emerging variance with conventional definitions, for he began to see that the individual's nature and his freedom are inextricably bound together. At the same time that Emerson began redefining the nature of the self, locating authority within, he also began to extend the conventional meanings of freedom. While he never completely relinquished the lure of the myth of success or the cultural lessons about the self, Emerson recast the myth of the self-made man after his own impulse to create a new self. Thus, like many Americans, Emerson regarded political freedom as a prerequisite for character formation, for becoming whatever one resolved to be within the social order. And like his contemporaries he knew that freedom validates morality, that unless one is a morally free agent his choices have no meaning. But having finally secured for himself a degree of economic and personal stability with his appointment to the Second Church pulpit and his marriage to Ellen in 1829, Emerson began to extend the usual meanings of freedom and of the self. Though one might expect that stability would find justification and validation in conservative "plagiarisms from the common stock" (*L* 1:207), Emerson flexed his thought, defining and inventing a self free of the constraints of the social order. Indeed, the direction of his thought was to suggest that one becomes a perfect character in proportion to one's ability to free himself from the chains of society (*JMN* 3:198–99) — a meaning different from his earlier pronouncement about the perfect character in Sermon No. XXVI. A risky undertaking, Emerson's thought involved not just an extension of conventional modes of character formation via habits and external change but also a metamorphosis of being generated by an inner conviction of invincibility.

In a letter to his Aunt Mary Moody Emerson, the young minister suggests the connection between freedom and character when he criticizes "flat & tiresome" men who "strive to hide all that is peculiar" and interesting about them, finding refuge, instead, in "the common stock of tho't & knowledge." By failing to "exhibit" the peculiarity of their nature, such men hide their talents and bind their identity and being to a necessity shaped and prescribed for them by the "common stock" (*L* 1:207). For Emerson, the antidote to conformity of thought lies within the self who realizes his intimate connection to the universe.

Indeed, as Emerson would have it, "you are the Universe to yourself" (*JMN* 3:144). Because the "Kingdom of God is within you," the individual is self-sufficient, independent of "the judgment of society," which is all too often fickle and deceptive (*JMN* 3:140). Releasing the self from the intellectual stranglehold of a collocation of narrow minds, Emerson's formulation also frees the self to *become*, for within the self resides the matrix of being, "the germ of a perfect character" (*JMN* 3:190), and within the self resides the power to shape individual character, to make fortunes, and to create the self.

Extending the meaning of free will beyond moral accountability, Emerson sketches in Sermon No. LIII a radical solution to one of the "great questions" of human intellectual endeavor—how "to reconcile the free agency of man with our dependence on God"—by positing the autonomy of a self in whom resides infinite possibility (*CS* 2:71). While Emerson never denies the traditional meaning of free will—that as moral agents humans have both the freedom to make decisions and the responsibility for them—he declares that the individual also has a moral responsibility to become an independent character. At the same time that he reminds the Second Church members, "Now, we know that we are free to all the purposes of moral accountability," and that he reiterates the Unitarian lesson that the trials of life educate and strengthen the individual, he also tells them that "our whole worth depends upon our freedom" (*CS* 2:71–72).

While Emerson's previous sermons had suggested that man learns morality *in* society, No. LIII urges the congregation to pursue moral and intellectual independence *apart from* society. Where he had declared in 1827, "In solitude [man] is weak; in society he is strong . . . In society his mind is expanded in its efforts to accommodate itself to the large minds which every hour brings before him," he now warns of the mediocrity and complacency of an "accommodation to the expectations of others" (*CS* 2:72). Although one may lead a seemingly virtuous life by following the habits and conventions of society, that person may also be a "sluggish servant of God's commandments," a "fashionist who goes to church because well bred people do," and his goodness, "borrowed [and] reflected . . . a dim and waning ray" (*CS* 2:72–74). The perfect character, to the contrary, is one who realizes his unique talents and individuality, independent of the whims and dictates of society. He wills himself into being by making his own decisions and by forming his own thought. Morality in this sermon has not so much to do with virtue (although that is always very important to Emerson); rather, it has to do with independence of thought: "A man is respectable only as far as his actions are his own" (*CS* 2:71). Emerson suggests here that the true character finds and exerts power in independence, for freedom "will not belong to you without you go and take it" (*CS* 2:71). In language riddled with images of manliness, competitiveness, and power, Emerson subverts the conventional moral advice that centered on virtuous and helpful habits. While Sermon No. XXIV had advocated cultivating habits of industry, temperance, honesty, and charity to combat the temptations of the world, No. LIII finds virtue derived "from mere propriety" to be "defective" and true virtue, derived from the internal resources of the self, to be "athletic . . . nursed by temptation, self existent, self-consulting, a tower of strength equal to the shock of great emergences" (*CS* 2:73–74). Simultaneously, he suggests that "only virtue is free, absolute, selfexistent" and that freedom is itself moral (*CS* 2:74).

Indeed, he claims for the individual who is morally accountable and independent of the pressures of society a similarity to God. Although Channing had preached in 1828, "In ourselves are the elements of the Divinity," he continued to maintain man's dependence on the parental God, explaining that as a child resembles the parent, so humans have "the likeness of a kindred nature" with God. Channing also advocated a program of "vigorous and conscientious" self-cultivation in order "to grow in the likeness of God." But where Channing had softened his "controversial, even heretical"[17] suggestion that man is like God by sounding the familiar rhetoric and doctrine of self-improvement, Emerson hints that man has the means and power to create the self and thus be *as* God. In a paragraph marked with revision and amended by a succeeding paragraph that is more conventional, Emerson points to the autonomy of the self. Having advocated human self-sufficiency in

17. Channing, *Selected Writing*, 150, 157. David Robinson, editor of *Selected Writing*, makes this comment about Channing's position, 145.

the face of the leveling tendencies of society, he also declares man's cosmic self-sufficiency:

> it seems to me that immortal life consists in the acquisition of virtue; that God is not alone self existent, but that every mind that he has made which feels the dignity of a free being and on the ground of its own convictions adopts this law of God's action, thereby becomes a sharer of his own eternal nature and thus hath the principles of its own life within itself. (*CS* 2:74)

By consolidating the accepted version that a person's virtue or conscience makes him like God with the ideological belief in the dignity of freedom, Emerson suggests that like God, man is a virtuous and free agent, a "sharer of his own eternal nature." Having declared the perfect character to be a social free agent, Emerson now declares him to be a cosmic free agent, free to create his own being from material inherent within himself. Emerson finds the principles of living not in social proprieties or habits or even in revelation but within, in "the <seeds>" of his own being. Although the edited version of this passage contains language more distant, changing the personal pronoun "he" to "it" and the generative "seeds" to the morally conventional "principles," the excised version nonetheless hints of a self who generates his own being and thus becomes more like God than Channing was willing to grant (*CS* 2:296).

In a kind of Nietzschean will to power, out of the reservoir of his own thought, then, Emerson wills into being a new kind of hero, a being he calls the perfect character. Unlike the socialized self of earlier sermons, the fictive hero that begins to emerge in the summer and autumn of 1830 is a being whose power is proportional to his independence from society. When Emerson told his journal in July 1830, "We contain in us probably the germ of a perfect character & a peculiar one," he meant something different than the perfection of character more conventionally ascribed to great men like Sir Isaac Newton (*JMN* 3:190). A review of the biography of Newton by David Brewster (1831) in the *Christian Examiner* demonstrates a more commonly held view of the perfect character. Of the various great men in history, Newton represented for Unitarians and Americans the paradigm of self-improvement. Claiming that Newton's character is "wanting nothing," the reviewer subdivides his character into the practical, the intellectual, and the religious. The practical character, he writes, entails "sagacity in action, which enables a man to act with efficient usefulness in the concerns of the world." The intellectual character has to do with bringing the mind "into vigorous and successful action." And the religious character is one who "does his duty to God and man with zeal, with energy, and with all his heart."[18] As the Newtonian example demonstrates, perfectibility was very much a pragmatic and social undertaking, and the perfect character was removed from the masses of men not in kind but in degree. Hence, the perfect character is the product of "the principle of improvement" and not the peculiar offspring of genius or fortune.

Yet when Emerson contemplated Newton and "the great men of the world," he found they "were those who did not take their opinions on trust, but explored themselves" (*JMN* 3:199). For Emerson, poised on a psychic precipice just prior to Ellen's decline in health and to his own descent into depression, "character" had more to do with freedom of thought than with material success or even conventional paradigms of morality. As he explored his own thought, he began to find that strength and meaning derive from inner resources rather than from external forms and rituals. Indeed, as he watched his wife struggle against the weakness of her body, he became convinced that essential meaning is internal and eternal, interconnected with universal forces, and not contained by the physical or external. Of the problem posed in Sermon No. LIII, the reconciliation of free agency with "our dependence on God" (*CS* 2:71), he began to find that the answer lay not simply with idiosyncratic assertions of will but instead in unity with the divinity whose nature man shares. Thus when he wrote in a September 27, 1830, journal entry, "I would have a man trust himself, beleive [*sic*] that he has all the endowments necessary to balance each other in a perfect character, if only he will allow them all fair play" (*JMN* 3:198), he meant both a declaration of intellectual independence from the small minds and common rituals of the mass of men and a declaration of alliance with the eternal force of God. By allying the self with God, by locating

18. *Christian Examiner* New Series, 21 (1832): 286–87.

the kingdom of God within the self, by realizing his "intimate connexion" with God (*CS* 1:290), Emerson finds the strength and authority to resist the will of the masses: "Let him scorn to imitate any being, let him scorn to be a secondary man, let him fully trust his own share of God's goodness, that correctly used it will lead him on to perfection, which has no type yet in the Universe save only in the Divine Mind" (*JMN* 3:199). The self that Emerson enjoins himself to trust is the God within the self, and perfection derives not from duty, usefulness, or behavior but from obedience to his "own reason": "In listening more intently to our own reason, we are not becoming in the ordinary sense more selfish, but are departing more from what is small, & falling back on truth itself & God" (*JMN* 3:199).

As he attempts to deny frailty and finitude by locating God within the self and by consummating the "perfect union" (*CS* 2:252), Emerson redefines the nature of the self, declaring it to be spirit—a participant and sharer of God's nature, a being who contains the germ of his own being—only lately corrupted by temptations of the flesh and an unthinking adherence to the conventions of the mass of men. Having found the self to be a spiritual partner of the universal forces, Emerson sets about redefining the nature of authority. Finding it to derive from the God-inspired, inner resources of self and will rather than from external, physical testimony, he declares to his congregation, "God is with us and in us, . . . The authority of conscience and the love of truth in us is the manifestation of Him" (*CS* 2:254). Unlike his Unitarian brethren who claimed with Channing that "the existence and veracity of God, and the divine original of Christianity, are conclusions of reason," Emerson found spiritual truth a matter of the spirit rather than of the reason or hermeneutical method.[19] Having centered the kingdom of

---

19. Channing, *Selected Writing,* 75. Mott, *"Strains of Eloquence,"* finds, "The 'God within,' Emerson's version of the Christian evidences, is the definitive theme of the sermons, a theme that did not emerge from one moment of insight but was treated in countless variations." Further, Mott notes, "In silently abandoning scriptural revelation as an external proof, Emerson had lost the confirmation of natural religion . . . and by locating revelation in the individual's direct experience of God, he was opening himself up to charges of infidelity." Indeed, Mott finds Emerson's habit of thought influenced by "Puritan concepts of the Spirit" (66, 69, 143).

God and the realm of the self within the soul, Emerson progressively refers questions of interpretation and validity to the heart's truth: "The Revelation of Jesus Christ . . . withdraws man from looking for his motives to the world, outward, and directs him to look within. It shows him a Divine Eye that cannot be deceived, that fixed within his soul, commands a perfect prospect of his whole being" (*CS* 2:246–47).

The "Oracle Within"

Discovering and inventing himself apart from the morass of society and the confines of the physical world, the potent being must finally relocate himself in society. Finding his voice, the "oracle within" (*CS* 2:254), as he finds himself, the perfect character has a crucial social role and position: he is to be the voice by which others discover the truth within themselves. By surrendering himself to the God-spirit within, the perfect character finds power and purpose as he finds "his own voice, manner, eloquence, and . . . action" (*CS* 2:265). As Emerson calls upon his auditors, both before and behind the pulpit, to "hasten to break down every barrier, to open every door and chamber of your soul, that this spirit of God from its hiding place in your inward parts may come forth as a flood, may circulate through every part of you that the union may become perfect" (*CS* 2:254), he finds a way by which to reembody that which he had disembodied. For at the same time that the orator-poet surrenders his ego to "the currents of the Universal Being," he brings to life in action and word the ineffable principles of living. The power that he gains thereby is not only soul energy but also real power in a world of real men where oratory was a mark of success and the means to political, religious, and practical power.[20]

Participating in his own culture's regard for the power of speech, the young Emerson, at the time he was beginning his "professional studies" (*JMN* 2:237), had hoped to "put on eloquence as a robe" (*JMN*

20. *Complete Works,* 1:10. Cheyfitz, *The Trans-Parent,* argues that for Emerson eloquence was a "masculine power." He quotes Emerson—"If I should make the shortest list of the qualifications of the orator, I should begin with manliness; and perhaps it means here presence of mind" (41).

2:242) in his bid for manliness, intertwining issues of selfhood with issues of eloquence. As with his emerging definitions of the self and authority, Emerson's definition of eloquence now insists on an inner attention to the voice within, to the voice that is the self. Rhetoricians had long followed Quintillian's correlation between eloquence and morality, teaching as did Hugh Blair, author of *Rhetoric and Belles Lettres,* that no man could be "truly eloquent, . . . who does not speak the language of his own conviction, and his own feelings" and that "The Preacher himself, in order to be successful, must be a good man."[21] But by asking the individual to become a persisting listener to the voice within, Emerson means something more than the conventional wisdom about moral eloquence. Rather, as his thought again turns to the power of consummation, to the perfect union, the perfect sympathy, he declares, "If a man would always as exclusively consult his own thoughts . . . he would always speak with . . . a force which would be felt to be far greater than belonged to him or to any mortal, but was proper to immortal truth" (*CS* 2:266).

What Emerson is after is a new definition of eloquence that plunges through and past external rhetorical displays and beyond a disembodied voice to reembody truth through the form and person of the speaker. Perhaps modeled after the example of Edward Everett or Orville Dewey, the Emersonian orator lets the "oracle" contained in his soul speak through him as if he were a mere instrument or organ "through which facts themselves speak" (*CS* 2:266). Earlier Everett had said of the "great minds" of the country, "They are the organs of the time; they speak not their own language, they scarce think their own thoughts; but under an impulse like the prophetic enthusiasm of old, they must feel and utter the sentiments which society inspires. They do not create, they obey the Spirit of the Age." Like Emerson, Everett finds the great thinkers and orators to be receptacles and instruments of truths higher and larger than their individual and limited talents. Similarly, Orville Dewey had written, "The voice is the principal organ of the soul." Moreover, Dewey granted to speech something palpable and real, something different than the "labors of the sculptor and the

21. Quoted in Cayton, *Emerson's Emergence,* 124–25.

painter" which he saw as artificial, for speech is embodied by the "in-struments . . . provided by nature, — the voice, the countenance, the eye, the lips, the hand, the whole frame." In other words, speech comes to life through the medium of the artist, the orator, whose human "frame" molds and propels the intangible inspiration.[22] For Dewey as well as for Emerson, oratory is "perfection in act," truth made real be-cause it is incarnated in the body and action of the orator. Whether Emerson had Everett or Dewey in mind, his own emerging definition of eloquence, like theirs, dances around the dialectic between body and soul. Inventing the orator as a perfect character, one who, like Jesus, listens to and gives form to the inner voice, Emerson attempts to recon-cile this persistent dialectic of his thought. Moreover, by sketching his hero in the form of an orator with the potential for transforming others into also being living instruments of truth, morality, and thought, Em-erson projects his own desires for morality and greatness onto the figure he creates.

What strikes one is that Emerson's energetic invention of the perfect character, a character endowed with freedom, authority, and eloquence, occurs at the same time he was mentally and emotionally preparing for Ellen's death. Working out some of the terms of consolation on the figure of the heroic character he was sketching, Emerson invents a hero who is empowered by detachment from the physical, social world and by the consummate union of like to like. As with the Ellen who will soon abandon her bodily form and become spirit, Emerson's hero abandons external evidence to discover himself and the authority for himself in the spirit that resides within. Indeed, he learns that abandon-ment is a condition for becoming a perfect character and for fashioning himself as a perfect character, that to become an independent, empow-ered self of the mind he must divorce himself from the body and give himself up to the voice within.

Perhaps in coming to these conclusions about the inner life of the self, Emerson had learned that external changes in life, from one profes-sion to another, do not of themselves bring about a "regeneration of

22. Everett, *Orations and Speeches,* 108. *North American Review* 29:64 (1829): 40–47, 65.

mind, manners, inward & outward estate" (*JMN* 2:242), that regeneration has more to do than with a change of clothes, the donning of the "manly robe" of the ministry (*JMN* 2:112). Perhaps his experience as minister had taught him that religious duties and habits do not make one godly, as his many injunctions against the "fashionists" who attend church regularly testify (*CS* 2:74). Perhaps his experience as minister had also taught him that true eloquence derives not from the "sophism" of learned men but from the sincerity and originality of the speaker who consults his "own thoughts" (*CS* 2:265–66). It may be that he was disgusted with Jacksonian politics and the materialism of his age, or that he had incorporated into his own thought that of the European Romantics, who, like Coleridge, taught that "all true and living knowledge proceed from within."[23] Whatever the case, and probably the case is a complexity of events and realizations, it seems pertinent that his criticisms of social forms coincide with the obvious deterioration of the external form of the woman he loved against all odds. It also seems pertinent that just months before Ellen was to die and when she was plagued by the evidence of her disease, Emerson should so steadily contemplate the meaning of "character" and that he should find that the secret of beingness lay not in external manifestations but rather in the uniqueness of the individual.

The Difficult Road of Self-Reliance

Shortly after Emerson wrote of the perfect character in Sermon No. XC, he turned his thought again to guilt, sin, and retribution in the sermons that finish out the year 1830, as he confronted the immediate task of finding consolation for his private loss. The task of inventing a fictive hero for his narrative of morality and freedom was dramatically interrupted by Ellen's death, and much of his energy was consumed in

---

23. Cayton's thesis in *Emerson's Emergence* is that Emerson developed a "natural organicism" to counteract the apparent decline of the social bond in early nineteenth-century Boston. How he did so is "the story of his interior response to the perception of decline in consensus in Boston during the 1820s" (57). *Selected Poetry and Prose of Coleridge,* quoting Coleridge's *The Friend.*

depression and in finding a way out of grief. Learning firsthand the costs of attachment and loss, Emerson emerged from the baptism of suffering a new man, tested and strengthened by his ordeal and braced with a philosophy that incorporated in profound ways lessons of self-trust and individuality. Indeed, Ellen taught him a meaning of freedom that extended the cultural lessons of freedom, for he learned firsthand the necessary freedom from the body. Because of his attachment to her, he learned in a passional way what he knew already, a detachment from the body and an allegiance to the internal, eternal self. And because of his attachment to her, he learned the lesson of consolation, to disengage and free himself from her physical form. This lesson of consolation, of freeing the self from external bodies, also played behind the project of self-formation that Emerson pursued in more energetic and original ways after the immediacy of his grief. When he again picks up the thread of his thought about the heroic self, the task of invention is more urgently a task of *self*-invention and the task of independence one of vocation.

Returning to a sustained discussion of the self-reliant character, Emerson extends his rejection of external authority to include the forms and rituals of religion. Having urged independence from society — from "accommodation to the expectations of others" (*CS* 2:72) — Emerson now urges religious independence. At stake for him is not merely rebellion from social and religious forms but also the value of individuality and the discovery of his own individuality. And as he has consistently done, Emerson continues to figure assertions of selfhood on and against the metaphor of the body — the physical body, the social body, and now the religious body. As Mary Douglas points out, "To insist on the superiority of spiritual over material elements is to insist on the liberties of the individual."[24] Insisting on individuality and freedom for the self, cutting ties to the physical, social, and religious bodies and institutions, and asserting "the superiority of the spiritual," Emerson also begins to assert his vocational freedom.

While all along Emerson had called for sincerity in worship, when he returns to discussion of the self after the crisis of loss, he begins to

24. Douglas, *Natural Symbols,* 162.

call for independence from the institutions of the church. Transformed by Ellen's death, Emerson now pursues a line of thinking consistent with his insistence that truth and meaning are contained within the interior resources of the individual rather than in external signs or institutions. Concerned that forms have taken the place of piety for many churchgoers, Emerson declares, "A good man needs no provocatives to piety, from the sympathy or the example of others. These are the crutches of weakness. It is matter of sad regret to see how low and dependent is the flame of devotion in us" (*CS* 3:97). Indeed, Sunday Christians who lean on "the crutches" of faith and are "religious by rote" (*CS* 3:202), practice an "effete superannuated" religion (*JMN* 4:27) sorely in need of vigor and true faith. To that end, Emerson encourages his congregation "to think, to study, to verify in each one's own experience every doctrine" (*CS* 3:201). Rather than rely on external evidence or the interpretations of others, self-reliant Christians are to verify doctrine from within themselves by trusting their own reason. Unfortunately, Emerson observes, men have for so long neglected their own reason that they fear it and have instead "been content to be religious by rote, to make piety to consist in giving a verbal assent to articles of faith, and in giving a bodily obedience to forms of worship" (*CS* 3:202). When Christians at last trust their own reason, Emerson argues, they will "receive truth immediately from God" and transform a "dead faith" into a "living faith" (*CS* 3:202). But because Emerson knows the difficulty in being truly religious in a complacent system, he advises, "The only way for a man to become religious is to be so by himself," and hence the self-reliant Christian is to find his faith in solitude, in his own closet where he can privately commune with the God within (*CS* 3:202). What Emerson seeks is a one-to-one relation with God, an original relation of like minds that is not made secondary by society or tradition. In an original relation to God, one without "crutches," the self becomes independent and strong. As Emily Dickinson would declare, "The Soul selects her own Society,"[25] so Emerson declared from his pulpit "that God is society enough" (*CS* 3:100).

Undercutting the traditions of both the church and society, Emerson

25. Dickinson, *Final Harvest,* 55.

gains strength in his society of one. With Ellen's death, he prescribes solitude, not only from the hubbub of society but also from the rites of traditional Christianity, as he insists upon heeding the voice within: "I believe when a man wholly opens his heart to the love of God and has no self-love, no motive but from on high, that man speaks with authority, . . . he becomes passive to the influence of God, and speaks his words" (*CS* 3:123). While many of Emerson's early sermons had to do with man in society and his duties and responsibilities to others, the sermons that came after Ellen's death insist on a solitude perhaps learned in mourning, on listening closely to the still voice of eternity, and on finding one's own truth, even though it may be contrary to the popular truths of society. Having found the world within the self, Emerson finds that self sufficient to itself and external forms superfluous if not actually dangerous to the heroic self who would follow the bent of his own genius. This new hero of Emerson's narrative is to go his own way, to see with his own eyes, and to listen to his own voice: "In order to remove the illusion, in order to see things as they really are, the objects of life must be accurately observed, and for this end the wise have always insisted much on the necessity of retirement and meditation, of a voluntary truce imposed upon the tumult of care and hope" (*CS* 3:133).

What Emerson is telling his congregation is pertinent to his own reassessment of his calling. At the same time that he was advising his congregation to "refuse to follow the multitude" (*CS* 3:133), he was coming to suspect that to realize his own talents and power, he must make his way outside the ministry. It seems that Emerson was preaching both to the Second Church congregation and to himself, for the private and public texts intersect and inform each other. As Wesley Mott contends, "Emerson's primary 'audience' became himself,"[26] and it seems that he used the public text to work out his private dilemma — how to be true to himself and yet maintain a position of power. Thus, the private insistence in his journal to trust his own reason, to put to use his own talents "or they will ruin the steward" (*JMN* 3:278), becomes a public call to self-reliance in the sermons. He urges his audi-

26. Mott, *"Strains of Eloquence,"* 109.

ence, himself included, "We must plant our foot and refuse to follow the multitude. We must insist on knowing what is the road and what is the object of the journey. And we must judge whether the object is good, and the road is the right one" (*CS* 3:133). To do otherwise, Emerson knew, is to commit "spiritual suicide" (*JMN* 3:278).

Yet despite the rhetoric of his private and public exhortations to strike out on his own, Emerson's optimism about the road, the journey of life, wavers. The dialectic between self-trust and self-doubt continues to inform Emerson's thought and sermons as he works toward a personal resolution that would apparently require quitting the security of the Second Church pulpit. Though he opened the springtime sermon, No. CXII, brightly enough, speaking of "the warmth of the sun [on] our soil, the sap . . . ascending in the vegetable tribes," another version of this opening stresses the alternate side of seasonal change, one still real to him:

> The spring is wearing into summer. Life is wearing into death. Our friends are forsaking us; our hopes are deceiving us. Our riches are wasting; our mortifications are increasing. A few more winters, a few more friends, a few more hopes, a few more defeats and our thread of life will be snapped and men will throw a little dust on our bodies/ breathless clay. (*CS* 3:132 and 330)

While Emerson may identify himself with the brave hero and with the promise of spring, he also identifies himself with the broken and forsaken man whose journey leads only to death. The harrowing scene of death, of failure and negation, plays behind the more positive depiction of rebirth; as with his willed consolation for Ellen's death, he wills himself, with difficulty still, to a vision of hope and renewal.

Indeed, the psychic dialectic of his own nature creates a discursive tension often evident in the cancellations and emendations of the sermon manuscripts. In his journal he sketches the elements of his own conflict, of his "unevenness of character," when he writes, "Every man is one half of a man[,] either benevolent & weak or firm & unbenevolent, either a speaker & no doer, or a doer & no speaker" (*JMN* 3:310). At this point he seems just such an uneven character, for as he complained, "Who opposes me, ↑who↓ shuts up my mouth, ↑who↓ hin-

ders the flow of my exhortation? Myself, only myself. Cannot I con-
form myself to my principles?" (*JMN* 3:312). Having convinced himself
of the indwelling God and located authority and truth within the self,
Emerson knew the dishonesty of following any but his own voice:
"Suicidal is this distrust of reason; this fear to think; this doctrine that
'tis pious to believe on others' words[,] impious to trust entirely to
yourself" (*JMN* 3:279). Yet at the same time that he could proclaim to
himself his intellectual and spiritual independence, he found himself
unwilling or unable to make the proclamation public: "In my study my
faith is perfect. It breaks, scatters, becomes confounded in converse
with men" (*JMN* 3:314). This obvious conflict between his private and
public selves, between conscience and duty, for a time kept him locked
in a psychic battle without apparent resolution. It was as if he were
waiting for the right time to declare himself to his public and to himself. Like the minister in a parable in his journal who must share a stage
coach with orthodox passengers who wish to talk of religious matters,
Emerson rationalizes his silence by convincing himself that the time for
public declarations has not yet arrived: "God is not in a hurry . . . God
will provide opportunities. Calmly wait" (*JMN* 3:303–4).

As Emerson understood, declaring his spiritual freedom risked his
position in the world. Though he strained at his ministerial duties,
complaining, "It is the best part of the man, I sometimes think, that
revolts most against his being the minister" (*JMN* 3:318), he was not
quick to discard the profession and livelihood for which he had so long
prepared. Indeed, his journal indicates that he required a Thoreauvian
frame of mind to make the leap from comparative comfort back into
poverty. Steeling himself in February 1832 for the anticipated split from
Second Church, he tried to convince himself that intellectual power
counts for more than temporal riches: "And mind does so far vindicate
itself that I think the man does not live so base who would exchange
the least intellectual power for the wealth of the world. I believe a hun-
dred dollars a year would support me in the enjoyment of what I love
best. Why toil I then for 20 times so much?" (*JMN* 3:325). Yet he still
does not make the break his private voice calls for.

Moreover, Emerson recognizes that freedom carries with it the danger of unanchoring the individual and leaving him floundering in an

anarchical state of existence. Although he warns against the Christian who pays only a "lip service, an eye service, an ear service" to a "religion consisting in a decorous regard for the institutions of worship" (*CS* 3:256), he knows that Christianity has enlightened and civilized people for centuries. And though he wonders in his journal, "Were not a Socratic paganism better than an effete, superannuated Christianity?" (*JMN* 4:27), he also worries about "the terrible freedom" and "frightful excesses our vices may run" without the constraints of social and religious institutions. Thus, he also knows that accommodation is necessary for the practical operation of society (*JMN* 4:30), even though he declares to his journal,

> I will not live out of me
> I will not see with others' eyes
> . . . .
> I would be free
>   (*JMN* 4:47)

His hesitations in immediately setting out on his own vocational and intellectual road, then, are personal and real, and play behind the texts of self-reliance, aggravating the dialectic between trust and doubt.

Nonetheless, despite the peril inherent in declaring intellectual, spiritual, and hence vocational freedom, the direction of his thought and life was to seek that freedom. He did this by balancing self-determination against anarchy, finding a "Celestial economy!"(*JMN* 3:315) that resolved the tension between conscience and duty, and by inventing an idealized, fictive hero whose duty is to follow his conscience and to act his thought—the sublime orator whose words are turned to deeds. At the same time that the fictive hero of the sermons of Emerson's last year in the ministry is his psychic double, shaped from his own passional and vocational impulses, this perfect character is a model made safe by fictive distance, enabling Emerson to work out, to some degree, the tensions and risks of his own self-transformation. In Sermon No. CXLVI, written in March 1832 shortly before his resignation, he proposes to his congregation a hypothetical situation that previews his own. In the narrative, Emerson tells of a "sincere man [who] has made up his mind that it is right for him to do something which the common opinion of good men disapproves." After careful consideration of the objections of the community, the man still feels that he must proceed: "if, at last, with the best light, and in perfect simplicity the man still approves his action, let him go and do it though he go alone" (*CS* 4:86). That this "sincere man" is an imaginative rendition of the private man who wrote the sermon is obvious; it is also apparent that Emerson appears to be imaginatively experimenting with the conditions and means of a self-reliance that would compel him to "cut & run" in his bid for manliness and freedom (*JMN* 3:325). Testing the personal quotient of self-reliance, Emerson returns persistently to the themes of self-reliance and freedom in the sermons and to the invention of a hero, the genuine orator, who realizes the authority of the self and the oneness between thought and action that Emerson strives to attain in his own life.

The New Man

Having declared the hero's (and his) freedom from sin, society, and the forms of historical Christianity, Emerson now declares his freedom from himself, not only from the frailty of the self but also from his "mean ego," to fully realize his potential as a cosmic free agent. Paradoxically, Emerson finds self-reliance to derive from a willing denial of self to the Vast Mind. More than encouraging the individual to listen to his inner voice, to trust himself, Emerson now proposes an apocalyptic union of self with God, from which the resurrection of a new self will occur. In a sense, Emerson has worked the psychological sublimation of the body to the will of the mind to its theological conclusion—the sublimation of the physical human to the mind of God. Rooted in Emerson's persistent distrust of the physical self, this new strategy demonstrates as well the vision of correspondence and unity that constituted his personal consolation for loss. Alan Hodder, in his comparison of Emerson's *Nature* with the rhetoric and vision of biblical apocalypse, reminds us that "the crucial event of apocalypse is the double one of destruction and creation." He cites Revelation 21:1–5 as the key apocalyptic text: "And I saw a new heaven and a new earth; for the first heaven and the first earth were passed away, . . . And he that sat upon the throne said, Behold, I make all things new. And he said unto me, Write, for these words are true and faithful." Hodder suggests a parallel between the progression of Revelation and that of *Nature:* "As in the Book of Revelation, the crux of *Nature* is the sequence of dissolution, when the world's 'outlines and surfaces become transparent,' and advent, when God will 'go forth anew into the creation.' And just as Saint John's Revelation culminates in the creation of a new heaven and earth, Emerson's culminates in his famous exhortation: 'Build, therefore, your own world.'"[27]

Similarly, Emerson proposes in the last sermons an apocalyptic union of self with God predicated by the annihilation of "Self-love" and the liberty of "doing what you please" (*CS* 3:207–8). As in the biblical version, a new order emerges out of the ruins of destruction, for with the negation of the selfish demands of the phenomenal self, a spiritualized, empowered new self comes into being. The truly free person is one like the fictive character of Sermon No. CXXIV who becomes master of himself because he surrenders to the universal God within the soul, not only trusting the voice of God within but also merging his identity with that of the Vast Mind:

> He acknowledges that he lives not by himself, but by the Infinite Father, and to him he bows not by compulsion, but eager, trusting, devoted affection. His affection is inquisitive about its object. He believes there's more perfection than he understands. He opens his heart to receive more life. He perceives the great truth that God is in him, and that he is no longer his own; as he rids himself of his vices he becomes more and more instinct with life from the Vast Mind that animates and governs the whole Universe. (*CS* 3:208)

Like the hero of this passage, a being much like Jesus of Nazareth who felt keenly his oneness with God, Emerson finds a new energy derived from the sublimation of the physical self to the world (God) within the soul. In apocalyptic fashion, Emerson too seems to have experienced a kind of spiritual metamorphosis that left him a new man, for he writes persistently now of a character who has "a new hold on

27. *Complete Works,* 1:10. Hodder, *Emerson's Rhetoric of Revelation,* 23–24.

existence," who "is born again," and who has a "new life" of "balance and energy" (*CS* 4:127). The language and imagery of Sermon No. CLII clearly indicate that Emerson has experienced a "conversion from a moral to a religious character" (*JMN* 3:186), a conversion that left him empowered and sure of himself, a conversion truer than the one of his southern journey, for it is engendered by his own peculiar vision and arises like the new apocalyptic kingdom out of destruction, negation, and loss. Indeed, the biblical paradigm of destruction and renewal parallels Emerson's personal experience of loss and resurrection from grief; and as the speaker of *Nature* demands, "Build, therefore, your own world," so the speaker of the sermons is in the process of building a new world vision and a new self based on his own version of correspondence and self-reliance.

The new man who emerges in the last sermons and months of Emerson's ministry is both the Emerson who can "dare . . . to lay out my own road" (*JMN* 4:47) and an idealized, fictive hero. The new man is "the image of God," a rare man whose thoughts "go deepest of all" and "stir the great deep within him" (*CS* 4:143, 146). He is a heroic self who is "aware of the grandeur of his nature, and conscious of the immortality of the soul" and a man who is "conscious of having really thought and acted" (*CS* 4:146). He is a man whose moral nature provides "the key by which the works of nature are to be read" and whose inmost thoughts are converted into deed (*CS* 4:144). He is free of "a wretched dependence upon human censure & human praise" (*CS* 4:388). This, then, is the hero of Emerson's narrative, a hero fashioned by Emerson from the seeds of his imagination and an image Emerson shapes for and of himself.

Merging both the real and the fictional in his farewell sermon to Second Church, Emerson describes and demonstrates this final version of the perfect character. More than a self-made man, this character, like Emerson, is a man-made self. When Emerson finally wrote Sermon No. CLXIV in October 1832, he had made up his mind to leave his church. He had asked himself in February, "Might I cut & run? Might I dignifiedly walk away & keep the man nor turn cat?" (*JMN* 3:325). And when he wrote his Aunt Mary of the pending resignation, he echoed the sentiments of the heroic, independent figure of the previous sermons: "I apprehend a separation . . . I can only do my work well by abjuring the opinions & customs of all others & adhering strictly to the divine plan a few dim inches of whose outline I faintly discern in my breast" (*L* 1:354). Like the genuine man of the sermon, he turned his thought into action by declaring his intellectual and spiritual independence and resigning from a situation that seemed to demand of him "spiritual suicide" (*JMN* 3:278) at the hands of tradition and conformity. On September 11, 1832, he had requested that he be dismissed from "the pastoral charge" (*L* 1:355–56), ostensibly because the congregation and he did not agree on the meaning and practice of the Lord's Supper. One would expect, then, that his sermon on the new, genuine man would be a strong statement of self-reliance. And it is, with some eloquent and forceful assertions about the man who "speaks what he thinks, [who] acts his thought," evidencing Emerson's decision to strike out on his own, both in his livelihood and in his thinking (*CS* 4:206). For that moment, Emerson seems to have embodied his own truths by voicing and acting his thought, to have become the self he had fashioned in his homiletic narrative.

Yet even at this moment of self-realization, the old dialectic with the self returns, making difficult the writing of this sermon. The manuscript evinces the usual emendations, as Emerson seeks to clarify, qualify, and economize his thoughts. But in some passages he seems to have difficulty getting his thoughts together, and the manuscript looks like a list of assets that men striving for success might "embrace" — the "mechanick arts," the "bustle of commerce," or the "gentle offices of compassion or instruction" (*CS* 4:414–15). A long section added in pencil in the middle of the text further attempts to describe the attributes of the genuine man — that he "believe in himself" and that "the development of the inward nature . . . [raise] it to its true place of absolute sovereignty" and speak "the voice of God" (*CS* 4:412). Emerson seems to have difficulty clearly distinguishing the successful man promoted by American nationalism and self-help manuals from the "true & entire" man (*CS* 4:410). Indeed, the unfocused addition demonstrates the dialectical tension evident in other sermons between the apparent and the ineffable, between Emerson's impulse to self-determination and the security of conformity. For as the emendation makes clear, it was easier for Emerson to describe what he does *not* mean than what he does mean about the genuine man:

> And this is my object in the present discourse to draw the picture of the Genuine Man —
>
> [I think very few such have ever lived]
>
> But it is essential that he shd. believe in himself because that is the object in view to <act on> raise up a great counterbalance to the engrossing <uses> of riches of popularity of the love of life in the man & make him feel that all these ought to be his servants & not <his> masters that He is as great nay much greater than any of these: to make him feel that <he may becom> whereas the consequence of most men now depends on their wealth or their popularity; he is capable of being & ought to become <su> a man so rich & so commanding by the simple force of his character that wealth or poverty wd. be an unnoticed accident that his ↑solitary↓ opinion & his support to any cause whatever would be like the acclamation of <a nation> the world in its behalf.
>
> This as we shall see is the secret of all true greatness the development of the inward nature the raising it to its true place to absolute sovereignty <preferring> ↑hearkening↓ this voice which to most men sounds so faint & insignificant above the thunder of the laws & the customs of mankind. And it is founded & can only be founded in religion. It can only prefer this self because it esteems it to speak the voice of God.
>
> This example of public life is only a glaring instance of the manner in which we are dazzled by circumstances but you & I <ar> ↑in↓ the most private condition are quite as apt to make the same mistake. A failure in trade is called ruin tho' it may only call out the faculties & resources of his character The death of a parent or <frie> ↑relative↓ on whom a family depends is esteemed an irreparable loss How many <fe> women are brot up in the belief that a↑n↓ <c> advantageous connexion in life is essential to their respectability & comfort & grow up in ignorance of their own resources. (*CS* 4:412–13 and MS)

The working manuscript testifies to Emerson's difficulty in composing the genuine man; the tentativeness and negativity of the paragraphs threaten to undermine the "sovereignty" of this new kind of self-reliant individual. Indeed, Emerson's very difficult task is not to describe the conventional hero of American go-aheadism; rather it is to create a new man, both the fictive hero of the sermon and the new man that Emerson is becoming. His task as he defines it is "the higher & holier work of forming men <free> true & entire men" (*CS* 4:410). As the national identity was figured by and formed by the mythic self-made man of the American dream, so too Emerson's identity was figured and formed by a character of his own making, this "true & entire" genuine man. What is at stake in No. CLXIV is not mere eloquence, though that always matters to Emerson, but self-identification, and that is one reason why writing this sermon was so difficult.

Moreover, the sermon is marked by an underlying doubt about his ability to become the man he has invented. One seemingly minor change takes on significance in the light of David Leverenz's study on man-making words. Emerson says, "But not only an inferior [he had said, "a little"] man is thus <frequently> often magnified <into a great man> but <in> men of real ability owe to this <trumpeting> ↑noise & pomp↓ the largest part of their eclat" (*CS* 4:411). Leverenz describes what I also find to be true about the Emerson of the sermons, that throughout much of his life he was involved in "the struggle for a feeling of power," a struggle that "reflects the fears of failure, the desperate rivalries for success, and the fluidity of a social frame in which power itself was uncertainly shifting from one group of men and one mode of manhood to another."[28] Emerson's sentence registers worry about such inferiority, and its numerous revisions suggest a concern with more than stylistic economy. Moreover, a subsequent change relates manliness to bravery, as Emerson speaks of the ungenuine man who is "not good enough — not <brave> ↑man↓ enough to go in & converse with that celestial scene. Very likely he is so utterly unacquainted with himself, — has lived so on the outside of his world, that he does not yet believe in its existence" (*CS* 4:412). Emerson, of course, was braving the displeasure of his family and congregation in abandoning a ministerial career; at the same time, he fears that he is not brave

28. David Leverenz, "The Politics of Emerson's Man-Making Words," 49, 53. Also see his *Manhood and the American Renaissance*.

enough to become a genuine man, to be himself. There is a disjunction between what he wills himself to be — the man of his ambition — and what he fears himself to be — a man of mediocre talents — between self-distrust and self-trust. The road to manhood, the road to selfhood, is fraught with pain and fear, as this sermon and the others that comprise its foreground testify. He laments in the sermon that a "Long & weary road . . . lies before him! Painful perhaps frightful convulsions . . . he must suffer before the twilight of that inner day can dawn upon his understanding!" (*CS* 4:412). Emerson excised this sentence from the sermon, perhaps revealing his fears about striking out on his own as well as his real effort to will himself to the power that he sought.

A paragraph added at the end of the sermon further demonstrates the personal dialectic that lies behind the sermon and Emerson's will to reify the self he has invented. As if he were talking to himself, urging himself to become the genuine man he has just described, he begins, revealingly, "<Now I am afraid that the> I said just now that to us was committed the formation of men" (*CS* 4:416). This unfinished musing suggests a hesitancy not only about the preceding discourse but also about his power to become the man he calls for — something that "cannot however be done by many To himself, to himself," he continues, "it is committed & if he fails to form it the conspiring world cannot do it for him" (*CS* 4:416). Again, the fear of failure undercuts the resolution, will power, and bravery needed to become a "man," for Emerson has risked his career and his idea of himself in the formation of this new man. He then declares that a man "should feel that he has a right to be original, to follow the dictates of his own judgment" (*CS* 4:416).

Emerson sounds as if he were still arguing not only with his family — Aunt Mary in particular, who wanted him to overcome his doubts and remain in the ministry — but also with the part of himself that feels "little" and "inferior," a part that needs to be buoyed up by persuasive argument. He supports his argument with a confident statement that man "derives his right from the Creator of the world who made him a new being, with some thoughts that never were in any other being with a plan & determination of character peculiar & novel in the universe." Yet the very next sentence undermines this assertion and also changes the pronoun to "you" — to the "you" that is part of Emerson's "me":

"But you are a stranger to that originality & strength for you never give it play. You depart from your own convictions & copy other people & say what they say — & so you have not found out what you are." You and your like, Emerson tells himself, present "the same tame <& timid mediocrity> & uninteresting mediocrity" (*CS* 4:417). He both fears and scorns what he has for so long felt himself to be; and yet that mediocrity might be a kind of security against the hard and painful road that the self-willed, self-formed man must take. While he generally assumes an affirmative voice in his sermons, this passage contains some telling negatives, beginning with "I am afraid" and ending in a line separated from the rest of the passage — "The genuine man never fears to avow his opinion" — reflecting not only his fears but also his doubts about speaking his mind (*CS* 4:416–17).

Whatever his doubts and fears, though, Emerson at this juncture in his life did become the new man he had invented, a man who acted on and acted out his thought. Despite the anxieties that underlie this sermon, the public occasion of the sermon required Emerson to compose himself — to pull himself together and to write himself. By announcing to his congregation the "Genuine Man," he was also announcing himself as a genuine man. Shaped within the text of this sermon and the ones that precede it, this new self is formed from Emerson's personal intersection with texts, particularly the cultural materials that described self-formation and the self-made man. At a time when the need to reconstitute himself was made pertinent by attachment and loss, Emerson's reading and rendering of the self-made man subverted the usual "error" that character is "quite external — like a dress ↑to wear↓" by finding "another standard of success," one that marked him as a man of the mind, indeed as an "original mind" (*CS* 4:416). Engaged in the project of becoming a new man at the same time that he was finding consolation in the idea of correspondence, Emerson formed a self-reliance that likewise was tinged with moods of attachment and sympathy, independence and freedom, and metaphors of the body. Diving into and beneath the surface of the body, the body of texts and the body as text, to discover himself, Emerson reconstitutes the self through a discourse that continues to speak to the figure behind the texts who first taught him who he was.

5

Emerson and the Mantle of Biography

The great value of Biography consists in the perfect sympathy that exists between like minds . . . We recognize with delight a strict likeness between their noblest impulses & our own. We are tried in their trial. By our cordial approval we conquer in their victory. We participate in their act by our thorough understanding of it. (*JMN* 5:11)

In a nation preoccupied with getting ahead, anxious about becoming successful, and engaged in glorifying and mythologizing the self-made man, it is only reasonable to expect that heroes from the past would play a role in the literature of self-cultivation and in the management of definitions of self. Indeed, in the guides and manuals for success written in the first half of the nineteenth century, one finds not only the recurrence of certain historical figures but also a consensus of the uses of those figures and a general agreement on the qualities that made those men heroic and worthy of consideration and imitation.

It appears that many of Emerson's contemporaries agreed with him that "There is no history: There is only Biography" (*JMN* 7:202). The writers of sentimental, conventional guides to self-improvement may not have had the theoretical interest of Emerson or Carlyle, who would echo Emerson's pronouncement by declaring in *On Heroes and Hero-Worship* that "Universal History, the history of what man has accomplished in this world, is at bottom the History of the Great Men who have worked here." Nonetheless, their rendering of the past often takes the form of biography. From the first, Americans looked at their history as biography, confusing fact and fiction and creating, or re-creating, history as myth. As often happens with interpretive history, its re-creation more often than not illustrates a contemporary concern of the author, thereby altering to some degree the "facts" of history (or biography) to illustrate current concerns and ideologies. Thus, the early Puritans tended to see themselves and their mission in the wilderness in typological terms, interpreting their experiences in the tradition of biblical exegesis. Cotton Mather's history of New England, structured around biographical sketches of the founding fathers, was intended "with a just Fear of incroaching and ill-boding Degeneracies . . . to prevent the Loss of a Country, so signaliz'd for the Profession of the purest Religion, and for the Protection of God upon it." Likewise, the biographical histories of the late eighteenth and early nineteenth centuries were intended "to retain the espirit of a social society."[1] The writers of these histories looked to the heroic figures of the recent past, especially the patriots of the Revolutionary War, celebrating their deeds and endowing some with mythic qualities, as Parson Weems did in his biography of George Washington. What the lives of Washington and the other patriots of American history illustrated was the greatness of not just a few men but of the nation as a whole. As it became more apparent that America's greatness and identity lay in its potential for prosperity and material success, writers turned their attention to the problem of attaining prosperity while at the same time maintaining virtue — social and personal. In the process, hawkers of success selected those men who exemplified the ideal of America; at the same time these advisers participated in the formation of an American self as they encouraged their audiences to imitate *men* of the past.

Using biography to illustrate and encourage successful and moral living seems to have been a happy choice, for the heroes were examples

1. Thomas Carlyle, *On Heroes and Hero-Worship and the Heroic in History*, 3. Cotton Mather, *Magnalia Christi Americana, Books I and II*, Book I: 115. Fred Somkin, *Unquiet Eagle: Memory and Desire in the Idea of American Freedom, 1815–1860*, 7. Somkin suggests the association of prosperity, progress, and virtue in both a "ritualistic identification with a spiritually heroic past" and with the actual prosperity of the nineteenth century, an association that conflated the actual and the ideal (15).

of character formation who also touched the hearts of readers. As public figures, their biographies were manipulated in advice manuals to effect change in the private self of audience members. The intersection between public and private, indeed, the incursion made by the public into the private realm of the self, is exemplified in the heroes, who were at the same time private men with families and public men with political and economic concerns. This intersection is also exemplified in the expected effect on readers, also both private and public beings, whose transformation as industrious, moral citizens would be created out of habits inspired by sympathy for the heroes and identification with them. In this way, heroes also represent the intersection of external and internal by teaching conduct and habit formation through the agency of the affections. We have already seen how the advice proffered to young men urged character formation by means of external changes—forming exemplary habits. And we have seen how Ellen Tucker warmed up the "cold" (*JMN* 3:72) Emerson for his own project of self-formation by teaching him sympathy, the sympathy of like minds. What we have yet to see is the role of biography in effecting the self-improvement of the mass of young men and of Emerson's own refiguration. By investigating from a different angle Emerson's conversion into a man-made self by means of his handling of (being handled by) cultural materials, and by looking at ways he appropriated the characteristics and identity of biographical characters in his private reshaping of the self, we will discover how public and private, external and internal influences intersect in his construction of a "new man" for the public—the genuine man, the representative man.

Public Uses of Biography

The underlying purposes for using biography shifted somewhat during the first half of the nineteenth century as the nation's economy became more industrial and less agrarian. During the early years of the republic (and continuing to some degree later into the century), educated men who enjoyed position and rank in society began to find themselves threatened by the restless masses of Americans who strove to make their own places in the strata of American life. In his Phi Beta Kappa Address of 1824, Edward Everett echoed these concerns when he said, "Society must be preserved in its constituted forms, or there is no safety for life, no security for property, no permanence for any institution, civil, moral, or religious." For the first generation of the nineteenth century, that of the Reverend William Emerson, writers used biography to attempt to maintain the social position of the gentleman by hearkening to the traditional values of duty, order, and social obligation. From his study of the appearance of heroes in American magazines, Theodore Greene finds evidence that biographies served three functions in the first decades of the nineteenth century: as testimony to the caliber of American society, as examples of morality, and as bulwarks against an encroaching egalitarianism. Because "success" meant something different in the early 1800s than it would in the 1830s, 1840s, and later in the century — because it was at first defined in terms of competence, independence, and morality rather than in strictly materialistic terms — the types of heroes and the uses to which they were put by authors stressed gentlemanly virtue and man's role in society. Thus Jeremy Belknap's series of biographies for the *Columbian Magazine* were advertised as celebrating men "who have, at any time, been instrumental to the foundation and prosperity of the United States." In 1808 a writer for the *Monthly Anthology* suggested the concerns of his generation when he declared, "The design of biography is to celebrate useful talents, to record patriotick labours, and to exhibit characteristick traits of virtue." Evidencing a budding nationalism, these writers also betray what is perhaps the most prevalent concern of biography, that it be useful. The word *useful* seems to have been a common adjective, reflecting as Everett does a utilitarian streak in the American mind-set: "All men should seek to cultivate and inform their minds, by pursuit of *useful* knowledge, as the great means of happiness and *usefulness*" (emphasis added). As the century progressed, the focus of biographers shifted to celebrate the self-made man, the individual who, by winning laurels and riches, promoted the nation's prosperity. Emphasizing those traits that have become almost synonymous with Americanism, Everett told his Franklin Lecture audience of "the great benefactors of our race; the men, who, by wonderful inventions, remarkable discoveries, and extraordinary improvements, have conferred the most eminent service on their fellow-men, and gained the highest names in history, — by far the greater part have been men of humble origin, narrow fortunes, small advantages, and self-taught."[2]

While contemporary ideology and sexism underlay much of what was said about figures from the past, authors generally had direct and immediate uses for biography, for they sought to shape and manage definitions of behavior, success, and self in the context of the national quest for identity and success. In doing so, they apparently neglected the women of the nation, who might find different terms for the self than those exemplified in male figures and celebrated in a male-dominated ideology. Seeking to do more than "celebrate," "record," and "exhibit" the "traits of virtue," inspirational authors hoped to lead Americans and America "forward to some better future" and focused on the effects of biography on the masculinized audience. The notions of material self-improvement, moral self-cultivation, and celebration of heroes conflated as Americans were urged to forge brighter and more successful lives for themselves from the examples of the past. Historical as well as contemporary figures were used to teach, inspire, and excite audiences to emulate in their own lives the positive qualities of the hero. This relationship between historical model and contemporary person was suggested by Emerson, who called "the great men of the world, the teachers of the race" (*JMN* 3:199). Much of what was said about the past rang of didacticism, but throughout, figures functioned as models and examples of "successful" living and as representatives of the potential of diligent readers who followed their lead. Finding the same kind of inspiration as did Plutarch when he said, "the virtues of these great men [serve] me as a sort of looking-glass in which I may see how to adjust and adorn my own life," writers turned biography to practical and personal ends, to preserve the masculine hegemony and to inspire personal behavior and self-definition within already prescribed, cultural formulas. Recognizing the role of sympathy, a writer for the

---

2. Everett, *Orations and Speeches,* 15. Theodore Greene, *America's Heroes: The Changing Models of Success in American Magazines,* 41. Quoted in Greene, *America's Heroes,* 38–39. Everett, *Speeches and Orations,* 290, 298–99.

Columbian Magazine avowed, "Nothing excites more powerfully to virtuous deeds, than the examples of those whom they have rendered conspicuous. Man generally desires what he finds applauded in others." For the American, greatness in others suggests not simply a distant and awestruck hero worship but also a kind of egalitarian imitation of greatness whereby the hero represents the potential of any person willing to follow his example, to adopt the accepted meaning of success. Suggesting this representative quality of biography, Edward Everett told the Working Man's Party on October 6, 1830, "It was no magic, no miracle, which made Newton, and Franklin, and Fulton. It was the patient, judicious, long-continued cultivation of powers of the understanding, eminent, no doubt, in degree, but not differing in kind, from those which are possessed by every individual in this assembly." Later in the century, Timothy Shay Arthur, author of inspirational literature, called for a new biography of self-made men "that we may know the ways by which they came up from the ranks of the people," suggesting, as did Everett, that one could similarly rise in the world by following and imitating the virtues and habits of the successful.[3] Realizing the value to self-cultivation and self-improvement of human examples over mere lists of virtues or encomiums to right behavior, advisers enlisted the affections in promoting the kind of behavior and self-concept deemed appropriate for this emerging, industrializing nation.

While insisting that the truly successful man is a Christian and a gentleman, the popularizers of success, themselves often Christian ministers, nonetheless pointed to specific traits of character that one must cultivate in order "to rise . . . in the world." Unsurprisingly, these are also the traits that heroic figures from the past were described to possess. Daniel Wise in *The Young Man's Counsellor* lists six elements of character that he feels the young man must cultivate: integrity, intelligence, industry, economy, energy, and tact. William Alcott, Henry Ward Beecher, and John Todd concur in the main with Wise's analysis

3. Greene, *America's Heroes,* 38. Somkin, *Unquiet Eagle,* quotes Gulian Verplanck on page 77. Quoted in Edmund G. Berry, *Emerson's Plutarch,* 20. Quoted in Greene, *America's Heroes,* 39. Everett, *Orations and Speeches,* 285. Quoted in Irvin Wyllie, *The Self-Made Man in America,* 19.

of success, adding specific habits of industry, such as rising early, and warning against the evils of indolence and temptation. To drive home his point about the importance of rising early, Alcott points to the examples of Franklin and Napoleon; Todd illustrates the point with Napoleon and William Cobbett, a favorite of manual writers for his prodigious industry. All of the inspirationalists stressed hard work and almost unceasing industry as keys to success; Edward Everett, for example, mentions the "amount of labor" that the "distinguished men" could perform and mentions "Demosthenes, Julius Caesar, Henry the Fourth of France, Lord Bacon, Sir Isaac Newton, Franklin, Washington, Napoleon." Because they are advocating individually generated success, these writers often used as examples those figures who were self-made, who became great because of their "self exertion": Alexander, Caesar, Charles XII, Napoleon, Alfred, Luther, Howard, Franklin, Washington, Rush.[4]

Emerson's Early Use of Biography

Like his contemporaries, the young Emerson used biography and references to historical figures in his sermons. While Henry Ware Jr. and others may have seen his use of secular heroes as out of place in the pulpit, Emerson, especially in the early years of his ministry, used biography in ways consistent with those of his contemporaries. Only as he confronted the accepted definitions of selfhood and worked toward an exit from Second Church did his use of biography veer from the conventional. Like his contemporaries, then, young Emerson used biographical figures, both sacred and secular, to illustrate the lifelong

---

4. T. S. Arthur, *Rising in the World: or, a Tale for the Rich and the Poor,* 186. Wise, *Young Man's Counsellor,* 41–42. Alcott, *Young Man's Guide,* advises that young men adopt as habits industry, economy, rising early, obedience, temperance, modesty, politeness, and cleanliness. Todd's list of habits includes early rising, system, finishing every task, punctuality, regard for truth, and self-improvement of the mind, manners, and faith. Henry Ward Beecher advocates industry and honesty as primary habits in *Seven Lectures to Young Men on Various Important Subjects.* Alcott, *Young Man's Guide,* 39. Todd, *The Young Man,* 153. Everett, *Orations and Speeches,* 267. Alcott, *Young Man's Guide,* 25–26.

process of "developing and unfolding . . . a potential inner virtue," and to depict a self-generated future success and virtuous living in the face of worldly temptation.[5]

Although Emerson sometimes used biography simply to ornament and enliven his sermons, he concurred with his contemporaries that biography should be "useful" in inspiring moral and successful living. In fact, he knew that biography attains meaning only in as much as it is appropriated by modern readers. In his first sermon, he asked his congregation:

> for what is the Past? It is nothing worth. Its value, except as means of wisdom, is, in the nature of things actually nothing. And what is the imposing present? what are the great men and great things that surround you? All that they can do for you is dust, and less than dust to what you can do for yourself. They are like you stretching forward to an infinite hope, the citizens in trust of a future world. (*CS* 1:60)

Like his secular brethren, he finds the value of the past to lie in its transformative use by the individual who would make his own future, for he understood that "we learn virtue almost as we learn our native tongue, by imitating the tones and actions of others" (*CS* 1:72). Recognizing the influence that "the pomp of wealth and power" (*CS* 1:87) exercise on most men's affections, he also warned that "we learn with the more fatal facility the example of vice" (*CS* 1:72). Because biographical figures have the peculiar benefit of embodying abstract ideas or lessons in a recognizable form, they can readily elicit an emotive and imitative response from an audience. It is important to Emerson, then, not only that "we learn virtue" but also that the inspiration of the "great men" leads to useful and moral living. Like his contemporaries, the young minister suggested that great men are to be admired and imitated, and they are to function as models, examples, representatives of the virtue and potential of each person.

---

5. Henry Ware Jr. complained that Emerson cited Scripture too little. In a letter to Ware on December 30, 1826, Emerson replied, "I have affected generally a mode of illustration rather bolder than the usage of our preaching warrants, on the principle that our religion is nothing limited or partial, but of universal application, & interested in all that interests man" (*L* 1:157). Robinson, *Apostle of Culture*, 13.

Early in his ministry, Emerson suggested that Jesus' life, which is "a model for ours," is instrumental in the "sublime sympathy" man has with his "maker" and in individual moral self-improvement, the "great and neverending progress to greatness in the effort to bring ourselves into his majestic likeness" (*CS* 1:146–47). In other words, biography's usefulness is that it makes one "better" (*CS* 1:282). In Sermon No. XXXVI, "Cultivating the Mind," Emerson urges that his congregation "get a little into the habit of reading valuable books" and states that "there are biographies of great and good men, and of bad men, by which you can hardly help being made better," giving as examples the lives of "Franklin, of Howard, of Wesley, of Dr. Johnson, of Washington, and of Napoleon" (*CS* 1:282). Suggesting, as do the more secular self-improvement manualists, that the man aspiring to improve himself not waste time but "in the intervals of business . . . read a few pages of the histories of Plutarch or of Robertson," Emerson notes that the effect of "some one heroic trait of Aristides, Luther or of Washington" would be to make one "feel differently & incomparably better" (*CS* 1:282). In fact, biography was often touted by moralists as the most useful and manly reading: "No branch of reading is more instructive than the biography of those, who, born in the humbler walks of life, have risen by their talents and virtues, to the highest grades of useful distinction." Biography's usefulness lay also, then, in its role in making one manly — virile, industrious, and moral — and in constructing and preserving a public male ideology.[6]

Biography's advantage for readers is the more keenly made because it is a felt benefit, one that makes its way into the individual's life first through "sympathy." Echoing the influence of John Locke on the impact of sense experience on ideas and the mind, Emerson indicates that the immediate impact of biography is on the emotions, the affections

---

6. Jasper Adams, *Laws of Success and Failure in Life: An Address delivered 30th October, 1833. In the Chapel of the College of Charleston before the Euphradian Society*, 13. Barish, *Roots of Prophesy*, summarizes the nineteenth-century attitude about biography or history as literary type when she says, "History was a respectable, intellectual, and manly pursuit" (121). In my "Stowe's Matriarchy and The Rhetoric of Domesticity," I demonstrate that advice for women failed to assert the need for self-cultivation in the same ways that advice to men did.

and sympathy of the individual, which in turn serve as intermediaries to the mind and the soul. Indeed, the impact of Jesus upon humans and their perception of moral truths is due in large part to the "attachment" that they have to the person of Jesus. In Sermon No. LX, Emerson suggests that ideas become real and meaningful only when first perceived through the emotions: "How vague and cold is our regard for patriotism, courage, purity, honesty, compared with our attachment to those qualities in the person of a friend. They are dead possibilities till they live in a soul" (*CS* 2:109). In ways that echo his own private attachment to "the person of a friend" and his subsequent transformation from a "cold" (*JMN* 3:72) man to one warmed by love and enlivened to the possibilities of his own soul, Emerson ponders the effect of public heroes on the private life of the self. At the same time reiterating the message found in cultural materials, Emerson also whispers a secret of his own heart's attachment to one who exemplified and made real the virtues of piety and sanctity. Though Sermon LX clearly refers to Jesus, one hears behind its explicit message the lesson of the heart Emerson learned most emphatically from Ellen.

One of the great benefits of biography, then, is that it embodies ideas in the form of humans for whom one can develop an emotional attachment and thereby readily learn truths of human nature and activity. Just such was the genius of the Supreme Biographer who advantageously embodied truth in the physical form of Jesus:

> When the Word was made Flesh, when the mind which was to contain and unfold by miracle and by doctrine the revelation of God was cloathed with a human form, was born of a Jewish woman, and sent out into the light of worldly life to have the sympathy and influence, the love and the hatred, the tears, infirmities, fear, and death of man, then, the inestimable advantage of a personal interest was imparted to the truth which he taught . . . The relation of Christ to the Revelation, as its actor, and representative, and proof, is, as the relation of a fact to a theory. (*CS* 2:109)

Jesus, then, is the Word made Flesh, truth humanized, idea made sense, a living example who "lived as he taught" (*CS* 2:110) and lived what he taught, a theory made fact in order that his human readers may reverse in the act of reading the process of incarnation and find from the fact the theory, find from the example the truth, find from the Flesh the Word. Jesus can be an effective "actor, and representative" of truth because humans form an emotional attachment and interest in him as a fellow, albeit greater, man.

Furthermore, like his contemporaries, Emerson suggests that the primary benefit of examining these examples of greatness is the self-knowledge that becomes, in turn, the vehicle for individual improvement, success, and perhaps greatness. In Sermon No. XXVII, first preached on November 23, 1828, he addressed a theme that was to accrue even more urgency later in his ministry, the necessity of knowing oneself. "My brethren," he said, "it is not enough considered by us how much it is the proper business of life to learn ourselves. We may read history, but this is what we learn there, or we learn nothing" (*CS* 1:227). The figures of history are not only "diagrams" of greatness but also illustrations of human "capacities and infirmaties" common to all and "by whose story I may learn how I might act and suffer" (*CS* 1:227). Interesting in this passage is Emerson's use of the personal pronouns "we" and particularly "I," which he rarely uses in these public texts, betraying not only how he reads history but his own striving for greatness and the role that biography played in the formation of his own character. Here, the heroes of the past are representatives of the human condition and their stories suggest the heights and depths that man is capable of reaching. But as is the case with so much of his sermonizing, Emerson's discussion of the benefit of biography reveals his own passional self. Thus we witness his own interior struggle between temptation and perseverance when he explains:

> When I am disgusted by the bloody annals of despotism and hideous profligacy, I learn, with alarm, to what depths of depravity, my passions will lead me, if I surrender myself to their solicitations. When I read the story of the martyrs of religion and liberty, I see how God has proportioned the strength of the body and the mind; and that my mind may be trained to such firmness of virtue, as to be superior to all torment which the body can bear and live. (*CS* 1:227)

The value of biography, then, is personal and utilitarian, both to the congregation and to Emerson, who would engage in a program of self-cultivation and would inspire himself to the greatness that as a young man he so longs for and often despairs of attaining. His reading of the "texts" of history — the biographical figures — and of Scripture concur with and feed his quest for a new, empowered self. For in the act of interpreting those texts and in conjunction with his move toward self-reliance, he also creates or invents a new self to make up for or disguise a self that he feels to be weak and unsatisfactory.[7] The effect of the great men who decorate and inform his sermons would be to inspire not only his congregation but himself to become "a more powerful being" (*CS* 1:282).

Emerson's Early Heroes

If, then, Emerson uses the heroes of the past as examples of greatness and models of the self, which heroes does Emerson mention and what characteristics do they exemplify? In the first half of his ministry, through Sermon No. LXXXIX, Emerson iterated the concerns of his culture and found inspiring those men who served society while maintaining the characteristics of a Christian gentleman. Taking his cue not only from the example of Jesus but also from the definitions of behavior current at the time, Emerson extolled strength of mind, faith, humility, and patience. The men he selects to illustrate these heroic traits emerge from three basic categories of heroes (though of course there are exceptions) — the religious figure, both from the Bible and from modern history; military or patriotic heroes; and men of scientific and geographic discovery. At this point in his life and thought, Emerson found in public figures definitions of the heroic self that not only confirm the social body but also represent it. Not yet registering his aversion to society, the young Emerson, himself just recently become a public man, partici-

7. Dennis Pahl quotes from J. Hillis Miller's "The Disarticulation of the Self in Nietzsche": "The various entities of the inner world making up a given person's 'character'—feelings, thoughts, volitions, the 'self'—is not a present document waiting to be read. It is created by the act of interpretation which reads it. Interpretation posits signs and reads them, in a single act, once more of autogeneration, autosuspension, and, ultimately, of autodestruction" (*Architects of the Abyss: The Indeterminate Fictions of Poe, Hawthorne, and Melville,* 26n).

pates in constructing a version of the self as one who discovers and preserves the larger, social body. Indeed, Theodore Greene observes that in the early republic, when the viability of the new nation was still tentative, the basic institutions of society—the state, military, and church—provided the major fields worthy of a hero. They were "the activities necessary to provide and protect a more perfect Union, establish justice, insure domestic tranquility, and promote general welfare."[8] Like the writers of the early republic, young Emerson was concerned with the individual's role in society and often chose as heroic types those who benefited mankind, affirming rather than transforming society and the social man.

Evidencing some of the concern of his father's generation that the successful man exhibit characteristics of the gentleman, Emerson tells his audience in Sermon No. VIII that "whatsoever anecdotes of ancient or modern fame have transmitted the memory of selfdevotion, of valor, of abstinence, of wisdom, of sacrifice,—all that is excellent in them is in strict coincidence with religion . . . The spirit of a gentleman and the spirit of a Christian . . . are one" (*CS* 1:111). And in Sermon No. XXXIII he extols the "power in gentleness," oddly enough giving the examples of Peter, Luther, and the Puritans, who lacked gentleness and yet performed great deeds. Emerson demurs by insisting that he does not believe that "the graces of the Christian character are ever incompatible with its most robust strength and highest majesty" (*CS* 1:261). Perhaps that is the danger of a Napoleon, that "Power becomes tyranny whenever its exercise is not tempered by kindness" (*CS* 1:262). The hero as gentleman is one concerned about his fellowman and capable of achieving a kind of sympathy and humility rather than one whose ego runs roughshod over others. Additionally, it seems, the gentleman-hero is a simple man of humble origins, for Emerson continually reminds his congregation, as he did in Sermon No. XLIV, of the humble origins of Columbus and Jesus and of the simplicity of Jesus and Newton.

While Napoleon, that enigmatic figure for nineteenth-century moralists, may illustrate the "perversions" of the gentlemanly qualities of patience and gentleness, he nonetheless exhibited an intriguing strength

8. Greene, *America's Heroes*, 52–53.

of mind (*CS* 2:39). Emerson grants Napoleon his great achievements and the "master[y] of himself" (*CS* 2:312) but cannot quite condone his character. Instead, he insists that true moral and mental strength arises from patience, meditation, and humility. Most of the men who exemplify moral power, "Socrates, Plato, Paul, Newton, Milton, Fenelon" (*CS* 2:229), have also been identified for their strength of conscience, (Sermon No. XXI), simplicity (No. XLIV), and patience (No. XLV). Indeed, Sir Isaac Newton's greatness is all the more exemplary because, even though he "knew so much more than his fellow-men," he yet exhibited a childlike simplicity and humility, even on his deathbed (*CS* 2:151). And while in Sermon No. LXXXIV Emerson claims that like the heroic mind "every mind needs only to have its attention thoroughly aroused to be made conscious that worlds of knowledge are open to it on every hand" and in brackets alludes to Columbus and the "discovery of Am[erica]," he makes explicit that the power of Newton's mind was trained and put to beneficial use by "certain habits of mind . . . of meditation — of patient thinking — of seeking for truth" (*CS* 2:233 and MS). Just as his fellow moralists have avoided characterizing Newton as a genius, one who inherited rather than cultivated his powers, so too Emerson participates in a democratic and pragmatic reading of Newton's powers. Like his fellow inspirationalists, Emerson's goal is to inspire self-cultivation in his auditors, and he accordingly portrays Newton as a model for shaping the lives of others less gifted.

The Common Denominator

Until midcareer, Emerson's notions about the hero exemplified the notions of his father's generation about gentlemanly traits, humility and simplicity, and service to one's fellowman. But Sermon No. LXXXVIII reveals the shift in his thinking that characterizes the second half of his ministry, that the "best & greatest men," like Paul and Fenelon, are convinced that "God is present" and in the human soul (*CS* 2:400, 252). The primary difference between the heroes just described and those to follow is that the new hero derives his strength from his conviction of unity with (likeness to) the spirit of God. His heroic quest is discovery of the self, and his adventures are played out in the inner terrain of the self. Converting the ideals of geographic and scientific discovery into the discovery of the self and the ideal of military prowess into control of the solitary body, Emerson redefines the terms of heroism as he looks progressively inward, finding the kingdom of God within the self, within *any* self. As he does so, it becomes apparent to him that greatness is not a social quest but rather a private one that all are capable of undertaking.

Indeed, in Sermon No. XC, the pivotal sermon, Emerson redirects his focus from the great men of history to the potential that resides within the individual. That this sermon indicates a new line of thinking for Emerson is evidenced by the difficulty he had in composing it, for the manuscript is marked with numerous additions and changes. In fact, the key sentence indicating the change in his thinking on heroes, "Every man has an idea of a greatness that was never realized," was added to the original draft (*CS* 2:266). Without the additions, the paragraphs mildly discuss the *character* of historical figures, while the emended version considers the *greatness* of the common man. He wrote: "If you name over men that have <created> the most decided <character> ↑greatness↓ you will find that they present very dissimilar ideas to your thought. <Socrates> Abraham, Moses, Socrates, Milton, Fenelon, these are all eminently good men yet how wholly unlike" (*CS* 2:264 and 403). Here, Emerson changed "character" to "greatness" in his discussion of the heroes of history. Yet in the next paragraph he undermines the greatness of these characters as he strengthens the character of the common man. By showing that the "great men" of history nonetheless have character faults and by finding God within the human soul, he builds the self's potential for greatness. Unlike the use of the hero as a model of greatness in Emerson's previous sermons, the hero in the revised version of No. XC becomes a symbol of the greatness that each person can achieve:[9]

9. Robert D. Richardson, *Myth and Literature in the American Renaissance,* 87, states that in *Representative Men,* Emerson "simultaneously cuts down the greatest of men to ordinary human size and then builds them up into representative figures, symbolic heroes in whom we recognize ourselves."

> But I honour more this image of God in human nature which has placed a standard of character in every human breast which is \<beyond\> ↑above↓ the highest copy of living excellence. ↑Every man has an idea of a greatness that was never realized.↓ Take the history of a great and good man, of Newton, or Franklin, or Washington, and explain all its details to the \<meanest\> ↑most obscure & ignorant↓ wretch that wears the human form, and ↑you shall find that↓ whilst he understands all its elevation he will be able to put his finger upon imperfections in \<their\> ↑that↓ life. Which shows that in his heart there is a greater man than any that has lived in the world. (*CS* 2:266 and 404)

Not without difficulty, Emerson is shifting greatness from a few characters of history as well as finding that the self's greatness lies in the idea that "the image of God" (eventually he will say "God") resides within the human heart. The man who understands that "the image of God" is within, who knows himself, "To him who has reached this wisdom how ridiculous is Caesar and Bonaparte wandering from one extreme of civilization to the other to conquer men, — himself, the while, unconquered, unexplored, almost wholly unsuspected to himself" (*CS* 2:267).

The great explorations and conquests, then, lie not on a geographical plane but in the interior landscape of the self. How very different is this notion of greatness from the early view that valorized man's benefit to society. It is self-centered rather than other-centered, psychic rather than military. Written in October 1830 as he teetered on the brink of despair, Sermon No. XC indicates the direction of Emerson's thought about self-reliance and greatness that was interrupted by Ellen's death and his immediate task of finding consolation. As with the other themes of Emerson's sermons, his thought on heroism and greatness derived from his own inward turning, to his casting off conventional ways of thinking. Moreover, as he had begun to write himself on the figure of the vanishing Ellen, converting her into a cipher for his own project of self-fashioning, so he begins to use biographical figures in a similar way. Assigning to the biographical figures the characteristics of the self that he was coming to regard as empowering, he begins to appropriate those characteristics in his own refiguration. From this point on, Emerson more or less steadily creates a hero whose main resource is his own self-trust rather than particular and external talents or feats of strength. And from this point on, Emerson's interest in the biographical hero becomes more and more personal as he grapples with his own ambitions and with the creation of a fictive hero and of himself as heroic. While Emerson is discussing character, he is at the same time forming his own character, and the virtues that he ascribes in the last two years of his ministry to the heroic figures are those that he would attain for himself. What Joel Porte observes of *Representative Men* is true also of the sermons: "Emerson did not want to worship great men but rather to use them — even to use them up in measuring his own stature and preparing for future growth."[10]

Thus, Emerson's interest in biography is more than intellectual; it is also intensely personal. From his youth Emerson had about him traditional examples of success — his father, the well-liked, cosmopolitan minister; the commanding figures of his ancestors who had also found success behind the pulpit; the legendary figures of American patriots, some of whom were on speaking terms with the Emerson family; and even his own brothers, Charles and Edward, who won the school prizes that he longed to win. Compounded with the regular dose of hero worship that a young boy schooled in Plutarch received and the general tenor of a country determined to make itself and its people successful, then, was the familial pressure to succeed. Combined with a sense of inferiority, strengthened no doubt by his failure at times to perform up to the expectations of his family,[11] this pressure is heard in many places in Emerson's journals as both a declaration of ambition and a reminder of humility. The journal entry for March 23, 1823, clearly illustrates the dual impulses of Emerson's early years as well as his identification of career with manliness:

> I am hastening to put on the manly robe. From childhood the names
> of the great have ever resounded in my ear. And it is impossible that
> I should be indifferent to the rank which I must take in the innumerable assembly of men, or that I should shut my eyes upon the huge

10. Porte, *Representative Man,* 305.

11. Quoted in McAleer, *Days of Encounter,* 16: Rev. William Emerson wrote to a friend, "Ralph does not read very well yet" — Ralph was a week short of his third birthday.

interval which separates me from the minds which I am wont to venerate. Every young man is prone to be misled by the suggestions of his own ill founded ambition which he mistakes for the promptings of a secret Genius, and thence dreams of an unrivalled greatness. More intercourse with the world and closer acquaintance with his own faults wipes out from his fancy every trace of this majestic dream. (*JMN* 2:112)

Looking forward to giving up his temporary employment as schoolteacher and to entering the ministry, Emerson told his journal, "My trust is that my profession shall be my regeneration of mind, manners, inward & outward estate; or rather my starting point, for I have hoped to put on eloquence as a robe" (*JMN* 2:242). Manliness, eloquence, and the ministry are conflated by the Emerson of 1823 and 1824: he hoped that by putting on the "manly robes" of eloquence associated with the ministry, he would find his success. Yet even though he was well thought of by the parishioners of Second Church, there remained for the young Reverend Emerson something unsatisfying about his career. Chafing against the intellectual constraints and his church's demands for his time, he complained to his journal on January 10, 1832, near the end of his term at Second Church, "It is the best part of the man, I sometimes think, that revolts most against his being the minister. His good revolts from official goodness . . . The difficulty is that we do not make a world of our own but fall into institutions already made & have to accommodate ourselves to them to be useful at all, & this accommodation is, I say, a loss of so much integrity & of course of so much power" (*JMN* 3:318–19).

Searching for intellectual freedom and for the power that would generate from a career cloaked in manliness and eloquence, Emerson looked to the examples of history for his answer. And as the sermons of the second half of his ministry reveal, he would become empowered not by putting on the ministerial robes, but by putting on the mantle of biography. In conjunction with relocating authority from a God on high to a God within the self, he redefined the historical quotient of greatness and simultaneously translated that quotient to himself. He found for himself, as he found for and in his favorite biographical figures, the power and authority of eloquence, and he began to identify power and himself with the poet rather than with the priest. In a sense, he finds himself, the self he wants to be, first by uncovering the heroic figures, finding that essential thing that makes for greatness, and then by wrapping himself in the mantle of their greatness, inventing or constructing a self as he interprets or deconstructs "texts."[12]

Emerson's vocational and philosophical task, from about December 1830 until he gave his farewell sermon to Second Church, centered around developing a strategy for doffing the minister's robes and yet retaining manly eloquence. How he went about this is seen most particularly in the change in his descriptions of Jesus, the historical figure with whom he most identified.[13]

Emerson's Christology

Following the lead of the new school of biblical exegesis coming out of Germany, Emerson tended to read Jesus as a historical figure whose life and teachings can be explained by using methods similar to historical and literary methodology. In this way, he found a Jesus whose origins were humble, whose life was simple, and whose teachings, while profound, did not necessarily mark him as part of the godhead. Whether due to an American habit of mind to praise the self-made man of humble birth, to a Unitarian impulse to emphasize the humanity of Christ, to the Plutarchan tradition of simplicity and innocence, or to an effort to imitate (and identify with) the man whose life became the

12. Jeffrey Steele, "Interpreting the Self: Emerson and the Unconscious," 102. Steele similarly discusses Emerson's "attempt at regeneration through self-presentation of images of power." For Gadamer, to understand a text "does not mean primarily to reason one's way back into the past, but to have a present involvement in what is said" and from that involvement to gain insight, which, he says, "always involves an element of self knowledge and constitutes a necessary side of what we call experience in the proper sense" (*Truth and Method*, 320). See also Pahl, *Architects of the Abyss*, for his discussion of the interplay between text and the search for origins. His discussion of Poe's "The Assignation" fits nicely with my own reading of Emerson's use of biography.

13. See Mott, "Christ Crucified," where he maintains that the figure of Jesus is "pivotal" to Emerson, and Porte, *Representative Man*, 115. See also Mott's extended discussion of the role of eloquence in Emerson's preaching and life during the ministerial years in *"Strains of Eloquence."*

model of Christian faith and deportment, Emerson continually refers to and makes a point of Jesus' humble origins.

In Sermon No. V, "Christ Crucified," in which, according to Wesley Mott, "the figure of Jesus became pivotal" to Emerson's "personal sense of mission," Jesus is portrayed as "the example of perfect innocence" and simplicity (*CS* 1:86). For a young man whose fortunes were yet to come and who knew too well the taste of poverty—who had waited tables at Harvard and whose widowed mother ran a series of boarding-houses—the lesson of Jesus' life, that strength comes from adversity, must have been particularly inspiring.[14] In this sermon, written almost two years before he had found a home at Second Church, Emerson holds up for praise the simple but hearty life of Jesus, scorning as effeminate the child born in the "lap of grandeur . . . cushioned on the soft embroidery of a palace amid kneeling nations and nourished safely up to an effeminate manhood" and scorning as horrible the "desolations" of the military conqueror (*CS* 1:87). In fact, Emerson suggests, the majesty of Jesus' life is proportionate to its simplicity: Jesus was "a despised Hebrew; among men reputed a carpenter's son; born in a manger; a man of sorrows and acquainted with grief, the associate of humble men and one who had not where to lay his head. . . . All that was simple and unpretending in his circumstances was made to show in stronger relief the majesty of his life" (*CS* 1:87–88). The detail and slow pacing of the passage indicate Emerson's own mental balancing of the terms of success and heroism. That he opts to praise the simple life indicates not only a distrust of materialism but also a personal iden-tification with the historical Jesus and with the current definitions of success that stressed a life of austerity and perseverance.

Though he does not always go into the detail seen in Sermon No. V, Emerson rarely neglects to remind his audience of Jesus' humble ori-gins or of the benefits of the simple life. In Sermon No. XIII, Emerson correlates human sympathy for Jesus' humble life with understanding

14. Mott, "Christ Crucified," 17. See also page 27, where Mott says, "Emerson's enthusiasm in embracing the heroic Jesus who overcame the adversities of sin, mu-tability, and the spite of men, achieving an inner peace and vision, . . . which Emer-son craved both personally and philosophically."

of his "office" or mission: Emerson rejoices "that he was not born in the lap of majesty and ostentation," for from Jesus' poverty "we feel . . . the artificial distinctions of life . . . and the dignity of the office he was appointed to bear" (*CS* 1:144). In Sermon No. XXXVI, in which Emerson hopes to inspire his congregation "to the cultivation of all our powers," amid the many references to heroic figures, Emerson reminds his audience that "Jesus Christ was not brought up in schools" (*CS* 1:278–79). Contrasting the outward appearances of success with the reality of a noble life concerned with truth rather than with ostentation and reward, Emerson points to the simplicity of the lives of Columbus, Jesus, and Newton (No. XLIV). In Sermon No. LX, in which Emerson again correlates human understanding with the affections, with sympathy and attachment, he notes that Jesus, "a Jewish peasant, the poor man's and the children's friend, who had not only no external dignity, but no house, set his hand upon society, and changed the face of the world, — for he lived as he taught" (*CS* 2:109–10). In these early sermons, then, we can see that Emerson praises the simple life, humility, and even poverty, for they both reveal and help to form the strength of character necessary to greatness. Participating in a reading of character that contributes to and confirms the new, emerging nation of workers, Emerson also participates in managing self-definitions for his audience by holding up the figure of Jesus as a model for human behavior. Sounding much like a conventional Unitarian or a popular inspirationalist, Emerson stresses the development of a good character and self-cultivation in terms of fairly external, and therefore largely imitable, means.

But beginning with Sermon No. LXXVI and particularly from No. C on, the figure of Jesus represents his attempts to realize the implications of finding the kingdom of God within the self. Testing out versions of the Christological figure, Emerson suggests that Jesus benefits modern man not simply by being a model of behavior but also by being a teacher and a representative of the kind (if not degree) of moral perfection that each person is inherently capable of attaining. In this way, Jesus becomes a symbol of the self's authority and autonomy and an embodiment of the self that one is capable of becoming. As a symbol,

Jesus is both "an end and an instrument," not only exemplifying the self's potential but also partaking, transformationally, in the creation or invention of a new self. Although Mott suggests the importance that the person of Jesus had for Emerson during the crisis that led Emerson to journey south in 1826,[15] the record of the sermons suggests that the figure of Jesus had an even more compelling appeal for Emerson in the later years of his ministry. Mention of the heroic qualities and person of Jesus occurs in seven sermons before the pivotal Sermon No. XC, and in fifteen sermons afterward. Indeed, the intensity of Emerson's identification with the historical Jesus corresponds proportionately to his own intense testing of different versions of the self, of self-reliance, and of compensation following Ellen's debilitating illness and death.

Emerson's evolving depiction of the heroism of Jesus demonstrates his testing and trying on of versions of the self and heroism, until Jesus finally represents a male, public version of the figure of Ellen Tucker. Like the figure of Ellen, the figure of Jesus participates in Emerson's personal, urgent task of self-discovery and functions in ways similar to Ellen. Both are guides and teachers of the interior self, the kingdom of God, pointing the way to Emerson's discovery of himself. Both are effective teachers because of the attachment, affection, and sympathy Emerson feels for them. And both are catalysts for Emerson's baptism, rebirth, and transfiguration as a new man. Transformed into texts or ciphers by and on which he writes himself, they project Emerson forward as an independent creator of words, acts, and self. Through their figurative guidance, he discovers that to be manly is to disengage the self from society, from the external and physical. He discovers that to be manly requires cutting himself off from the public versions of masculinity and attaching himself to the private sphere of the heart. These are the lessons he learns from Ellen, and the lessons he learns in his evolving constructions of Jesus.

Oddly enough, while Emerson has excoriated the feminine or effeminate as degenerate and unmanning, he finds his manhood/selfhood in the figure of a woman and in a feminized version of Jesus as keeper of the heart. Even so, Jesus represents something more to Emerson

---

15. Langer, *Philosophy in a New Key,* 53. Mott, "Christ Crucified," 17–18.

than the figure of Ellen could. For while Ellen teaches Emerson the eloquence of prayer and piety, it is through his configuration of Jesus the orator that Emerson learns and acquires the true eloquence of the embodied voice. As Emerson uncovers the genius and genesis of Jesus' voice, he finds his own voice, listening intently to himself and incarnating the voice of the inner oracle in his own word and deed. Though the figure of Ellen glances behind the sermons, doubling with and subtly eroticizing the figure of Jesus and the union, oratory, and vision that he represents, it is Jesus who occupies the public space of the sermons. Jesus both doubles with the figure of Ellen and is a separate entity on and through which Emerson discovers, constructs, and writes the self and himself.

The new Jesus that Emerson invents exemplifies the autonomy, authority, and eloquence that he seeks in his own self-invention. In Sermon No. LXXVI Emerson explains that Jesus' rhetorical power derives not from the learning of a Paul or from subtle reasoning or dogmatism or from eloquent, "insinuating arts of address." Rather, it derives from the authority of truth. Jesus' rhetorical style, like his life, was simple because he spoke as he lived, from the authority of his "divine commission" (*CS* 2:192). Indeed, Emerson asserts, his "soul was filled with heavenly knowledge" and "his character was consistent, part with part, and the mighty work of his hand was justified by the mighty word of his mouth." Jesus becomes for Emerson the teacher whose lessons of "the supreme kind of truth" are articulated eloquently in his discourses as well as in his character. In No. LXXVI, Jesus' role as teacher and his "miraculous powers" still derive from his special powers of understanding and his peculiar relationship to the truth rather than from the truth and power potentially available to all (*CS* 2:193). But as Emerson continues to shape the figure of Jesus, he discovers that Jesus' powers are not peculiar to him but are accessible to others, rare though they may be, who also listen closely to the God within. He finds as well that Jesus is not only an example of the greatness available to all but a catalyst for the greatness of others who, like Washington and Howard, "love him much" (*CS* 4:62). As the shape that Jesus is taking under Emerson's hands suggests, the terms of heroism and greatness are shifting for Emerson, becoming ever matters of the inner self, of the authority and eloquence that derive from self-trust. He noted in his journal on September 27, 1830, "The great men of the world, the teachers of the race, moralists, Socrates, Bacon, Newton, Butler, & the like, were those who did not take their opinions on trust, but explored themselves and that is the way ethics & religion were got out" (*JMN* 3:199). For Emerson at this time, greatness is correlated with "listening more intently to our own reason" (*JMN* 3:199), and the usefulness of great men rests in their capacity to teach others to be persistent listeners of the self and to ignite the transformation of those who "love [them] much."

This line of thought leads Emerson to a subversion of the traditional hero, one who benefits society by "directly touching our worldly goods." In his stead, Emerson proposes a new kind of hero, "the Divine Teacher of our souls" who leads man to "a nobler freedom than the mere absence of external chains" (*CS* 3:66). Of course, Emerson is suggesting the greater power and benefit of Jesus, but he also suggests that the true hero affects the internal self rather than the merely external person. Working with the theme of intellectual and political freedom in Sermon No. C, Emerson made a change in the manuscript that suggests his own burgeoning intellectual independence. Following his declaration that Jesus will lead man to "a nobler freedom," Emerson wrote, "He will break the chains of the mind" (*CS* 3:298). He evidently thought "mind" too philosophically radical for his congregation and substituted the more conventional word "sin" in its stead (*CS* 3:66). Sin is not at all the topic of this sermon; rather, it is freedom and independence of the individual. Perhaps even here Emerson is toying with the idea of his own independence from the "chains" of traditional institutions and thought. Indeed, the next sermon suggests that the heroes of the past can "help" (not just "teach") less noble men to reach a similar plane of greatness, that their powers of greatness can be translated to others bold enough to declare, "It is now our turn" (*CS* 3:72).

In Sermon No. CXVII, Emerson is almost "bold enough" to ascribe to himself the qualities of greatness as well as the cost of greatness, solitude (*CS* 3:356). Emendations in the manuscript draft of this sermon reveal the conflation of the "you" that can represent either the congregation or the "you" that is Emerson's alter ego, or both, to the more distant "they" of past heroes. For example, he wrote: "↑The biography of almost all distinguished men may shew you that↓ In proportion as <you> ↑they have↓ raise↑d↓ <yourself> ↑themselves↓ to extraordinary acquirements and extraordinary virtues <you> ↑they have↓ outstrip↑ped↓ the affections of <your> ↑their↓ fellowmen" (*CS* 3:171, 357). Where the original impulse had been personal, the finished text is distant. Nonetheless, the sermon indicates an author who identifies with and longs for "extraordinary acquirements & extraordinary virtues." Moreover, the confusion of the pronouns demonstrates Emerson's appropriation of the heroic in his shaping of himself as a self-made man / man-made self, as one who has "raised" himself to greatness. And when he has found that the cost of greatness is solitude and loneliness, he justifies the asocial and withdrawn behavior with the example of Jesus who also "was alone without any that understood him or entered into the great purposes that swelled in his bosom" (*CS* 3:172). The solitude that he would more actively advocate in later years is here still painful, and necessary, to the man who only five months previously had lost his wife. The corollary, then, between Jesus and himself is pungently personal and hints of his relation to Ellen, of the loss of the one who "understood him," and of the role each plays in his project of self-formation.

Indeed, what he learned about subsuming his identity in the person of another, of the role of consummation in finding oneself, he applies in the lesson of Jesus and in the authority of his voice, subtly eroticizing them. In Sermon No. CXIX Emerson suggests that when "Jesus had lost all self-love, had made all subservient to God's will," that when his will was unified with the greater one of God, then he was able to participate in the authority and greatness of God and thereby realize his own autonomy and power (*CS* 3:180). Emerson suggests that out of the denial of the self in the mystical union of self with an Other, and out of making transparent the personal ego, arise in apocalyptic fashion new authority and power. Emerson makes it clear in No. CXIX that "the authority" does not belong to Jesus "as a person, but to the truths which he uttered" (*CS* 3:180). Nonetheless, in sketching a Jesus on whom authority and power indeed are conferred, he hints that power and authority may also be conferred on other orators who give themselves up to the voice within. The "organ" of ethereal truths, Jesus as orator appears in this sermon as an early prototype of the Poet, a figure that Emerson will later create and try out in his own life.[16] What No. CXIX demonstrates is the underlying, personal project in Emerson's discovery of Jesus' greatness and eloquence. As Emerson locates the source of Jesus' eloquence, he is also at the task of finding his own voice. And inasmuch as Emerson personally identified his own power-making with eloquence and poetical truth-saying, the figure of Jesus gradually transformed into a symbol of Emerson's own projected and imagined self.

In fact, after he describes the origins of Jesus' special powers of eloquence and truth, Emerson confers those powers on the nondivine man: "The delivery of the same truth would invest the humblest created spirit with the same authority" (*CS* 3:180). Like Edward Everett's hero who represents the potential of each person, Emerson's Jesus is here a representative of the human potential. In both cases, that potential is largely associated with the power of oratory. In fact, during the nineteenth century, that "oral age," the speech was a "known and respected art" and the literary sermon was a trademark of Unitarian preaching. The Reverend Chandler Robbins, who replaced Emerson at Second Church in 1832, proclaimed sermon writing to be "one of the highest arts," for it demands the exertion of the minister's "highest faculties" and gives scope for his genius, knowledge, and imagination. And as David Robinson reminds us, the Unitarian pulpit was "one of the major vehicles for the development of the art of eloquence." The man who delivered the great speech was much revered by his contemporaries and to him were conferred honors due a hero. Edward Everett, himself a favorite of the podium and an early hero for Emerson, told the Phi Beta Kappa Society in 1824 that "The character, energy, and resources of the country, are reflected and imaged forth in the conceptions of its great minds. They are the organs of the time; they speak not their own language, they scarce think their own thoughts; but under an impulse

---

16. See Porte, *Representative Man,* 115, where he says that in "The Poet," Emerson identifies Christ as "the poet or orator whose thought is finally ejaculated as Logos, or Word" and "is obviously a version of himself, the Christ/Preacher/Poet who is charged with showing 'that the Ought, that Duty, is one thing with Science, with Beauty, and with Joy.'"

like the prophetic enthusiasm of old, they must feel and utter the sentiments which society inspires. They do not create, they obey the Spirit
of the Age." In words that Emerson later echoed and respiritualized,
Everett, who was voted into Congress as a result of this speech, presents as a national hero the orator whose voice articulates the truths of
a greater Other, "the Spirit of the Age." The orator is a man of power
who, in the Plutarchan tradition, subdues his audience and conquers
his hearers, but he also derives power from his ability to make his voice
an organ of truth, whether of the age or of all ages.[17]

To make his mark through eloquence, then, was an aspiration that
Emerson learned not only from his reading of the character of Jesus but
also from the emphasis placed on oratory during the early nineteenth
century. As a young man looking forward to the time when he would
"be legally a man," Emerson had found that the ministry best matched
his "strong imagination" and "keen relish for the beauties of poetry,"
and he wrote that "in Divinity I hope to thrive. I inherit from my sire
a formality of manner & speech, but I derive from him or his patriotic
parent a passionate love for the strains of eloquence" (*JMN* 2:237–39).
Influenced by his own facility with language, the example of his father
and forebears, and the general respect for the orator, the young Emerson had hoped that by putting on "eloquence as a robe" he would also
assume the success and power of the orator, and that his ambitions
would be met. At first he identified that robe of eloquence with his
father and the men of his family who had preceded him to the pulpit,
finding in them early models for his own life. But as the sermons indicate, eloquence was more closely identified with the person of Jesus
and the authority and power consequent of his being "the organ of the
All wise and Almighty" (*CS* 3:180–81). Jesus becomes simultaneously
the heroic figure cut from the cloth of Emerson's own ambitions
and the kind of hero whom Emerson aspires to become. Biography and
poetry commingle in Emerson's formation of both a fictional self and
his own self.

This interplay between the figure of Jesus and the self that would

17. Russel Nye, *Society and Culture in America, 1830–1860,* 137–38. See also George
Willis Cooke, *Unitarianism in America: A History of Its Origins and Development,*

engender a heroic, Emersonian self is effected in the remaining sermons by a simultaneous humanizing of Jesus and deifying of man. Having made the point in Sermon No. CXIX that Jesus' authority derives from his selfless unity with God, in Sermon No. CXXIV Emerson declares a similar relationship between God and man. He argues that those who are morally free, "who speak what they think & act as they & not others chuse," while there may be very few, "yea, if one be found," find their freedom, paradoxically, in unity with God (*CS* 3:375, 207). Self-reliance derives from a reliance on and unity with the God within. In a passage pocked with emendations, Emerson unfolds his radical thesis:

> He [the free person] ↑acknowledges↓ <feels & rejoices to feel> that he lives not by himself, but by the Infinite Father, and to him he bows not <with reluctance> ↑by compulsion↓, but eager, trusting, devoted affection. ↑His affection is inquisitive about its object. He believes there's more perfection than he understands.↓ He opens his heart to receive more life. <It is> He ↑perceives↓ <feels> the great truth that God is in him, and that he is no longer his <mself> ↑own↓ <but onewith> ↑as he rids himself of his vices he becomes more and more instinct with life from↓ the Vast Mind that animates & governs the whole Universe. (*CS* 3:208 and 377)

Like Jesus, this man can declare, "I and my Father are one" (*CS* 3:180). And like Jesus, the rare, genuine man finds his self-reliance and thus his power and authority from the humble union of the self with "the Vast Mind." What Emerson is suggesting here, what he suggested also in conjunction with Ellen, is that one comes to himself, and comes to know himself, through a consummating union with an Other, through the sympathy that exists between persons of like mind. Implicit as well is Emerson's sense that personal ambition must be subsumed in humility, an attitude he identifies as necessary for success. Emerson may indeed have felt himself on the horns of a dilemma — to personally aspire to power and yet to understand the necessity for denying the self and the self's aspirations. Making a virtue of his own situation and of what he finds to be the source of Jesus' power, he offers as examples of heroic

---

415–16. Quoted in Nye, *Society and Culture*, 139. Robinson, *Apostle of Culture*, 31. Everett, *Orations and Speeches*, 25. Berry, *Emerson's Plutarch*, 111.

success men like Vanini and Pestalozzi who understand the unity and correspondence of being, that "All is in all" (*CS* 3:222).[18]

Emerson further merges the example of Jesus with human greatness as he reiterates the lesson of No. CXXIV—the unity of beingness. When he tells his congregation of the strength of admiration and attachment, "that the mind was made . . . to go out of itself and apply its affections to some other being," Emerson suggests a secular, social correlation to the spiritual union of self and Other (*CS* 4:31). This correlation is heightened as Emerson locates heroism and human greatness in the Christian attributes of love, loyalty, and honor. Secularizing religion and spiritualizing hero worship, he declares in Sermon No. CXXXVII "an unexpected coincidence of sentiment between these heroes of the world and the heroes of the gospel" (*CS* 4:32). Just as religion is to acquaint the worshiper with his finer qualities, so secular heroes "acquaint us with our own powers and wants" (*CS* 4:33). In language highly charged with both religious and erotic implications, Emerson declares that from man's admiration and affection for the hero, he discovers "that the soul was made to go beyond itself for its objects; to apply itself to more than its own benefit; to lose itself in the love and seeking of infinite good. They point at and prophesy a higher principle to be the love and object of devotion to the soul, that is, God" (*CS* 4:33). Sounding much like he did in Sermon No. CXXIV when he discussed the self's union with God, Emerson suggests a similar unity between the self and the hero and a similar empowering of the individual. The union between the self and the hero, like the union between the self and God, is the catalyst and means to an empowering transformation of self. In both cases, the transformed self realizes and makes real his union with a greater Other, marking in word and action the terms of his new, heroic self.

Imaginatively projecting the self and himself on the greater image of the hero, as his confusion of pronouns in No. CXVII suggests, Emer-

---

18. In Sermon No. CXXVII he cites Vanini, accused atheist who on his death pyre picked a straw from the pile to prove the being of God, and Pestalozzi (Sermon Nos. CXXVII and CXXVIII), who based his system of education on the maxim, "All is in all."

son seeks a translation of power from the hero to the self. More important, the hero is one in whom the individual finds and becomes his greater self. Jesus as hero is the example of perfection toward which humans strive, and by loving him (identifying with him) the individual participates in his power and perfection and is thereby transformed into a heroic character: "He did such a thing in the spirit of Washington, in the spirit of Howard" (*CS* 4:63). More than a representative of the individual's potential, the hero here is a symbol of the self's power and is both a transformative and a transformational symbol, effecting and rendering power. A journal entry for August 12, 1832, suggests this dual role of the hero as a symbol of individual power and as a means to power. Contemplating, perhaps, a book of heroic portraits, Emerson says, "I would draw characters, not write lives. I would evoke the spirit of each and their relics might rot . . . I would walk among the dry bones & wherever on the face of the earth I found a living man I would say here is life & life is communicable." Like a symbol, the hero speaks of the life which, while not always obvious in the "dry bones" of the conscious, everyday world, is nonetheless present. But, Emerson suggests, the hero is more than a symbol of greatness; he is the means to greatness just as partaking of the Lord's Supper is the means to grace: "Jesus Christ truly said my flesh is meat indeed. I am the bread. For of his life or character have the nations of the earth been nourished" (*JMN* 4:35). As in the religious ceremony, the human soul or spirit is nourished (empowered) by the person of Jesus and partakes in a transubstantive identification with the greater figure. In her discussion of primitive ritual, Susanne Langer says of the feast that it "not only dramatizes, but actually negotiates the desired acquisition."[19] So too with the figure of Jesus for Emerson; he represents and effects the attribute of power for and to Emerson. As Emerson imaginatively consumes Jesus into his own rendering of the quotient of greatness, he is himself transformed in the process.

19. Langer, *Philosophy in a New Key*, 141. Langer notes that the sacramental quality of eating is due to the "kinship among those who eat together, and the even closer connection — identification — of the eaters with the eaten." She further suggests that as groups become more sophisticated, it is not the food but the animal *characteristics* that constitute the ritual's fare.

Yet even as Emerson projects a transformation of power and great-ness from the hero to the self, he remains unsure of his ability to act the hero, and as with his discussions of self-reliance, a dialectical tension undergirds his affirmations: "It is good to act with the brave and the industrious, — but what can it do for those who are excluded from ac-tion, who are only called to suffer?" (*CS* 4:32). As a little poem in-scribed at the end of Sermon No. CXXXVII hints, he fears that he will not be able, like Jesus and like the true hero, to act his thought, which is becoming increasingly radical and unconventional:

> There is no such thing as atheism
> But only choice of theisms
> The whole structure of man is theistical
> Witness the universality of Admiration
> (*CS* 4:317)

Underscoring his discussion of heroes and hero worship lies a theology about which he no doubt realizes the radical import for his congrega-tion and for himself. Thus arise his doubts about his own courage to speak of his "choice of theisms" in a public discourse, an act that he nonetheless recognizes to be vitally essential to his own heroic great-ness. While Emerson has intellectualized the qualities of heroism, he knows that finally the hero, and he, must act and that the solitary man must come out from his private closet and exert his own influence in the social world. "Great powers," he tells us in Sermon No. CXLIII, "demand to be put in action" (*CS* 4:68). Like Jesus and the fictive genu-ine man, Emerson too must act his thought and shape his external cir-cumstances to meet his inner directive. Hinting that he will find his power and greatness in a profession other than the ministry, Emerson tells his February 5, 1832, audience, "Even now we sometimes see an individual forsake all the usual paths of life and show men a new one better fitted than any other to his own powers . . . Every man is uneasy until every faculty of his mind is in freedom and in action" (*CS* 4:68).

Having pushed the issue of the celebration of the Lord's Supper to his resignation from the Second Church pulpit, Emerson portrays in Sermon No. CLXIV, the farewell sermon to his congregation, a new kind of hero, a self-made man whose accomplishment is the creation of a new self. The genuine man of the sermon is both a fictional representation of a new kind of heroism and a symbolic representation of himself as he is at this moment and as he aspires to be. Born from two parents, the Emerson who aspires to greatness and the Emerson who fears his inadequacy, this figure is the distillation of the personal and heroic characteristics that Emerson has come to admire and that project his own talents and hopes. Rejecting finally the conventional hero as exemplum of greatness, Emerson portrays a Christlike, almost Nietzschean, hero who finds truth within himself, and in uttering that truth he becomes the embodiment of his message. Nietzsche said of the Dionysian man: "He feels himself a god, he himself now walks about enchanted, in ecstacy, like the gods he saw walking in his dreams. He is no longer an artist, he has become a work of art."[20] Different and more than the milder Unitarian "character," this self is an entirely new man who, through "steadily fixing the eye upon [the] higher self," has arrived "at a precise notion of a genuine man such as all good & great persons have aimed to be, — such as Jesus designed to be & to make many become" (CS 4:412). Like Jesus, the new man believes in himself and derives his greatness and "sovereignty" from within himself rather than from external or material means (CS 4:412). Self-reliant and God-reliant at the same time, this new hero, like Jesus, speaks for and from God in words as well as in action. In language very similar to that which he used to describe Jesus in previous sermons, a "character, whose words went with his actions" (CS 3:264), and the rare if indeed impossible hero described in No. CXXIV, Emerson here describes the genuine man as one who "acts always in character because he acts always from his character. He is accustomed to pay implicit respect to the dictates of his own reason & to obey them without asking why. He therefore speaks what he thinks. He acts his thought. He acts simply & up to the highest motives he knows of" (CS 4:413). The similarity between Jesus and this new, genuine man is, I think, intentional, for Emerson has been steadily identifying Jesus as the primary hero of history, and at the same time he has been steadily identifying himself and his own role as poet and priest. The difference between the heroic self of No.

20. Nietzsche, *The Birth of Tragedy,* edited by Kaufmann, 37.

CXXIV and that of No. CXLIV indicates that this hero is not impossible and that despite doubts evident below the surface of the text of this farewell sermon, Emerson, at least for this moment, embodies the hero whose words and actions are unified, who "acts his thoughts," and like Jesus represents an incarnation of the Word.

Fascinated always with the heroes of history to the point even of compiling a series of essays on representative heroes in 1850, Emerson, at the crucial point when he was making up his mind as to who and what he wanted to be, found the great men more than inspiring, for he made himself over by partaking in and assimilating for himself their qualities of greatness, heroism, and power. At the same time that he was discovering a new philosophy based on self-reliance learned from his appropriation of cultural materials and tested in the fire of grief, Emerson found in the figure of Jesus the means for shaping a hero and himself in ways that the private figure of Ellen could not. For he was able to write out and enact the lesson of Jesus in public, formal, and more conscious ways than he could the private, passional urges that lay behind and propelled his intellectual movement. Using the medium of Jesus in his project of self-discovery, Emerson found his own voice, the vehicle by which he too could become a representative man for his time, one who knew his private heart and enacted that wisdom in public acts of language. In this way, Jesus is a more appropriate metaphor of the self, for he projects Emerson forward into the public sphere and into a quest that in Stanley Cavell's words converts the discovery of the private self into "founding a nation, writing its constitution, constituting its citizens."[21] As the Lord's Supper Sermon demonstrates, self-discovery does indeed have public implications and responsibilities that Emerson understood and enacted.

---

21. Cavell, *This New Yet Unapproachable America*, 93.

6

The Lord's Supper Controversy

"I have sometimes thought that in order to be a good minister it was necessary to leave the ministry. The profession is antiquated. In an altered age, we worship in the dead forms of our forefathers. Were not a Socratic paganism better than an effete superannuated Christianity?" (*JMN* 4:27)

"Is it not true that our power does increase exactly in the measure that we learn how to use it?" (*JMN* 3:320)

Probably the most discussed sermon of Emerson's ministry is the one he delivered on September 9, 1832. "The Lord's Supper" (No. CLXII) has long been recognized as a key sermon to understanding Emerson and his vocation, for it marks the end of his ministry at Second Church and the beginning of his ministering at large. Although Henry Nash Smith, following Henry James's lead, sees Emerson's ministry as a period of "'painful probation' through which Emerson had to pass before he could discover his true vocation as artist and thinker," Emerson's vocational unrest should be seen, Wesley Mott tells us, "not as a rejection but as an extension of his 'ministry.'"[1] Indeed, Emerson continued to be an "Apostle of Culture," to use David Robinson's words, whether

1. Henry Nash Smith, "Emerson's Problem of Vocation: A Note on the American Scholar," 225. Smith opens his essay: "Among the many fine perceptions of Henry James's essay on Emerson in the *Partial Portraits* is his allusion to the period of 'movement, experiment and selection . . . of effort too and painful probation'

he spoke behind a pulpit or a podium. The Lord's Supper sermon, then, marks both an ending and a beginning: an ending of the homiletic narrative and a foreground to the narrative more familiar to readers of American literature.

Long admired by readers, the Lord's Supper sermon was the only one printed during Emerson's lifetime and the only one included in *The Complete Works of Ralph Waldo Emerson*. Often viewed as an example of Emerson's talents or as the mark of his vocational shift, the sermon has often seemed to readers to be something more than it initially appears to be. Many, indeed, realize that Emerson only used the controversy over the celebration of the Lord's Supper to formalize his religious thought and to actualize the separation from organized religion toward which he had been moving for some time. It is, moreover, a sermon made interestingly complex by Emerson's mixed purposes in writing it and by the import of the subject matter, the Lord's Supper, on those purposes. In addition to being an argument about the means of celebrating a religious ritual, the sermon is also a declaration of Emerson's selfhood. As such, it hints that the issue of selfhood is complicated with the issues involved in its topic, the Lord's Supper; with discovering meaning within rather than in external forms; with writing and publicity; and with the intersections between the individual and the texts that impinge on self-concept, behavior, and belief.

The Hermeneutics of Interpretation

Many modern readers of the Lord's Supper sermon have been struck by its carefully crafted argument and by Emerson's use of Quaker texts and ideas about the sacrament. Gay Wilson Allen says, "This was one of Emerson's most closely reasoned and concisely expressed sermons. He could be an able debater when he wanted to be, in spite of his

---

through which Emerson had to pass before he could discover his true vocation as artist and thinker." Mott, *"Strains of Eloquence,"* 170. Of the Lord's Supper Sermon, Mott says, "Emerson explained his resignation from the Second Church pulpit, . . . in terms that simply carried out certain implications of Puritan typology," specifically the "Puritans' craving for the *spiritual substance* of sacraments" (159–60).

protests that he never argued." John McAleer finds that the "consecutive logical reasoning" and "concise phrasing" of the sermon owe to Emerson's heavy borrowing from other texts, noting that "the most important sermon Emerson ever gave . . . was also his most derivative." As other scholars have done, McAleer mentions Emerson's use of Thomas Clarkson's *Portraiture of Quakerism,* which he had borrowed from the Boston Athenaeum on June 11, 1832, and his use of other Quaker texts, William Sewal's *History of the Quakers* and Henry Tuke's *Memoirs of the Life of Fox,* both of which he had taken with him on his retreat during the summer of 1832 to New Hampshire to recover his health and think through the positions he would take on the Supper and his career. Some scholars suggest the influence of Miss Mary Rotch of New Bedford, who in 1827 quietly left the church in which Emerson was preaching when the Lord's Supper was about to be observed. Indeed, it has been suggested by Emerson as well as others that he became "more of a Quaker than anything else," observing the Quaker objection both to the Lord's Supper and to public praying.[2] The Quakers' deemphasis of preaching and of external means to grace and their attention to the still voice of God and the Inner Light must have registered with

2. Gay Wilson Allen, *Waldo Emerson,* 191–92. McAleer, *Days of Encounter,* 120, 122. See also Mary C. Turpie, "Quaker Source for Emerson's Sermon on the Lord's Supper." Gay Wilson Allen, *Waldo Emerson,* 224–25. Allen says, "It is not unlikely that [Rotch's] example influenced him in the controversy which forced him to give up his pastorate of the Second Church." McAleer, *Days of Encounter,* 120. McAleer quotes Emerson's cousin, David Greene Haskins, from *Ralph Waldo Emerson: His Maternal Ancestors with Some Reminiscences of Him.* For alternate views of the Lord's Supper sermon and controversy, see Cayton, *Emerson's Emergence,* who argues that Emerson was rejecting "formalism in religion" and challenging his congregation to practice "true religion" based on "their own internal sentiment" (130–33). Barish, *Roots of Prophesy,* consistently argues that food and eating are symbols of deprivation for Emerson and finds that the sermon came at a time when he suffered diarrhea: "The sharing of food symbolically representing a dead person, however holy the ritual, now seemed repellent to him" (230). Grusin, *Transcendentalist Hermeneutics,* finds the sermon composed of two parts: "The first, longer section of the sermon contains the Quaker-derived exegesis with which he supports his claim that Jesus had not instituted the Supper as a permanent rite. The second part of the sermon anticipates the counterargument that . . . it should be celebrated anyway for the 'undoubted occasion of much good' that it had provided for the Christian world" (22). See also Hodder, *Emerson's Rhetoric of Revelation,* 55–56.

an Emerson also intent on listening to the voice within. Certainly, the clues he left in his journal suggest the influence of Quakerism and George Fox, whose story he summarizes in connection with his "hour of decision" (*JMN* 4:30–33).

Moreover, the Lord's Supper sermon is a striking example of Emerson's use of hermeneutical exegesis to frame an argument for his Unitarian audience, even if Barbara Packer finds it to be "an odd pastiche of Unitarian rationalism and higher critical attempts to reinterpret Jesus's words at the Last Supper by imaginatively reconstructing the cultural context out of which they arose." Seeming to follow the Unitarian precept for biblical interpretation, "that the Bible is a book written for men, in the language of men, and that its meaning is to be sought in the same manner as that of other books," Emerson uses rational methodology to interpret the passages relevant to the traditional Lord's Supper celebration. His intent appears to be that of Schleiermacher, to clear up misunderstandings about the texts by considering the textual, historical, cultural, and linguistic conditions of the Scripture and of the situation that it recounts. To that end, Emerson reveals the textual discrepancies of the synoptic Gospels about the supper and Jesus' injunction, "This do in remembrance of me," demonstrating that "It is found in Luke alone, who was not present" (*CS* 4:186–87). He asks his audience to follow him in an imaginative reconstruction of the original supper and the moods that may have informed Jesus' purpose in calling his disciples together one last time, suggesting that Jesus did not mean "to impose a memorial feast upon the whole world" (*CS* 4:187). Emerson next considers the historical evidence of the Jewish celebration of the Passover, arguing that "the supper *was* the passover" and not a separate event nor one substantially different than another local custom, washing the feet, a ritual not celebrated by modern Christians (*CS* 4:187). Reminding the congregation of Jesus' typical use of parables and symbols, Emerson further suggests that when Jesus "calls the bread his body, and bids his disciples eat," he means only that "we should live by his commandment" (*CS* 4:188). After having approached the Bible, which Channing professed to be a book "which demands a . . . frequent exercise of reason," Emerson examines the history of the church and its early misinterpretation of the ceremony.[3] He argues that though the Lord's Supper was good for the early Christians, "it is not suited to this day" (*CS* 4:191), reminding his congregation of the rite's Trinitarian bias and its inappropriateness for the New England mind accustomed to freedom and unaccustomed to "express our thoughts or emotions by symbolical actions" (*CS* 4:192). Thus, Emerson's sermon has all the appearance of a well-constructed argument that uses the rational methodology familiar to its audience. Indeed, it seems as if Emerson has marshaled his evidence and presented it in ways that would be particularly effective for a Unitarian audience schooled in the classics and the problems of interpreting ancient texts, and that followed the ongoing reinterpretations of the Lord's Supper evident, say, in the *Christian Examiner.*

But was Emerson's purpose in this discourse to persuade his audience to abandon or rethink their celebration of a ceremony he found to be outmoded and inappropriate? Clearly the answer is no, for the church had already decided not to accept Emerson's proposed changes in the administration of the Lord's Supper. In May 1832, Emerson had gathered some of his parishioners at his house so that he might explain his misgivings about the Lord's Supper. Then in early June, possibly on June 2, Emerson had written a letter that was considered by a committee of seven, stating that he could not continue to administer the Lord's Supper as a sacred ordinance but would administer it as a memorial service.[4] The committee members reported on June 16 that they held Emerson in "undiminished respect" and recognized his right to private judgments in matters of religious belief, but they "cannot regard it as the duty of the Church to consent to any change in the mode of administering the ordinance." On June 21, the committee's decision was confirmed and a letter was written to Emerson informing him of their ac-

3. Packer, "Origin and Authority," 83. Grusin, *Transcendentalist Hermeneutics,* also provides commentary on how the Transcendentalists, Emerson, Thoreau, and Theodore Parker, used the higher criticism. Channing, *Selected Writing,* 72. See Gadamer, *Truth and Method,* 162–63. Channing, *Selected Writing,* 73.

4. Quoted in McAleer, *Days of Encounter,* 119, from *The Letters of Charles Eliot Norton.*

tion (*L* 1:352n). Apparently, then, his sermon, which has so much the appearance of an argumentative discourse that marshals the resources of Quaker texts and Unitarian methodology, was not aimed at convincing the Second Church audience to change the Lord's Supper ceremony. Indeed, Emerson may have guessed even before he pursued the issue that his congregation would not follow him. Further, Emerson apparently knew that he would not persuade his audience even at this late date and despite whatever arguments he might muster in his favor, for with his announced resignation at the end of the sermon, Emerson leaves members of Second Church no room to reconsider their decision.

If Emerson's purpose was not to persuade his audience, what then was it? It was to declare, to himself and to a public audience, who he was: a man who conforms his public life to meet his private judgments, a man who acts his thoughts. The purpose of the discourse, the real logic of it, is not to persuade his audience of the inappropriateness of the traditional Lord's Supper celebration nor is it to showcase his exegetical expertise; rather, it is to declare and bring into being a new self, the self he had been shaping and fashioning for some time. Thus with Emerson's rejection of the traditional commemoration of the Lord's Supper, he declares not only his vocational freedom from the ministerial duties at Second Church but also the freedom to determine himself, to choose who he will be. That he opts to make this announcement of self in this particular sermon and at this particular time is due less to timing than to the appropriateness of interpreting the ritual as part of his reading of the self. For embedded in this ritual are the issues of externality and internality, of authority and voice, of flesh and spirit, of public and private, of unity and splitting off, that have consistently danced around Emerson's sense of self and manhood. The Lord's Supper and Emerson's approach to it provide symbolic ground on which Emerson consolidates these issues, replaying in code his liberation from the body — the physical body, the social body, and the religious body — and his identification of himself as a man of the mind.

The Lord's Supper sermon, then, is more appropriately an act of writing and speaking that involves the author in bringing into being a new self and in authorizing his own self-determination. Rather than being predominantly an example of persuasive discourse, it is what James Kinneavy calls expressive discourse. According to Kinneavy, expressive discourse involves the project of self-formation: it "involves a man with the world and his fellows to give him his unique brand of humanity." It is the kind of discourse by which the author "expresses and partially achieves his own individuality,"[5] and which includes autobiography, declarations and manifestos, diaries, and apologias. Like other discourse types, expressive discourse has distinct features, style, and logic that distinguish it from persuasive, referential, and literary discourse and that more closely align with Emerson's purpose in writing this sermon than do the features of persuasive or argumentative discourse.

A necessary condition for the expressive project is a rejection of the past (in Kinneavy's working example of expressive discourse, the Declaration of Independence, this is achieved by repudiating an unsatisfactory colonial past). So too Emerson surveys the historical traditions of celebrating the Lord's Supper only to reject and repudiate them as irrelevant to him and his present reality. Much of the argument of the sermon is backward-looking, surveying the ancient texts and traditions as well as, implicitly, his own previous acceptance of the rite, but the real direction of the sermon looks forward to the new self and the new religion that Emerson is in the process of forming. Behind the sermon lie not only his earlier statements about the Lord's Supper but also a previous self whose thought echoed the mores and beliefs of a religion and culture he had by now subverted. Earlier, in March 1829, on the occasion of his appointment to Second Church, Emerson had preached that one of the duties of the Christian minister is the administration of the Lord's Supper, which he called a "melancholy memorial" of the "dying love of Christ" and a "symbol of a holy affection" (*CS* 1:238–39). In Sermon No. L, Emerson had described the ceremony as "a means of improvement" held "to make those who partake of it better" (*CS* 2:58), an attitude in concert with contemporary notions that the Lord's Supper is of "the most useful, serious, and affecting nature" and is "a means of promoting and confirming holiness." But in the Lord's Sup-

5. James L. Kinneavy, *A Theory of Discourse: The Aims of Discourse,* 396, 398.

per sermon, Emerson announces a new mode of commemoration, more effective because it is personal, "pleasing, affecting, religious" and "true" (CS 4:192). With his rejection of the ritual, Emerson rejected a morality based not on the essence of Godliness but instead on materialistic motivations for self-improvement in which usefulness and profit for the individual and the community at large were valued. From the same impulse that had motivated Emerson to invert the myth of the self-made man and its barrage of manuals and lectures for self-improvement, he is now subverting what one contributor to the *Christian Examiner* called the "social compact" theory of worship for a personal worship of the divinity within, a worship that required no public ordinances or rites, even if they were regarded as "merely aids to religion."[6] In essence, Emerson is rejecting an external form of worship, the celebration, and he also is symbolically rejecting a mode of interpretation that emphasizes the external and social self and that considers self-improvement to be a "useful" way of promoting one's moral and secular success.

Emerson even repudiates the truthfulness of the hermeneutical method that he imitates in his exegesis of Scripture, for his reason is based not on the dry forms of method but on the logic of the self. As Sartre points out, "For human reality to be is to choose oneself," and in this sermon we hear Emerson actively choosing himself as one who rejects not only the tradition of the Lord's Supper but the whole rationalist, practical tradition of the Unitarians, who arrived at their religious conviction "at the bar of reason" rather than by searching the passional sources of the self. As we have seen, the direction of Emerson's interpretive method during the course of his ministry was inward. For Emerson, "Internal evidence outweighs all other to the inner man" (*JMN* 3:214). Indeed, Mott points out that for Emerson, "the reality of the indwelling God could not be explained. It could only be felt."[7] At

6. *Christian Examiner* 4:1 (1827): 82, 4:2 (1827): 112, 5:2 (1828): 111.

7. Quoted in Kinneavy, *Theory of Discourse,* 403. Kinneavy draws on Sartre's model of the self, among other models, to demonstrate the purpose and logic of expressive discourse. *Christian Examiner* 3:1 (1826): 2. Mott, *"Strains of Eloquence,"* 105.

the same time that Emerson is rejecting old interpretive methods and announcing new ones, we hear him declaring who he is, one who is convinced of the authority of his own self—"This mode of commemorating Christ is not suitable to me. That is reason enough why I should abandon it" (*CS* 4:192). While the sermon does show how Emerson uses texts and cultural materials to shape his discourse, more important, the sermon demonstrates how Emerson uses those texts in subversive ways to mark and declare his own thought and individuality.

In fact, Emerson is rejecting the past altogether, not only because its methods and interpretations are old-fashioned or inappropriate but because it is dead. He saw the past as having no life for the present generation. He knows now what he would so memorably state to the Phi Beta Kappa Society in 1837, "Each age it is found, must write its own books; . . . The books of an older period will not fit this." His criticism of much of the Judeo-Christian tradition is not only of external forms of worship and evidence but of a deadening adherence to the past. Indeed, Emerson's interest is with now, with a "new reality" based not on the dead forms of the past but on a present and living relation to God, and with the future, the potential of the self to be reached through spiritual metamorphosis. As Wallace Stevens wrote, "It is one of the peculiarities of the imagination that it is always at the end of an era. What happens is that it is always attaching itself to a new reality, and adhering to it." This sermon, then, is concerned with now, with beingness in the time of now, as well as with a specific point of time that for Emerson on September 9, 1832, was now. Though scholars may place the Lord's Supper sermon at the end of their narrative (as I have done) or at the beginning, for Emerson the sermon represented a distinct moment—a moment between times. What mattered to him was the nowness of the sermon, that point that is, like every act, between "the end of an era" and "a new reality." For it is at the point of now, the period of transition, where power and reality lie and where the self exists. Painful as it may have been for him to leave a congregation he loved so well, Emerson was compelled (again) to break attachments to the past in order to be a new man and to realize the power of his being. As with truth, power is "a-being" and exists between times: "Life only avails, not the having lived. Power ceases in the instant of repose; it resides in the moment of transition from a past to a new state."[8]

Further, Emerson seeks a religion whose forms are not divorced from the spirit that had originally caused them to become significant. The problem, he thought, was that the spirit had escaped the vessels of rite and ceremony, leaving them lifeless and without meaning (*CS* 4:193). Having spent so much of his intellectual and passional life in anxious dialectic between the flesh and the spirit, attempting to sublimate the flesh's demands to the spirit's will, indeed, to find meaning in the spirit rather than in the body, he now seeks a reunion of the two. Having disembodied the self, he now seeks to reembody truth in the forms of language—verbal, symbolic, and animate. Emerson now says of religion what he has repeatedly said of Jesus (and the sublime orator): that as instrument he gives form to the voice within, that he acts his thought, that he is the Word made Flesh. He contends that "only that life was religious which was thoroughly good" and not one whose "sacrifice was smoke and forms were shadows" (*CS* 4:193). Emerson seeks a religion and a hero that are living incarnations of the spirit and of the word, whose union of body or form with spirit is willed by the spirit and not by the flesh with its concerns for eating and drinking—actual or symbolic. He had repeatedly demanded of the body that it "reduce [itself] to the soul. Make the body the instrument thro' which that thought is uttered" (*JMN* 4:15). Likewise, he now demands of the forms of religion: "The Kingdom of God is not meat and drink; but righteousness, and peace, and joy in the Holy Ghost" (Romans 14:17). That he found the concern with eating and drinking in the Christian celebration disconcerting derives in part from his constitutional and learned alienation from appetite, and in part from his relocation of the kingdom of God within the soul and his subsequent dismissal of public, external forms of ceremony. But Emerson's discussion of body or form here is not simply disgust but is rather a realignment and resignifying of the physical as "instruments thro' which that thought is uttered." Like the truly perfect character, who gives utterance to the truth

---

8. *Complete Works,* 1:88. Wallace Stevens, *The Necessary Angel: Essays on Reality and the Imagination,* 22. *Complete Works,* 2:69.

within and who gives form and substance to the ineffable, the ritual as form derives significance only from the truth it embodies. That is what was wrong with religious tradition and with current practice; they were "*all* body" (emphasis added) and not spirit embodied and living through the form. By resignifying body or form through incarnation, Emerson breathed new life into religion, resignifying the self and himself as a vessel of the spirit and as an instrument through which the spirit is given voice. As the occasion of the discourse demonstrates, Emerson acts out his words, incarnating not only his words in action but also his own being in language that embodies the who I am in the what I say. In this way, language, "one of the agents of our incarnation," has a tangible role in the project of self-formation.[9]

Because language, particularly one's own language, is so intimately involved in self-formation, so intimately a part of Emerson's self-concept, expressive discourse also involves "the struggle for style," for a voice peculiarly one's own. Oddly enough, in the Lord's Supper sermon we predominately hear a style and tone notably different from previous sermons that tended toward the metaphoric and inspirational, sermons that indicate more clearly the direction of his style than does this sermon. But I think Emerson is demonstrating to himself and to the alert members of his congregation that if he acted against his conviction and spoke in words not his own he would be a "secondary man," untrue both to the spirit and to the form and language that make tangible the ineffable. In September 1830 he had written, "Every man has his own voice, manner, eloquence, & just as much his own sort of love & grief & imagination & action. Let him scorn to imitate any being, let him scorn to be a secondary man, let him fully trust his own share of God's goodness, that correctly used it will lead him on to per-

---

9. In *Transcendentalist Hermeneutics,* Grusin makes a case for the correlation between Emerson's understanding of temperance and his rejection of the Lord's Supper, that both derive their "value not from a merely formal observance, but from [their] ability to effect moral improvement in those who participate" (25). Barish, *Roots of Prophesy,* also finds a connection between the physical and the symbolic acts of eating and drinking, but she suggests that personal nausea prevented him from eating symbolic flesh. Kinneavy, *Theory of Discourse,* 403. Kinneavy here quotes Georges Gusdorf.

fection which has no type yet in the Universe save only in the Divine Mind" (*JMN* 3:198–99). Emerson knew that his voice, identity, and salvation derive from a one-to-one relation with the God within the self and that any imitation displaces the self from itself. Apparently adopting in Sermon No. CLXII the discourse style of the larger community of exegetes, Emerson actually rejects it (and the message it articulates) as "destitute of all authenticity."[10] Instead, he projected a self who had established in his own mind and in previous sermons a new value system founded on a morality marked by "boundless charity" and the "deep interior life" (*CS* 4:193) rather than by rites and formalities. Consequently, he establishes in the self-forming passages of the sermon a private dialect and a private logic distinguished by assertiveness and intimacy, personal pronouns appearing here more frequently and directly than has been his wont. He declares, for instance:

> I have therefore been compelled to consider whether it becomes me to administer it. I am clearly of opinion that I ought not. This discourse has already been so far extended that I can only say that the reason of my determination is shortly this — It is my desire, in the office of a Christian minister, to do nothing which I cannot do with my whole heart. Having said this, I have said all. (*CS* 4:194)

There is an idiosyncrasy in the abrupt, personal, and declarative style of this passage, an emotive component, that is at odds with the style and tone of the so-called more carefully reasoned earlier sections of the sermon. This section creates not simply a new style but a new being, one who identifies himself as an independent thinker who takes his being, the invention of himself, into his own hands. Indeed, as the voice of the personal passages must struggle against the voice of the community, so too must the private Emerson engage against the larger community — its morality, traditions, logic, and style — in his project of self-formation. Moreover, as Emerson finds his own tongue he makes public and formal the self he has fashioned in subterfuge behind the sermons and in his private encounter with himself. As the Lord's Supper

---

10. Kinneavy, *Theory of Discourse*, 405, 430. Kinneavy again quotes Gusdorf, who argued, "The struggle for style is the struggle for consciousness."

sermon indicates, then, what is at stake for Emerson is not just his style but his selfhood; it demonstrates that finding his voice, the voice within and the style of his writing, is complicated with his discovery and articulation of the private self that must become a public self as well.

That rejection of the past is requisite for the formation of a new self is apparent. What is also apparent is that rejection of a past life or self is painful. Kinneavy writes, "Repudiation of the past and anguish are inescapable aspects of the For-Itself," the authentic self. The self-in-process not only must avoid the "danger of bad faith"[11] (a precaution that often entails an intensely agonizing effort to be true to the new vision of the self) but also must contend with the loss of former alliances and positions, the disappointment of others, and the insecurity of the future. Indeed, the occasion of Emerson's sermon was agonizing in terms of personal distress as well as vocational insecurity.

Even though Emerson apparently "chose" as early as May to make of the Lord's Supper ordinance a controversy in which he and his congregation were forced to draw alliances, he nonetheless continued to struggle with himself about the matter. In a sense, he interiorized the conflict between the social world with its religious and vocational expectations and the newly discovered world of the inner self as he wrestled with his own conscience, debating with himself whether he was being "too conscientious" about the Lord's Supper ordinance. Coming finally to a point of crisis forced by his inner conflict, he wrote to himself on July 15, during his retreat to the White Mountains:

> The hour of decision . . . Let me not bury my talent in the earth in my indignation at this windmill. But though the thing may be useless & even pernicious, do not destroy what is good & useful in a high degree rather than comply with what is hurtful in a small degree. The Communicant celebrates on a foundation either of authority or of tradition an ordinance which has been the occasion to thousands, — I hope to thousands of thousands — of contrition, of gratitude, of prayer, of faith, of love, & of holy living. Far be it from any of my friends, — God forbid it be in my heart — to interrupt any occasion thus blessed of God's influences upon the human mind. (*JMN* 4:30)

11. Ibid., 406.

Here, Emerson wonders whether his personal dissatisfaction with the ordinance might be overcome for the better good of his congregation and for his own talents as a preacher. He wonders whether he is being obstinately petulant and unaccommodating, noting, "The most desperate scoundrels have been the over refiners." Yet despite the misgivings, he understands that he must be true to himself: "But this ordinance is esteemed the most sacred of religious institutions & I cannot go habitually to an institution which they esteem holiest with indifference & dislike" (*JMN* 4:30). He finds that he cannot lie to himself or to others, that he must be true and sincere, another mark of the expressive purpose of discourse.[12]

Although he opts to follow his conscience, to remain sincere to his vision, the decision is painful not only in terms of psychic strain — the "strain of duty" (*JMN* 4:40) — but also in physical anguish, for during this period of decision making, he suffered so much from diarrhea that he had to forego his usual duties and retreat to the mountains for the summer to attempt to recover his health. He wrote on August 11, "A stomach ache will make a man as contemptible as a palsy. Under the diarrhoea have I suffered now one fortnight & weak am as a reed. Still the truth is not injured" (*JMN* 4:33). At the same time that the attack of diarrhea is real enough to Emerson, physical evidence of his psychic crisis, it enacts Emerson's symbolic conflict with the body that informs his earlier diatribes on the appetites, his experiments with dieting, and the theme of Sermon No. CLXII. Even after his summer-long retreat and absence from the pulpit, he continued to be so plagued by his "obstinate" malady after the crisis with his church had passed that Charles reported him to be physically reduced, to be "very feeble," and "very thin & . . . very weak" (*L* 1:357n).

Difficult also for Emerson was the loss of regard from and contact with members of his congregation and the strain within his own family about his decision. His Aunt Mary Moody Emerson in particular wanted him to overcome his misgivings, retain the ancestral tie to the pulpit, and leave a name to be "enrolled with the Mathers & Sewalls of that venerable City" (*L* 1:353n). Indeed, severing that tie was no easy

---

12. Ibid., "sincerity is a basic characteristic of expression."

task for the young man. Though he had learned the necessity of cutting the self off from the physical, the conventional, the social, and the ritual in order to realize the self's potential, it still remained a difficult task. Not only would he risk his career and ambition by following the will of his heart, but with his resignation he would lose the kind of intimate contact reserved for a pastor and the collegiality of his fellow clergymen. Emerson was generally well liked by his congregation, and in bidding farewell to his duties as pastor he was in effect bidding farewell to friends in the church. In his letter to William, Charles, who had stayed with Waldo through much of the crisis, wrote of the congregation, "They part from their pastor, whom many of them tenderly love, & all respect, with heavy hearts. And Waldo looks very sad. He would have been glad to have been well these few last months & done more for those to whom his attachment seems the stronger when the bonds of it are just snapped" (L 1:356n). Although the Second Church committee had written of the high and continuing esteem for their minister, some members of the congregation were quite alarmed by Emerson's recent actions. One woman who was accustomed to speak with him about theological matters told Emerson, "Ye have taken away my Lord, and I know not where ye have laid Him." That he was moved by the incident is demonstrated in his comment years later, "That was one of the most touching comments on my decision." Moreover, rumors and whispers were apparently circulating in the larger community about the minister's mental stability. A neighbor of John Jay Chapman's grandmother reported, "Oh, have you heard? The new minister of the Second Church has gone mad."[13] The theological issue thus had a personal quotient that surely made more painful an already agonizing decision and that played behind the sermon, giving its sincerity an emotional edge.

Finally, of course, Emerson's resignation left him without a livelihood, without a career in a country obsessed with getting ahead. Although he was eventually able to fall back on the inheritance from Ellen, he would not actually receive any of it until May 1834. But at the time of his resignation, he did not know what to make of himself. As

13. Quoted in McAleer, *Days of Encounter,* 124, 125.

he indicated to William, he toyed with several ideas: "Shall I pester you with half the projects that sprout & bloom in my head, of action, literature, philosophy? Am I not to have a magazine." He did not know, and in fact he doubted, that he could get the support from contributors necessary for the production of a magazine or newspaper. In fact, his health was still so troubled that he doubted he would have the strength for such an undertaking. He knew, then, that for the time being anyway, his separation from Second Church would occasion him "perhaps some, (possibly, much) temporary embarrassment." But for the moment, he would enjoy the relief from the "strained cord" that had bound him to the church and the "peace & freedom" of the disassociation from the body, the religious, social, and physical body, that he had willed for himself (*L* 1:357–58).

While all along Unitarians had been preaching character development and American success mongers had been selling the idea of the self-made man, Emerson's sermon, indeed the sermons of the last year of his ministry, demonstrates a metamorphosis of self that was truer because it was interior. The achievement of Emerson in the Lord's Supper sermon, then, is not merely rhetorical but is rather an achievement of the self-determination toward which Emerson had been progressing for much of his ministerial career. Working with texts and in the text of the homiletic narrative, he had come to realize that power derives not from social position or from performance but from self-trust and in the individual's handling of the forces that would manipulate him. He had learned that truth resides not in external forms (bodies, texts, or rites) but in the ineffable voice that speaks to and through the true self. These lessons are enacted in Emerson's interpretation of the Lord's Supper and in this sermon, a metaphor, as it were, for the larger body-and-spirit controversy that informs and intersects with not only the celebration but also the issues of selfhood and manhood that confronted Emerson. The sermon is thus also a metaphor for Emerson's achievement of individuality, since by "insist[ing] on the superiority of spiritual over material elements . . . [Emerson] insist[s] on the liberties of the individual."[14] Declaring the primacy of the heart of religion over

14. Douglas, *Natural Symbols,* 162.

its forms, Emerson used the vehicle of the sermon to declare and publicize his own independence and autonomy. In essence, the Lord's Supper sermon is the distillation of all he has learned about the self during the long process of his ministry, especially of what he learned from his passional intimacy with Ellen and his contest with death.

Final Thought

What Emerson also learned in his sermon of resignation is that the self is always in process, always "a-being," and that the risky project of life is to skate on the thin surface of the present. Having emerged from his ministry a new man, Emerson nonetheless learned that he must continue to contest definitions, that he must continue to battle self-doubt, that life is never settled and "all are learning the art of life" (*CS* 4:210). Indeed, when he returned to Boston after his refreshing European jaunt of 1832–1833, he had already begun to work toward a new sense of self as teacher rather than preacher. Speaking once more to his friends at Second Church, almost a year after the Lord's Supper trauma, he told them, "The greatest gift of God is a Teacher and teaching is the perpetual end and office of all things" (*CS* 4:210). Almost simultaneously he began a new stage in his career as a lecturer. Though the self that he announced at the end of his tenure at Second Church is not the self that he continued to identify himself as, the work of self-fashioning that he undertook and the thought that emerged from this period laid out the route that his subsequent thinking and being would take.

# Works Cited

Abrams, M. H. *Natural Supernaturalism: Tradition and Revolution in Romantic Literature*. New York: W. W. Norton, 1971.

Adams, Jasper. *Laws of Success and Failure in Life: An Address delivered 30th October, 1833, in the Chapel of the College of Charleston before the Euphradian Society*. Charleston, S.C.: A. E. Miller, 1833.

Alcott, William A. *The Young Man's Guide*. 2d ed. Boston: Lilly, Wait, Colman and Holden, 1834.

Alexander, Archibald. *A Sermon, preached to the Chapel of Nassau Hall*. Princeton: Princeton Press, 1826.

Allen, Gay Wilson. *Waldo Emerson*. New York: Viking Press, 1981.

Allen, Joseph. *The Sources of Public Prosperity, a Discourse Delivered in Northborough, April 9, 1829, on the Day of the Public Fast*. Worcester, Mass.: Griffin and Norrill, 1829.

Arthur, T. S. *Rising in the World: or, a Tale for the Rich and the Poor*. New York: Baker and Scribner, 1848.

Arvin, Newton. "The House of Pain." In *Emerson: A Collection of Critical Essays*, edited by Milton R. Konvitz and Stephen Whicher. Englewood Cliffs, N.J.: Prentice-Hall, 1962.

Barcus, James E. "Structuring the Rage Within: The Spiritual Autobiographies of Newman and Orestes Brownson." *Cithara* 15 (1975): 45–57.

Barish, Evelyn. *Emerson: The Roots of Prophesy*. Princeton: Princeton University Press, 1989.

Barzun, Jacques. *Classic, Romantic, and Modern*. Garden City, N.J.: Anchor Books, 1961.

Beecher, Henry Ward. *Seven Lectures to Young Men on Various Important Subjects*. Boston: J. P. Jewett, 1846.

Bercovitch, Sacvan. *The American Jeremiad*. Madison: University of Wisconsin Press, 1978.

Berry, Edmund G. *Emerson's Plutarch.* Cambridge: Harvard University Press, 1961.

Bishop, Jonathan. *Emerson on the Soul.* Cambridge: Harvard University Press, 1962.

Bloom, Harold. *Poetry and Repression: Revisionism from Blake to Stevens.* New Haven: Yale University Press, 1976.

Buell, Lawrence. *Literary Transcendentalism: Style and Vision in the American Renaissance.* Ithaca: Cornell University Press, 1973.

Burke, Kenneth. *The Rhetoric of Religion: Studies in Logology.* Berkeley: University of California Press, 1961.

Burnap, George W. *Lectures to Young Men, on the Cultivation of the Mind, the formation of Character, and the Conduct of Life.* Baltimore: John Murphy, 1840.

Burns, Rex. *Success in America: The Yeoman Dream and the Industrial Revolution.* Amherst: University of Massachusetts Press, 1976.

Carlyle, Thomas. *On Heroes and Hero-Worship and the Heroic in History.* London: Ward, Lock & Co., 1900.

———. *Sartor Resartus: The Life and Opinions of Herr Teufelsdrockh.* Indianapolis: Odyssey Press, 1937.

Cavell, Stanley. *In Quest of the Ordinary: Lines of Skepticism and Romanticism.* Chicago: University of Chicago Press, 1988.

———. *This New Yet Unapproachable America: Lectures after Emerson after Wittgenstein.* Albuquerque, N.M.: Living Batch Press, 1989.

Cawelti, John G. *Apostles of the Self-Made Man.* Chicago: University of Chicago Press, 1965.

Cayton, Mary Kupiec. *Emerson's Emergence: Self and Society in the Transformation of New England, 1800–1845.* Chapel Hill: University of North Carolina Press, 1989.

Channing, William Ellery. *William Ellery Channing: Selected Writing.* Edited by David Robinson. New York: Paulist Press, 1985.

Cheyfitz, Eric. *The Trans-Parent: Sexual Politics in the Language of Emerson.* Baltimore: Johns Hopkins University Press, 1981.

Christ, Carol P. *Diving Deep and Surfacing: Women Writers on Spiritual Quest.* 2d ed. Boston: Beacon Press, 1980.

———. *Laughter of Aphrodite: Reflections on a Journey to the Goddess.* San Francisco: Harper & Row, 1987.

Coleridge, Samuel Taylor. *Selected Poetry and Prose of Coleridge.* Edited by Donald A. Stauffer. New York: Modern Library, 1951.

Cooke, George Willis. *Unitarianism in America: A History of Its Origins and Development.* Boston: American Unitarian Association, 1902.

Cox, James. M. "Ralph Waldo Emerson: The Circles of the Eye." In *Emer-*

son: Prophesy, Metamorphosis, and Influence, edited by David Levin. New York: Columbia University Press, 1975.

Dante (Dante Alighieri). *The Divine Comedy.* The Continental Edition of World Masterpieces. Edited by Maynard Mack et al. 3d ed. New York: W. W. Norton, 1974.

Douglas, Mary. *Natural Symbols: Explorations in Cosmology.* New York: Pantheon Books, 1982.

Eliot, T. S. *Ash Wednesday.* In *T. S. Eliot: Collected Poems, 1909–1962.* New York: Harcourt, Brace and World, 1970.

Emerson, Ralph Waldo. *The Complete Sermons of Ralph Waldo Emerson.* Edited by Albert J. von Frank et al. 4 vols. Columbia: University of Missouri Press, 1989–1992.

———. *The Complete Works of Ralph Waldo Emerson: Miscellanies.* 12 vols. 1904. Reprint, New York: AMS Press, 1968.

———. *The Journals and Miscellaneous Notebooks of Ralph Waldo Emerson.* Edited by William H. Gilman. 16 vols. Cambridge: Belknap Press of Harvard University Press, 1960–1982.

———. *The Letters of Ralph Waldo Emerson.* Edited by Ralph L. Rusk. 6 vols. New York: Columbia University Press, 1939.

———. Unpublished Manuscript Sermons. Houghton Library of Harvard University.

Everett, Edward. *Orations and Speeches on Various Occasions.* Boston: American Stationers' Company, 1836.

Foucault, Michel. *The History of Sexuality: An Introduction.* Vol. 1. Translated by Robert Hurley. New York: Vintage Books, 1990.

Frost, John. *An Oration, Delivered at Middlebury, before the Associated Alumni of the College, on the Evening of Commencement, August 19th, 1829.* Utica, N.Y.: Hastings and Tracy, 1829.

Gadamer, Hans-Georg. *Philosophical Hermeneutics.* Translated and edited by David E. Linge. Berkeley: University of California Press, 1976.

———. *Truth and Method.* New York: Seabury Press, 1975.

Geertz, Clifford. *The Interpretation of Cultures: Selected Essays by Clifford Geertz.* New York: Basic Books, 1973.

Gougeon, Len. *Virtue's Hero: Emerson, Antislavery, and Reform.* Athens: University of Georgia Press, 1990.

Greene, Theodore P. *America's Heroes: The Changing Models of Success in American Magazines.* New York: Oxford University Press, 1970.

Grusin, Richard A. *Transcendentalist Hermeneutics: Institutional Authority and the Higher Criticism of the Bible.* Durham: Duke University Press, 1991.

Halttunen, Karen. *Confidence Men and Painted Women: A Study of Middle-*

class Culture in America, 1830–1870. New Haven: Yale University Press, 1982.

Haskins, David Greene. *Ralph Waldo Emerson: His Maternal Ancestors with Some Reminiscences of Him.* Boston: n. p., 1887.

Hawes, Joel. *Lectures to Young Men, on the Formation of Character.* 3d ed. Hartford, Conn.: Cooke & Co., 1829.

Hodder, Alan D. *Emerson's Rhetoric of Revelation: Nature, the Reader, and the Apocalypse Within.* University Park: Pennsylvania State University Press, 1989.

Howe, Daniel Walker. *The Unitarian Conscience: Harvard Moral Philosophy, 1805–1861.* Middletown, Conn.: Wesleyan University Press, 1970.

Irwin, John. *American Hieroglyphics: The Symbol of the Egyptian Hieroglyphics in the American Renaissance.* New Haven: Yale University Press, 1980.

Jacobson, David. "'Compensation': Exteriority beyond the Spirit of Revenge." *ESQ: A Journal of the American Renaissance* 33:2 (1987): 110–19.

James, William. "The Will to Believe." In *The Writings of William James: A Comprehensive Edition,* edited by John J. McDermott. Chicago: University of Chicago Press, 1977.

Jameson, Fredric. *The Political Unconscious: Narrative as a Socially Symbolic Act.* Ithaca: Cornell University Press, 1981.

Jay, Paul. *Being in the Text: Self-Representation from Wordsworth to Barthes.* Ithaca: Cornell University Press, 1984.

Johnson, Thomas H., ed. *Final Harvest: Emily Dickinson's Poems.* Boston: Little, Brown and Co., 1961.

Kalinevitch, Karen Lynn. "Ralph Waldo Emerson's Older Brother: The Letters and Journal of William Emerson." Ph.D. diss., University of Tennessee, 1982.

Kinneavy, James L. *A Theory of Discourse: The Aims of Discourse.* New York: W. W. Norton, 1971.

Langer, Susanne K. *Philosophy in a New Key: A Study of the Symbolism of Reason, Rite, and Art.* New York: New American Library, 1942.

Lensink, Judy Nolte. *"A Secret to Be Buried": The Diary and Life of Emily Hawley Gillespie, 1858–1888.* Iowa City: University of Iowa Press, 1989.

Leverenz, David. *Manhood and the American Renaissance.* Ithaca: Cornell University Press, 1989.

———. "The Politics of Emerson's Man-Making Words." *PMLA* 101 (January 1986): 38–56.

Loving, Jerome. *Emerson, Whitman, and the American Muse.* Chapel Hill: University of North Carolina Press, 1982.

McAleer, John. *Ralph Waldo Emerson: Days of Encounter.* Boston: Little, Brown and Co., 1984.

McGiffert, Arthur C., ed. *Young Emerson Speaks: Unpublished Discourses on Many Subjects.* Port Washington, N.Y.: Kennikat Press, 1938.

Mann, Horace. *A Few Thoughts for a Young Man: A Lecture, delivered before the Boston Mercantile Library Association, on its 29th Anniversary.* Boston: Ticknor, Reed, and Fields, 1850.

Mather, Cotton. *Magnalia Christi Americana, Books I and II.* Edited by Kenneth B. Murdock. Cambridge: Belknap Press of Harvard University Press, 1977.

May, Samuel J. *Discourse: Slavery in the United States.* Boston: Garrison and Knapp, 1832.

Melville, Herman. *Moby-Dick.* Edited by Harrison Hayford and Hershel Parker. New York: W. W. Norton, 1967.

Michie, Helena. *The Flesh Made Word: Female Figures and Women's Bodies.* New York: Oxford University Press, 1987.

Milder, Robert. "Emerson's Two Conversions." *ESQ: A Journal of the American Renaissance* 33 (1st quarter 1987): 20–34.

Mott, Wesley T. "'Christ Crucified': Christology, Identity, and Emerson's Sermon No. 5." In *Emerson Centenary Essays,* edited by Joel Myerson. Carbondale: Southern Illinois University Press, 1982.

———. *"Strains of Eloquence": Emerson and His Sermons.* University Park: Pennsylvania State University Press, 1989.

Nietzsche, Friedrich. *Basic Writings of Nietzsche.* Translated and edited by Walter Kaufmann. New York: Modern Library, 1966.

———. *The Complete Works of Friedrich Nietzsche.* Edited by Oscar Levy. 18 vols. 1909–1911. Reprint, New York: Russell and Russell, 1964.

Nye, Russel B. *Society and Culture in America, 1830–1860.* New York: Harper and Row, 1974.

Olney, James. *Autobiography: Essays Theoretical and Critical.* Princeton: Princeton University Press, 1980.

Packer, Barbara. "Origin and Authority: Emerson and the Higher Criticism." In *Reconstructing American Literary History,* edited by Sacvan Bercovitch. Cambridge: Harvard University Press, 1986.

Pahl, Dennis. *Architects of the Abyss: The Indeterminate Fictions of Poe, Hawthorne, and Melville.* Columbia: University of Missouri Press, 1989.

Pascal, Roy. *Design and Truth in Autobiography.* London: Routledge and Kegan Paul, 1960.

Poe, Edgar Allan. "To Helen." In *Complete Tales and Poems of Edgar Allan Poe.* New York: Modern Library, 1938.

Pommer, Henry F. *Emerson's First Marriage*. Carbondale: Southern Illinois University Press, 1967.

Porte, Joel. *Representative Man: Ralph Waldo Emerson in His Time*. New York: Oxford University Press, 1979.

Reed, Sampson. "Oration on Genius." In *The Transcendentalists: An Anthology*, edited by Perry Miller. Cambridge: Harvard University Press, 1950.

Reynolds, David. *Beneath the American Renaissance: The Subversive Imagination in the Age of Emerson and Melville*. Cambridge: Harvard University Press, 1989.

Richardson, Robert D., Jr. *Myth and Literature in the American Renaissance*. Bloomington: Indiana University Press, 1978.

Roberson, Susan L. "Advice to Young Men in Ante-bellum Nineteenth-Century America." *Journal of the American Studies Association of Texas* 22 (1991): 1–10.

———. "Stowe's Matriarchy and the Rhetoric of Domesticity." In *The Stowe Debate: Rhetorics in Uncle Tom's Cabin*, edited by Mason Lowance, Jr., Ellen Westbrook, and R. C. DeProspro. Amherst: University of Massachusetts Press, 1994.

Robinson, David. *Apostle of Culture: Emerson as Preacher and Lecturer*. Philadelphia: University of Pennsylvania Press, 1982.

———. "The Sermons of Ralph Waldo Emerson: An Introductory Historical Essay." In *The Complete Sermons of Ralph Waldo Emerson*, edited by Albert J. von Frank, vol. 1. Columbia: University of Missouri Press, 1989.

———. *The Unitarians and the Universalists*. Westport, Conn.: Greenwood Press, 1985.

Scott, Donald M. *From Office to Profession: The New England Ministry, 1750–1850*. Philadelphia: University of Pennsylvania Press, 1978.

Shea, Daniel B. *Spiritual Autobiography in Early America*. Madison: University of Wisconsin Press, 1988.

Smith, Henry Nash. "Emerson's Problem of Vocation: A Note on the American Scholar." In *American Transcendentalism: An Anthology of Criticism*, edited by Brian M. Barbour. Notre Dame: University of Notre Dame Press, 1973.

Smith-Rosenberg, Carroll. *Disorderly Conduct: Visions of Gender in Victorian America*. New York: Oxford University Press, 1985.

Somkin, Fred. *Unquiet Eagle: Memory and Desire in the Idea of American Freedom, 1815–1860*. Ithaca: Cornell University Press, 1967.

Sontag, Susan. *Illness as Metaphor*. New York: Vintage Books, 1977.

Steele, Jeffrey. "Interpreting the Self: Emerson and the Unconscious." In *Emerson: Prospect and Retrospect.* Edited by Joel Porte. Cambridge: Harvard University Press, 1982.

Stevens, Wallace. *The Necessary Angel: Essay on Reality and the Imagination.* New York: Alfred A. Knopf, 1951.

Taylor, Isaac. *Character Essential to Success in Life. Addressed to those Who Are Approaching Manhood.* Boston: Wells and Lilly, 1820.

Thacher, James. *An Essay on Demonology, Ghosts and Apparitions, and Popular Superstitions. Also, an Account of the Witchcraft Delusion at Salem, in 1692.* Boston: Carter and Hendee, 1831.

Tocqueville, Alexis de. *Democracy in America.* Edited by Richard D. Heffner. New York: New American Library, 1956.

Todd, John. *The Young Man. Hints Addressed to the Young Men of the United States.* 2d ed. Northampton, Mass.: n. p., 1844.

Turpie, Mary C. "Quaker Source for Emerson's Sermon on the Lord's Supper." *New England Quarterly* 17 (March 1944): 95–101.

Whicher, Stephen. *Freedom and Fate: An Inner Life of Ralph Waldo Emerson.* Philadelphia: University of Pennsylvania Press, 1953.

Wider, Sara. "What Did the Minister Mean: Emerson's Sermons and Their Audience." *ESQ: A Journal of the American Renaissance* 34 (1988): 1–21.

Winslow, Hubbard. *The Young Man's Aid to Knowledge, Virtue, and Happiness.* 2d ed. Boston: Crocker & Brewster, 1839.

Wise, Daniel. *The Young Man's Counsellor: or, Sketches and Illustrations of the Duties and Dangers of Young Men.* New York: n. p., 1850.

Wright, Conrad. *Three Prophets of Religious Liberalism: Channing — Emerson — Parker.* Boston: Beacon Press, 1961.

The Young Man's Own Book. Philadelphia: Key, Mielke and Biddle, 1833.

Index

Permissions

Formal acknowledgment is made as follows to libraries and publishers for permission to quote from copyrighted material:

Passages from *The Journals and Miscellaneous Notebooks of Ralph Waldo Emerson,* 16 vols., edited by William H. Gilman et al., are reprinted by permission of The Belknap Press of Harvard University Press, Cambridge, Mass. Copyright © 1960-1982 by the President and Fellows of Harvard College.

Passages from *The Letters of Ralph Waldo Emerson,* vol. 1, 1813-1835, edited by Ralph L. Rusk, are reprinted by permission of Columbia University Press, New York. Copyright © 1939.

Passages from Manuscript Sermons of Ralph Waldo Emerson are reprinted by permission of the Ralph Waldo Emerson Memorial Association and of Houghton Library, Harvard University.

"Advice to Young Men in Nineteenth-Century America" was originally published in *Journal of the American Studies Association of Texas* in 1991, and is reprinted in part by permission of the publisher.

"The Private Voice behind the Public Text: Two Emerson Sermons" was originally published in *ESQ: A Journal of the American Renaissance* in 1986, and is reprinted in part by permission of the publisher.

"Young Emerson and the Mantle of Biography" was originally published in *ATQ* 5:3, September 1991, and is reprinted in part by permission of The University of Rhode Island.